# THE RUDE STORY OF ENGLISH

# THE RUDE STORY OF ENGLISH

TOM HOWELL WITH ILLUSTRATIONS BY GABE FOREMAN

McCLELLAND & STEWART

**Library and Archives Canada Cataloguing in Publication**

Howell, Tom
The rude story of English / Tom Howell ; Gabe Foreman, illustrator.

Issued also in electronic format.
ISBN 978-0-7710-3983-6 (pbk.)

1. English language – Obscene words – History.
2. Swearing – History. 3. English language – Slang – History.
4. English language – History. 5. English language – Etymology.
I. Title.

PE3724.O3H69 2013 427 C2011-904429-3

Typeset in Caslon by M&S, Toronto
Printed and bound in the United States of America

McClelland & Stewart,
a division of Random House of Canada Limited
One Toronto Street
Toronto, Ontario
M5C 2V6
www.randomhouse.ca

1 2 3 4 5 17 16 15 14 13

# Contents

*Part Two:* RISE OF THE POETS



*Part Three:* THE TONGUE THAT ATE ITSELF

*Part Four:* COMPANY

**rude** *adj.*

- illogical
- of low intelligence
- harsh or unkind
- unexpected
- barbarous and uncivilized
- inexpert
- unmannerly, impolite, deliberately discourteous
- improper or taboo because invokes sex, defecation, genitalia, etc.
- boisterous, rough
- involving hardship or discomfort
- robust, vigorous
- unmusical
- bad-smelling
- raw, untreated, unfinished
- of inferior quality
- lacking elegance or literary merit
- rugged and wild
- makeshift
- sturdy (but ugly)
- large in amount
- inexact
- rudimentary
- in the manner of a sketch

PART ONE

# The Hero

## I. THE NOT-RUDE NOT-STORY OF ENGLISH

The story of the English language is actually quite cool. It contains some sad parts, but these are well dispersed among moments of beauty, hilarity, pauses for thought, lessons for us all, and ambiguous moral themes. It is, as the saying goes, all over the place. I picked up the tale piecemeal, reading parts in books and hearing other parts virally, by word of mouth, word of radio, word of PowerPoint, word of museum, and sometimes by word of silly song. In my experience, when somebody attempts to fit the whole storyline together into a single form, two big problems stick out. One, no hero. Two, not rude enough. The rough, barbarous, fragrant folks of olden times who began unravelling the yarn we now call "English" liked their stories to be full of rudeness and heroism. They wanted battles with monsters, meetings with mentors, wild sea voyages, magic, and a lonely character's tumbledown luck. I think they were on to something.

There's a good reason why stories about English tend to be unheroic. It's the numbers. Five billion humans today speak this language, plus all the dead ones who used to, and, on top of that, parrots. Each speaker has (or had) a different story about how English found them, depending on what boat they/their ancestors climbed into (or perched on), or which gang of thugs showed up in boats to pester which grandparents/put them in a cage, etc., and a single hero can glue together only so many plot lines.

A central myth began to take shape two hundred years ago in the hands of scholars who called themselves "philologists." Their name looks as if it could mean either "lovers of study" or "students of love," depending on which end is the head and which the tail, but no, *wrong*, philologists were instead "phillers" of the "log," lovers of the word. Their job involved reading the handwriting that has survived from days of yore, translating all the ancient words, and tracing what amounted to career paths that connected old speech to modern, or old to even older. The scholars would observe how a single word had switched jobs over time, either taking on a new meaning or losing an old one, and how its outward appearance changed, usually in tandem with travels through space or time. Such threads of tale could be entwined to link our present moment with our past, and so it is due to the philologists' efforts that English has any story at all.

Sadly, rather than finishing their work by sewing the different word-careers into a neat, metred, rhyming epic tale, the philologists fell victim to a plague of science envy. Roughly eight decades ago, most rebranded themselves as "linguists," a name that is all tongue and no love, and they began wearing the used lab coats they'd found outside the chemistry department. The linguists set to dissecting various puzzles of speech into tinier and tinier pieces until no determined amateur could tell the bits apart, let alone put them all back together again. As a result, a properly informed account of English's life is now too difficult to tell around the campfire or at bedtime or while smoking pot at a housewarming, or wherever our crucial myths are supposed to live these days.

I never bash experts. I wouldn't know what to bash them with. I'd probably pick the wrong thing, like a chair, only to find out that's exactly what experts are trained to fight with, and I'd be wriggling on my back before I saw them move. However, the story of English needs all the help it can get – any idiot can see this and several have volunteered already. I'm only piping up because I made two astounding discoveries, in the Christopher Columbus sense of finding things other people already knew about, and I believe my discoveries can cure our language's anguish in the story department.

One century ago, in that golden age when philologists roamed the earth, the cream of their species found jobs with major dictionary projects such as the famous *Oxford English Dictionary*. In halls and offices filled with paper, pens, dust, and oak lecterns, the scholars conferred and created professional norms, such as a practice of telling the truth most of the time. They couldn't *always* stick to facts, because they lived in a dirty, messed-up world riddled with gaps. Ninety-five per cent of the universe is made of types of gap – dark matter, anti-matter and so on – and the same physics govern the realm of words, so upon finding a gap in the knowable universe, a philologist would attempt to fill it using a piece of wisdom handed down to him or her by elders in the form of a law. "Grimm's Law" was one. "Verner's Law" was another. As with physical laws, these rules extrapolated from past experiences and observations, helping a scholar predict the existence of objects, sounds, activity, and other forces that lie beyond the ken of a naked human eye. The wording of the laws doesn't matter right this minute because what counts is the result of philological practice, the slow spinning out of a semi-fictional parallel universe, which has been nicknamed the "asterisk reality." This is their profession's second-most inspiring and poetic artwork, after the *Oxford English Dictionary* itself.

I grew up knowing about the *Astérix* reality, the world of the books populated by cartoon Gauls and Romans engaged in unevenly plausible scenarios drawn from facts and other speculations. The asterisk reality is exactly the same thing. In a philologist's handwriting, an asterisk mark signals where material has been concocted to plug a hole in real-world evidence. For example, when someone at Oxford's dictionary department wanted to show that our modern word "arse" once had a job as an ancient Greek word, "orsoz," the scholar needed to imagine a scene in which a German princess two thousand years ago was sitting on something locally known as her "ars-oz." No documents exist to prove this occurred so the philologist added an asterisk in front of the word – **ars-oz* – and stuck it in the dictionary under the "arse" entry in a paragraph recounting the word's life story. Generally, depending on the number of nearby facts available, and on how clever/lazy the philologist was, an asterisk might stand for anything from "as good as true" to "probably-maybe" to "whatever, time for lunch."

"The * is the sign of the reconstructed form," explained Tom Shippey, who gave the asterisk reality its nickname. "It was proposed by August Schleicher in the 1860s and used widely ever since. In this entire process the thing which was perhaps eroded most of all was the philologists' sense of a line between imagination and reality. In a sense, the non-existence of the most desired objects of study created a romance of its own."

"Romance" is typically a divisive word. It's a red stoplight to the hard-headed, but to a certain strain of artist or poet or sophomore or lover, it's the other variety of red light, the type that means, "Come closer," or perhaps, "Desired object of study – right this way."

Soon after I discovered philology's looking-glass world, I also learned that it contains an asterisk hero who is perfect for the story of English, a demigod-like figure with one foot in the real universe and the other foot lost in dark matter. The hero's existence, stretching that word for the moment, owes much to one of the alt-reality's minor contributors, J.R.R. Tolkien, the same person who helped write *The Lord of the Rings* movies. He worked at Oxford's dictionary department for two years, 1919 and 1920, until he grew tired of trying to remain plausible and wandered off to write about hobbits instead. While in the office, J.R.R. mostly investigated English words that began with the letter *w*, such as "wolf" and "warg" and "wallop," from which he invented the ancient French verb **waloper* (to wallop someone, obviously). He also doodled fake Saxon riddles in the margins. Even after quitting the dictionary, J.R.R. carried on philologizing and asterisking, going past mere words to imagine the people who spoke them – and from these speculations emerged his stories of quests, elves, warriors, rings, and scary people on horses. Tolkien had read the old epics and knew that all good adventures need a single, socially isolated hero, so he collected several of these characters and kept them in reserve for later use in his fiction. Among the candidates was a man named Hengest.

Tolkien didn't magic this man out of nothing. I remember Hengest from my high-school history classes in England. The ancient warrior had somehow gained a reputation for discovering Britain on behalf of the Angles, a tribe in northern Germany, thereby inventing the English language. (The word "English" may refer to the speech of Angles who crossed the water, but nobody uses it to name the German dialect spoken by those left behind on the mainland.) This historic coup makes Hengest highly desirable as an object of study, but he's a horrendously tough fish to hook back up into the world of facts. J.R.R. certainly tried his darndest.

The professor based all of his asterisk-facts regarding Hengest on two poems, named *Beowulf* and *The Fight at Finnesburg*, ancient works from an oral tradition, set down on parchment a thousand years ago. The poems put Hengest in the company of Jutes, whose tribe supposedly lived next door to the Angles on what's now labelled the Jutish peninsula of modern Denmark. But there's a wrinkle. The Jutes' name was once pronounced "yooten," which also happened to be a Germanic word for magical giants. Strangely, the particular gang of Jutes that joined Hengest on his trip to Britain left no trash for modern archaeologists to dig up, raising the question of whether they were indeed magical giants or just very large humans with supernaturally tidy habits. Having visited the Danish province of Jutland myself, where I cultivated a rapport with the locals, I find the second interpretation easy enough to believe. However, if that's wrong and Hengest's original life story *did* feature giants, any sober-minded adult might suspect the whole crowd of characters belongs to a fairytale. It's hard to tell from scraps of parchment. They almost never declare themselves as fiction or non-fiction.

J.R.R. chose to believe that Hengest lived in real history and that the "yooten" were real Jutes from Jutland. Working from the claims of anonymous poets, the author-philologist sketched out a figure who was "a masterless man, seeking warlike employment and any opportunity that luck might present to him."* Hengest (or **Hengest*, really) seemed to be an expert swordsman, and, even more excitingly, the true prince of the Angle tribe, although he suffered a falling-out with his own people and became a loner. In this regard he resembled Aragorn, the wandering king of *The Lord of the Rings*, who travels far from home under a fake name.

* *Finn and Hengest*, by J.R.R. Tolkien. The book was compiled from the professor's notes by a younger colleague, Alan Bliss.

Ostracized, Hengest sailed to Britain in 449 AD "primarily as a mercenary but soon changed his purpose," as Tolkien put it. The warrior decided to settle down on the island, make babies, and invite his fellow thugs to do the same. Events were conspiring to give our language a great foundational hero.

Sadly, before Hengest could assume his full asterisk-self, urgent duties distracted J.R.R. Tolkien. The famous scholar's beautiful plans for Hengest gradually sank under piles of other asterisks, along with student papers, grocery lists, orcs, etc. I consider this to be a grim moment in the story of English because it seems to me that Tolkien, too, was on to something.

## 2. THE HERO AND HIS BROTHER, 430 AD

In most cases, a person's fundamental traits will begin to show at an early age.

"I am Hengest, the Stallion."

"Me too."

"No, you are Horsey, the Horse."

"But I want to be the Stallion, like you!"

"Shut up and give me a piggyback."

Hengest had a twin brother. Naturally, an economy of piggybacks developed between them. A skeptic will say we can't know anything about this, but we can. For instance, we know that the two boys either gave each other piggybacks *equally* or they did not. We may also split the possibilities in three: (a) Hengest gave more piggybacks; (b) no, his twin brother did; or (c) both boys gave each other the same number. A show-off could keep carving the odds, drawing lines through the brothers' long-lost piggybacking relationship to account for blips due to growth spurts, quality versus quantity of rides, which would be foxtrotting before we can walk. Piggybacks occurred – that's an *a priori* truth about able-bodied twin boys. Beyond this fact, even the simple detail of who most often carried whom exists outside the proper historical universe, though it does exist nonetheless because, luckily, we have heard about another, more romantic universe where one's knowledge depends less on direct evidence than on one's desire to know. It's an improper place for data-gathering, but the asterisk reality serves a storyteller's needs very well. Over there if I *want* hard enough, I can find out about Hengest's piggybacks. This requires some magic and wishful thinking, and yet the mirror-world isn't just arbitrary. It has rules too.

Ferdinand de Saussure, the co-parent of modern linguistics, based his account of human language on a paradox. A word can mean whatever we want it to mean. And, at the same time, it cannot. For example, no reason exists in nature why the phrase "messed up" can't be someone's word for a wooden dildo. It could even grow into a mainstream, worldwide English term. "Please put my messed-up where it belongs, back in the bedside drawer," someone could say. "Also, don't look at me like that." Freedom of meaning matters for words just as much as free will matters for humans. On the other hand, freedom is a fiction. "Messed up" cannot mean a wooden dildo because we have prejudices about words we've met before, about how English grammar works (roughly), and about how silly and random we'd like our next moment in the universe to feel. We're familiar with the word "mess" and the ending *–ed*, and most of us have a sense of what "up" does in situations like this. An English word's job prospects depend on its previous work experience, its peers and social contacts, along with the needs, wants, and fetishes of nearby people (and parrots), not to mention the forces exerted on all of these things by the financial markets, the availability and size of nuclear weapons, the warmth of the ocean, and, who knows, the plans of a pan-dimensional poet. A word is therefore both free and determined, or, to use Saussure's words, "arbitrary" and "motivated."

The life of any human shares something with the life of a word, but for a human in the asterisk universe, the connection is tighter. He or she lacks some of the anchors that encumber us mundane people. An asterisk-human could do anything, including magic, except that the pushes and pulls of logic, memory, and experience still buffet the person around. For example, **Hengest* is stuck with being "Hengesty," a word I coined two seconds ago, but into which Tolkien's sketched-out ideas are already piling meaning, faster than the eye can see. Unless a drastic new power arrives to twist the steering-shaft, a Hengesty person is someone who, roughly speaking:

(a) looks and sounds like a standard epic hero
(b) is of little or no value to proper historical scholarship, due to lack of evidence
(c) fascinates a word-lover with a hyperactive imagination, e.g., J.R.R. Tolkien

As with all words, a single utterance of "Hengesty" can mean one of these senses, or two, or all of them together (at least, in the mind of the person speaking). Or it can attempt some new meaning that surprises my current definition. **Hengest* the hero is a spirit of the asterisk world, wriggling within the same Hengesty constraints and exploiting the same loophole, that is, the ability to defy expectations. And Hengest the real, living, piggybacking kid in northern Germany is a helpless, time-bound figure of circa 430 AD who can do almost nothing to stop a modern person, like me, from inferring that he behaved Hengestly as well.

My definition of "Hengesty" needs to grow, because Tolkien isn't the sole source of ideas on Hengestness. In the fifth-century Angle tongue, "Hengest" literally meant "stallion," and today a man in modern Germany may still be called "der Hengst" if he enjoys plenty of hot, wild, sustained sexual intercourse. To people who know this fact, a Hengesty person might also be:

(d) like a stallion, e.g., well endowed, strong, or sexually accomplished

Hengest's twin brother was Horsa. My school history textbooks told me it meant "horse" in Angle-language, though I later learned they had ignored a crucial point. "Hors" named the garden-variety animal, while the additional letter *a* marked the diminutive, a form many English-speakers now build with a letter *y*, turning Jim into Jimmy or Ron into Ronny. In modern English, "Horsa" would be "Horsey." Tolkien and my school textbooks all agreed that the boys' names were probably adopted as *noms de guerre* rather than acquired at birth, which is good news because it yields a clue about the sibling dynamic. "Stallion" is macho and heroic. "Horsey" is cute and lesser. We can spot, I think, which brother held editorial control. The power imbalance pushes out a fifth potential sense of "Hengesty":

(e) given to displays of power, such as assuming the role of stallion to another's diminutive horse

"In this peculiarly difficult line of enquiry," wrote J.R.R. Tolkien on the first page of his Hengest notes, "one has frequently to begin with a temporary theory." I take inspiration from this. We won't get a final, permanent answer to the question, "Which brother received more piggybacks?" However, what we already know can motivate, for the time being, several theories. Like pool balls after a break, some will move faster than others, such as the theory that leaping on someone's back and demanding to be carried, perhaps while swirling a sword in the air, would be more Hengesty behaviour, while giving a piggyback would be more Horsey-ish. Stallions usually climb upon horses, not the other way around. (I watched several online videos to confirm this.) A person in need of this tiny detail from the childhoods of two ancient Angles could pick arbitrarily from the scenario options given at the start of this chapter, disregarding the laws of momentum. But such a person could never build the asterisk reality. Over there, in between the facts of the matter, everything exists due to forces of motivation, influenced by the gravity of the real world and the memory of what's happened to date. The true asterisk-answer is that the brothers' economy of piggybacks ought to have been unequal, extrapolating from the little data we have. Hengest took, Horsey gave. Furthermore, twins in general may be identical or mismatched – well, Hengest and Horsey were the latter sort. Until a new source of information redirects the story of English, the asterisk boys travel on divergent paths to opposite poles, one stronger and one weaker, like a pair of chickens growing up together. (I know about these things because, as a child, I kept two chickens as pets.) Apart from their nicknames, no direct real-world evidence about the historical Hengest or Horsey exists until they reached adulthood. Temporarily then, here are their portraits at age fifteen, once the lopsided dynamic had some time to achieve its stark, visible effects:

*Figure 1.1* – Hengest (with brother), early fifth century AD

## 3. BALANCE, 435 TO 448 AD

There was a woman too. Tolkien glossed right over her, which will surprise no one familiar with his books, but she's also missing from the oldest written accounts of England's early days – namely, the *Anglo-Saxon Chronicle* and the work of a monk called the Venerable Bede.* This woman skirts the edges of Welsh folk tales, often in the subtext where they mention a nameless cause of stupidity by their people's ancient leader, Vortigern, who must have been bewitched. ("Welsh" was the Angles' label for southern Britain's native people. It meant "foreign and/or Latin-speaking.") In the twelfth century, Geoffrey of Monmouth finally put the woman's name in writing, along with some of her backstory, in a book called *The History of the Kings of Britain*. He nailed the multi-epochal, popular style that today would get a scholar onto public television. Readers loved it, pirated and plagiarized it, such that handwritten copies of Geoffrey's work landed in private libraries as far away as Rome. *The History of the Kings of Britain* told its international audience that Hengest had a daughter named Rowena. Or Renwein, Rhonwyn, Rhona, Rowen, Rawen, or Rouhn, depending on which copy one looked at. Here lies a problem with handwritten manuscripts. Naturally, Geoffrey's original has gone missing.

"Rowena," "Rhona," etc., do not mean anything in the old Angle tongue, but in Welsh they resemble a word spelled

* The authentic spelling of this name is in doubt. Writings by ancient monks are notoriously prone to errors and inconsistencies.

variously as "rhawn," "roan," or "rawn," meaning "horsehair." Since Hengest's daughter grew up in northern Germany, she ought to have had a German-Angle name rather than a Celtic-Welsh one. Geoffrey, a French immigrant to Wales, heard about Rowena from Welsh legend-keepers seven centuries after the events, giving the oral historians plenty of time to put a local spin on the original word. Horsehair is a suitably Hengesty choice of baby name, given the father's known taste for ranking family members in a horse-related hierarchy, although the element of hair needs an extra piece of motivation to make sense.

The many mix-ups between copies of Geoffrey's work have led scholars to doubt him, especially because he seemed to dither over a major detail. He followed up *The History of the Kings of Britain* with a biography called *The Life of Merlin*, in which he refers repeatedly to Rowena as Hengest's *sister*, not daughter. One modern critic called this an "inexplicable oversight," but I wonder about this. Even if Geoffrey or his copyists erred from time to time, it doesn't follow that every startling detail in his stories must be wrong, any more than it's proven a man's daughter cannot also be his sister. The point is not inexplicable and therefore not necessarily an "oversight" either. We all read *Oedipus*.

Scholars who decide that Horsehair was either Hengest's daughter or his sister are taking what Geoffrey actually wrote and throwing it aside, based on – what? – a sense of propriety? The literal scenario stored by the written record is *both/and*, not *either/or*, adding an important new aspect to the potential meaning of "Hengesty":

(f) engaged in taboo sexual activities, e.g., incest

"Hen, meet your daughter," said Hengest's mother, I suppose, some months after our hero reached sexual maturity and began to explore.

"And as for you, Duck –" continued Hengest's mother, turning to the hero's twin.

"His name's Horsey!"

"Sorry. *Horsey*, you have a brand new sister. Also a niece."

The baby screamed.

"I've always wanted to be an uncle," said Horsey.

"Why is it furry?" Hengest demanded to know.

A good question. Perhaps their mother figured the baby's fur derived from a mutation, due in part to its short-circuited genetic inheritance. This sounds weirdly insightful for an ancient person, but incest taboos must have cropped up for some reason, the most obvious being amateur speculation about genetics.

"She'll just need to shave regularly," said Hengest's mother. "It's not a big problem."

Hengest gave a disgruntled sniff.

"We will call it Horsehair," he said.

Asterisky dialogues dance over the past's surface, gesturing at the gist beneath. My temporary theory is that the woman's strange name signified a real-life attribute. A word can paint a thousand pictures. However, in the case of Horsehair, they should all look roughly like this:

*Figure 1.2* – Horsehair, sister-daughter of Hengest, circa 448 AD

## 4. A FAUX PAS, 448 AD

Now the fighting begins.

The hero earned his warrior stripes at the age of twenty-five, as told in *Beowulf* and *The Fight at Finnesburg*. Both poems date from around 950 AD in written form, having survived five centuries of oral retelling, a miracle that implies poet after poet must have thought this story important. "*The Fight at Finnesburg* is in fact the only surviving pagan narrative poem in Old English," wrote Tolkien's friend, Alan Bliss. He believed that Hengest's adventure at Finnesburg once formed the heart of England's tribal story. A major point in favour of this (aside from the tale's lack of competition) is the way the plot motivates our hero to leave mainland Europe.

*Beowulf* runs hundreds of lines long. *The Fight at Finnesburg* has just forty-eight lines left, having suffered from library cutbacks throughout history, e.g., under the Vikings. It used to be much longer. J.R.R. Tolkien had to make do with a quoted passage in a notepad from the 1700s, a text full of gaps and errors, having been copied from a single leaf of an otherwise missing book, all now lost and gone forever, notepad included. Too bad, because *The Fight at Finnesburg* re-enacts Hengest's adventure in real time, blow for blow, whereas *Beowulf* just sums up the conclusion, as if we'd heard the episode a thousand times before.

The lonely scrap opens with a soliloquy from a prince or chief named Hnaef. He'd spotted a problem.

| | |
|---|---|
| *Hnæf hléoþrode ða,* | Up jumped Hnaef, the warlike |
| *heaþogeong cyning* | young chief, and said, |
| *"Né ðis ne dagað* | "Neither is this the dawn of |
| *éastan,* | the east, |
| *ne her draca ne fléogeð* | nor is there a dragon flying towards us, |
| *ne her ðisse healle hornas ne byrnað,* | nor are the gables of this hall burning, |
| *Ac –"* | nay –" |
| *[. . .]* | "Get to the point, Hnaef," said a warrior.* |
| *"Ac her forþ berað feorhgeniðlan, fyrdsearu fuslicu!"* | "Nay, mortal enemies approach in ready armour!" |

* Okay, I added this line. Someone had to say it.

Hnaef was Hengest's boss in 448 AD, although Hnaef didn't self-identify as an Angle. He ran a tribe called the Half-Danes, living off a profitable rape-and-pillage operation in the north end of Jutland. All I know about the Half-Danes is (1) they couldn't choose whether to be Danish or not-Danish, which suggests a waffling, fence-sitting nature; and (2) nevertheless, they became powerful enough to conquer parts of Jutland and employ Hengest, supposedly an Angle prince. Hnaef was paying Hengest to protect him and Frithuwulf (Hnaef's nephew) on a trip to the land of Frisia to see King Finn, who was Frithuwulf's dad, also the husband to Hnaef's sister, Hilda.

Then things got complicated.

I mentioned that Hengest travelled with Jutes (or giants). For this adventure, he hired a gang of Jutish thugs to be part of Hnaef's escort service. When the crew arrived safely at King Finn's fortress and sat down to dinner, a disaster took place. It concerned politics.

The Half-Danish occupation of Jutland had, fittingly enough, split Jutish society in two. The leaders of one wing fled from their peninsula while the other wing signed on to help the oppressors, à la Vichy French, and Hengest's thugs belonged to this traitorous camp. Unfortunately, many of the Jutish escapees and resistance forces turned out to have holed up at this very Frisian fort.

"That's awkward," Hnaef probably thought.

Being a Half-Dane, perhaps he allowed himself a counter-proposal. Maybe the scenario wasn't awkward. Maybe this gave everyone a chance to let bygones (and ongoing rapes and pillages) be bygones?

As shown above by Hnaef's long-winded battle cry, no, the situation was awkward and worse. Soon after midnight, the exiled Jutes crashed into Hnaef's sleeping quarters at a hall on Finn's property, aiming to kill their fellow countrymen. When our hero finally climbed out of bed to join the fray, he made his epic-poetic debut:

| *Hengest sylf* | Hengest himself |
|---|---|
| *hwearf him on laste* | followed them to the doorway. |
| *Swurdleoma stod,* | The swords shone |
| *swylce eal Finnsburuh fyrenu wære.* | as if Finnesburg was on fire. |
| *Ne gefrægn ic næfre* | Never have I ever |
| *wurþlicor æt wera hilde* | heard of sixty brave warriors |
| *sixtig sigebeorna sel gebæran,* | putting on a better show. |
| *Hig fuhton fif dagas,* | For five days they fought |
| *swa hyra nan ne feol drihtgesiða,* | so well that no defenders fell. |
| *ac hig ða duru heoldon.* | No, they held the doors. |

Sadly, that's about it for *The Fight at Finnesburg*. The other surviving lines refer to someone as "the hardy warrior" feared by an attacker named Guthere. Possibly this was Hengest. The scrap of poetry also reports the dying and/or boasting of Sigeferth, Guthlaf, and Eaha – Jutes on one side or the other (it's hard to tell). A raven of death flew in a circle, the poet observed. Most noticeably, Horsey earned no mention at all. Did he have a stomach flu that day, perhaps? To be kind, an excuse for Horsey's absence might be among the lost portions of the military dispatch, but based on what we have, the brothers' lopsided write-ups can only fuel my theory that Hengest was the more warrior-like of the two, while Horsey chose quieter hobbies. Often a gentle child will struggle to shine as his rougher sibling hogs the stage, a general truth that motivates me to fill a few gaps in the fragmentary Finnesburg scene, as follows:

"[*chop*], [*chop*], [*chop*]," said Hengest with his sword.
"Hengest, can I?" said Horsey.
"[*chop*], [*chop*], [*fricasee*], [*chop*]."
"Can I chop some?"
"[*chop*], [*chop*], [*stomp*], [*crunch*], [*chop*]."
"Hengest? I'd like a go."
"[*chop*], [*chop*]."
"Heng –"
"Shut up, Horsey. I'm busy."

Even if Horsey's pestering made it into the original poem, centuries of oral editing would doubtless have cut him out, since he didn't kill anyone or boast about doing so.

The rest of the story depends on *Beowulf*, a poem that mostly concerns monsters. Its anonymous author took a break halfway through the supernatural action and plugged in a short history lesson, reminding listeners that Hnaef the Half-Dane met his death in the Finnesburg battle (perhaps because he was focused on delivering his speech when he should have been killing people). Hengest took command, chopping down his leftover opponents, and then the hero paused for a rest.

"They made a solid pact of peace, Finn and Hengest," states the *Beowulf* poet, bluntly. A period of calm ensued. Winter set in, its maw inhaling the Netherlandic coast where the land of Frisia lay. In their crowded barns, herds of Frisian cows farted for warmth during what, for cows, is the friendliest season. Time passed. "Then spring came," the *Beowulf* poet wrote, "and that wretch Hengest wanted to go. But first he needed revenge. So he painted the hall red with the blood of his enemies."

The original poem's word for "wretch" was spelled "wrecca," or elsewhere "wraeca," and it meant something more complicated and Byronic than its modern version. An ancient Angle wretch wandered the lonely path of an exile, separated from his or her tribe, and was therefore obliged to venture far and discover new places. A more flattering modern translation of "wrecca" would be "epic hero." Nevertheless, Hengest's bloodthirsty revenge left him wretched in the ordinary sense too. His outburst of violence included dicing up King Finn, the chieftain on whose dime Hengest and his Jutes had lived and eaten for several months. This turned out to be a profound social gaffe.

Warriors in those days lived by hospitality alone, wandering from place to place, demanding dinner and a spare bed. There were certain rules governing guest/host behaviour. For instance, when Hengest took advantage of King Finn's largesse all winter long, the hero was expected to swear an oath not to murder the old man. All scholars today agree that such warriors' oaths counted as sacred in ancient semi-nomadic cultures. When Hengest broke his word and divided Finn into bite-size portions (and then, for good measure, kidnapped Finn's wife, Hilda, and took her to Jutland), he stepped well outside the established codes of guest etiquette. Worse than cruel, it was impolite.

The story of what Hengest did to King Finn travelled far. We know this because it ran the deadly gauntlet of forgetfulness through to the present day, of course, but more germane to the hero's short-term needs, the rumours spread geographically too. Tolkien asterisked the outcome at the end of his Hengest notes:

> The terrible sack was long remembered. What happened to Hengest immediately afterwards we do not know, but it seems likely that, Frisia and the North being no longer good places for him, he took his *heap** on a new adventure across the straits: to Kent [in Britain]. You may read his character how you will.

Tolkien's final sentence seems to offer future storytellers a broad permission. Nevertheless, the tiny morsels of story he reconstructed from the poems put limits on Hengest's character even as they added to it. For my purposes, the definition of "Hengesty" now includes:

(g) disrespectful to widows
(h) likely to break sacred oaths
(i) deadly to the hand that feeds him (or her)

* A *heap* was literally a "pile of thugs" in Old English. Tolkien is referring to the Jutes (or giants).

As J.R.R. saw it, the northern Europeans decided they'd had enough of the motherfucker, excuse their language. The story of English then falls to the likes of Geoffrey and the Venereal Bede,* who both tell us that the unloved prince rented three boats on the coast of Jutland, filled these with a heap of mercenary Jutes, Angles, and Saxons, plus his nerdy twin Horsey and his teenage sister-daughter Horsehair (omitted by Bede but featured by Geoffrey). The hero rowed off into the sunset, looking for a new home where nobody would know his name.

## 5. THE FIRST WORD, 449 AD

Until he landed on a British beach, Hengest spoke the Germanic dialect of an Angle warrior. After the first footfall, he spoke a different language, ours, even though he was not aware of it, and even though it sounded the same as ever to his fellows on the boat. I have more or less figured out what he said.

First, though, a parable.

A history teacher at my high school liked to overuse the phrase, "We just don't know," which he said seriously and emphatically.

"Did Thomas More privately regret his stand against Henry VIII? *We just don't know.*"

It became a joke for us.

"Are the wet spots on his shirt caused by nipple sweat or is he lactating? *We just don't know.*"

* See earlier note.

I believe the teacher wanted us to achieve a Zen state regarding the chasms of ignorance on which we'd erected our spindly personalities, which was a generous impulse and one that contrasted with most teachers, who preferred to inspire shame. Another man, being paid to make us appreciate poetry, lost his temper one day and shouted at our class, "I can't understand how you go through life knowing so little!" Today, I find it beautiful that a teacher of history tried to impress us with the mysterious while our poetry teacher complained about our lack of memorized facts.

My parable of the teachers is not about good and evil. The history man was kind, but he risked destroying the more unorthodox parts of our curiosity. If I had asked him about the way English started, his bias would have steered me into the abyss of unknowns. Perhaps Hengest stuck his foot on the beach and uttered a term that never met the right manuscript, or never got snagged in the net of a scholar's asterisks. Perhaps, damn my pencil marks, Hengest never existed outside epic poems. Perhaps the expanse of space-time we call the English language should be seen as edgeless, rather than beginning on a specific patch of sand. Well, the key word is "perhaps." The cruel-seeming poetry teacher may have had our interests at heart when he demanded that we keep adding to ourselves, fast and desperately. According to *his* biases, we are what we know and what we're still trying to know. To give up on the first word of our language is to give up a piece of our potential.

I was pleased to find a number of similarly biased souls who take the question of a first English word seriously – as a quest in the original sense – and who, in their books, papers, and thoughts, willingly charge off to behold the great yonder. The linguist David Crystal has answered the call in his own way in a book called *The Story of English in 100 Words*, and before offering up my solution, I will quickly re-dance his steps.

Eighty-odd years ago, digging under the eastern Angle territories in Britain, some shovels turned up a buried urn. The shovel operators summoned the pot experts, who said the urn looked much like other urns they had seen, especially those designed in southern Denmark and northern Germany during the early- to mid-400s, which was exactly when and where Hengest's family came from. The East Anglian urn contained twenty-five knucklebones, providing solid evidence of a hideous finger-chopping rampage, except that twenty-four of them previously belonged to sheep. The other knuckle came from a deer.

If you didn't know sheep and deer have knuckles then that's good, because I didn't either, despite growing up near a sheep farm. The animals walk on their equivalent of our third and fourth fingertips (or tiptoes), with their knuckle joints sitting up inside their ankles. Death ensues, at which point the tiny knucklebones dry out into chess pieces, or lopsided dice, or throwing jacks, or whatever one's imagination makes of them. A deer's bones are slightly bigger than the sheep's equivalent, large enough to provide a writing surface, and upon the single deer knuckle in the Anglian urn, a human hand once scratched out the following:

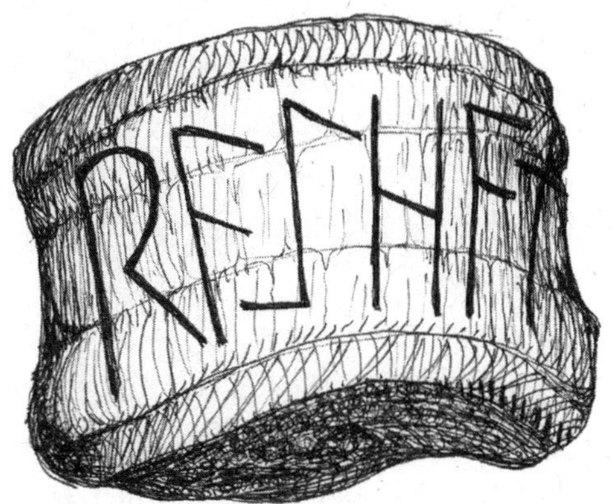

*Figure 1.3* – Deer knuckle found in pot, approximately 1,500 years old

This is the oldest written word in English. My inner wisdom tells me the word is "rfshft," for which I could suggest definitions based on a mixture of onomatopoeia and gut instinct. Luckily, professional experts had a go at guessing too, so we know my inner wisdom is wrong and that the marks are Germanic runes rather than bad Roman handwriting. In our alphabet, the word would be spelled "raihan," which one can render into modern English using the science of linguistics.

Angle descendants once said an "ay" or "aw" sound where many now say an "oh." People in Britain have always tended to drop the letter *h* from their words and file down the endings so that, over time, a word like "raihan" could degrade into "rowy," which, if you say it ten times while hopping on one foot, settles to "roe," the modern name for a species of woodland deer possessing four legs full of knuckles. (It's also a word for fish eggs. Ignore this.) Generations of spelling choices recorded on paper and parchment link the modern "roe" back in time as far as an old word spelled "raha," which is pretty close to "raihan."

"I can't imagine 'raihan' could mean anything other than 'roe,'" says David Crystal at the end of his word-finding mission. "We'll never know for sure, but in my opinion this is as close as we can get to the origins of English."

It's a fine answer. And a fine dodge too, pretending that the first *written* word of English has anything to do with the real object of the quest we sent him on, which was, ahem, the *first* word, no qualifiers.

Before letting Dr. Crystal off the hook though, I must point out a trap in the world of ideas known as "boring-bias." This is the tendency to rate what is less exciting as more likely to be true. The dull word "roe" slips past our suspicions because its appearance on a roe bone looks as unremarkable as finding "100% Danish Clay" stamped into an urn. However, the latest studies on the causes of Alzheimer's prove that it is physically dangerous to ignore delightful possibilities in the world around us, or to apply routines without exercising the mind. Crystal makes a gesture toward delight by speculating that the knucklebone could be a crucial piece in a game called "Find the Roe." He doesn't asterisk the scenario in detail, although I think I get the idea. An Angle child would use the sheep knuckles to form a trail into the woods, as if laying breadcrumbs. At the end of the trail, he or she would hide the big deer knuckle, and the job for playmates would be to follow the sheep knuckles successfully and "find the roe." Since life is hard and death is easy, a typical woodland could offer zillions of old deer bones that might confuse the game, and therefore a wise adult carved "roe" into the winning piece to preclude disputes. Games work metaphorically, so I guess the players were re-enacting a deer hunt, but still – spoilsport that I am – I don't see the cathartic joy in yelling out, "Hooray, a roe bone." Perhaps the treasure itself wasn't the goal. Maybe a good round of Find the Roe let young Angles spend quality time with their uncles, passing the hours until dinner, and so on. But we needn't settle for this if we don't want to.

Determined to avoid boring-bias, a man named Charles Wrenn once ventured forth along much the same breadcrumb trail as Crystal took. He, too, wanted to find the first word of English. Wrenn had inherited J.R.R. Tolkien's job in Oxford as the Rawlinson and Bosworth Professor of Anglo-Saxon, arriving a few years after the urn of knuckles showed up. In the same way that J.R.R. toyed with Hengest, Dr. Wrenn slowly chewed over the runes for years without telling anyone. Finally, in 1962, days before his retirement party, Wrenn published a story about the famous knucklebone. Like Crystal, he figured it was a game piece, but having fished around in his own private urn of Dark Ages trivia, Wrenn pulled out a different crumb. He noted that ancient Germanic people often mixed their letter *h*'s with an extra *w* sound, as in "why" and "what," which they actually pronounced as "hwy" and "hwat." If "raihan" similarly contained a *w* sound in its middle, then an "attractive conjecture," as Wrenn called it, was to see the runes as spelling out the word "rahwhan." This means nothing to most of us, but scholars know it as a magic word in Ancient Norwegian, a bit like "abracadabra." It was spoken as "rah-huh-wah-han," with a throat full of phlegm, and elsewhere in its word-life, "rah-whan" formed the first element of "Ragnarok," which was the name Norwegian storytellers gave to a coming apocalypse, the day when all their gods would explode.

"Rah-huh-wah-han" or "abracadabra" are great solutions to the rune puzzle, much better than "raihan" or "roe," and yet, wistfully this time, I hold my applause. Remembering Occam's advice that the simplest answer ought to be assumed, I spot a more basic option being ignored (as usual) here, in the person of Hengest's oft-overlooked sister-daughter. If Hengest counts as the father of the English language, she was the mother, being the first English-speaking woman on the island of Britain. She also took blame for messing up British chief Vortigern's judgment, in an adventure I will soon speak of, so she mattered to the Celts as well as the Angles. No one needs to gargle the vowels and consonants of "raihan" and "rahwhan" for long periods to produce the Celtic-British-Welsh translation of "Horsehair," already heard and seen variously as Rowen, Rowena, Renwein, Rhonwen, Rhaun, Roan, rfshft. In fact, it's a bit shocking to see the sexism at work here, such that in all my reading of Google previews, no historian has suggested the ancient runes might just be one more local attempt to spell this woman's name. "Find Rowena" promised a more passion-filled chasing game in Dark Age Britain than finding an old roe bone. Indeed, given her vexed place in Welsh and Angle culture, I expect a metaphorical hunt-and-rescue could get brutally competitive if children from each ethnicity formed the teams.

But that's not what I came to tell you about. Even the attractive conjecture of "Rowena" cannot fulfill a quest to find the beginning of the English language. This written word did not come first. It came *fairly near the start.*

"King Richard, here is not the Holy Grail but a goblet coming from thereabouts and somewhat later. Satisfied?"

"Of course I'm not satisfied. Go back and get me the Holy Grail, please."

And so I close the chapter on this distracting matter of what professional scholars have come up with so far. The point is, they fall short.

## 6. THE BOAT, 449 AD

Hengest arrived by boat. Intrepid sailing historians have built a replica and tested it out, proving that the vessel was powered by a mixture of sail and oars. The oars are no surprise but the sailing aspect had long been doubted because sail technology came so late to the Germans and Danes. In the fifth century, only a small avant-garde among them owned seagoing sailboats, and these were the coastal folk, especially the Jutes (or giants), who made a great leap forward when they fashioned a keel and changed the standard local boat hull. Their new shape mimicked the so-called "acute elliptic" variety of plant-leaf – wide and flat in the middle, narrow and pointy at the tips. Together, the keel and hull lowered a Jutish boat's centre of gravity, protected it from crosswinds, and allowed the Jutes to tug their Germanic cousins into the club of ocean-worthy peoples.*

Even so, the first Angles, Saxons, and Jutish migrants took between twenty-four hours and two weeks to complete their journeys across the water to Britain, depending on weather and route. In the best-case scenario, Hengest's crew must have arrived after being confined round-the-clock in a vessel with no privacy, no deck, no cabins to hide in, no space even for a picnic table. Potential ran high, I would imagine, for resentments. From the hero's point of view, his status surely felt precarious amid his crew of Jutish sailors, who would have begun to question the pecking order established on dry land. A great historical slogan to this effect – H.R. Loyn's line that "a sea voyage is perilous to tribal institutions" – emerged directly from that professor's study of Angles and their colleagues, and there's every reason to believe H.R.'s insight would have pertained right from the moment the warriors shoved themselves off the European coast. From the Jutes' point of view, they laboured under an untrustworthy boss who didn't know what was going on and who (based on my understanding of Hengestness) probably refused to help with the rowing. Strong as he was, he preferred to be carried.

So much for the on-board dynamic. If the boat matched others buried in Dark Age Jutland, it measured twenty-three metres by four and carried forty people. Here's what it looked like, approximately:

* If Jutes really were giants, this would have given them an incentive to improve boat stability.

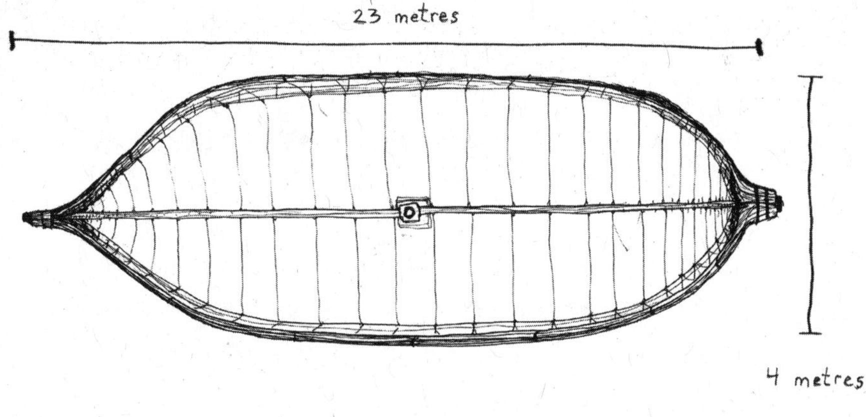

*Figure 1.4* – Hengest's boat, plan view and cross-section, 449 AD

According to the Venereal Bead and derivative historians, Hengest's landing spot was a sandy beach near a place called Ebbsfleet, decorated today with a commemorative Viking warship after an expensive and face-palming error by the regional tourist board, which confused Angles with Vikings. (The Vikings arrived several hundred years later from Norway.)

I've taken a look at the beach. The coastline has surely changed since Hengest's youth due to the melted North Pole, cliff erosion, and so on, but the gradient looks consistent enough that I can asterisk the relevant sandbar's cross-section fairly safely:

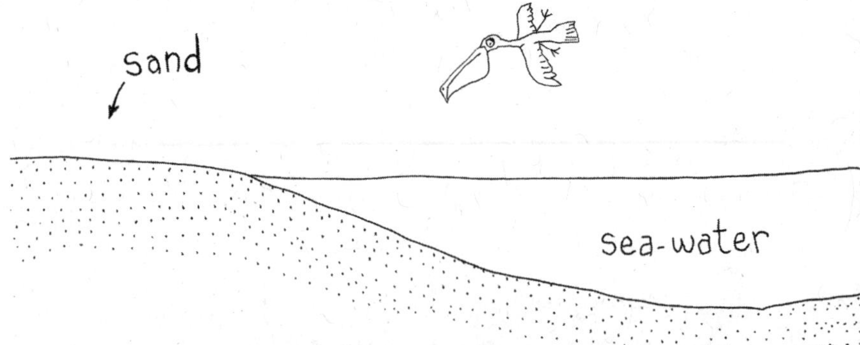


*Figure 1.5* – The landing spot near Ebbsfleet

Historians of sail infer from the shape of an ancient Jutish boat that it would make its landing bow-first onto the sand, at which moment a volunteer would jump off holding a rope and pull the craft out of the water. Thanks to Newton's Three Laws of Motion, we can reconstruct the scene in some detail.

The boat approached under oar at a speed of, say, four knots. Everyone on board had just experienced the longest voyage of their lives. While no one sensed the full global-historical significance of their arrival, any hero with an eye for marketing would know to set his feet on the ground before his colleagues did, thus giving his name pride of place in future epic poems. It's important to remember that complex forces of this sort operated alongside the so-called "simple forces," such as the momentum shown in *Figure 1.6*.

*Figure 1.6* – Angles, Jutes, and Saxons approach Britain at a speed of, say, four knots.

Newton's Third Law predicts that every action entails an equal and opposite reaction. When the vessel's slim prow shunted onto the sand, Britain resisted the new arrivals' momentum, aggravating the normal upward thrust of ground beneath a heavy object. In graphical terms, the boat's forward thrust-arrow stimulated a reverse-arrow pushing back against the prow.

Pay attention, please.

The push-back was temporary. It dwindled and drained from the prow as the boat decelerated at a rate inversely proportional to the total braking force divided by the boat's mass (Second Law, obviously). Meanwhile, the volunteer who was holding the rope and feeling eager to jump from the prow so as to single-handedly discover Britain caused an asymmetricality that would affect the boat to the tune of one gentle rotation, governed by gravity. This rotation struck a wall when ocean water returned from its displacement to push upward against the hull, leading to a rapid exchange of forces during which the volunteer might be expected to function as (i) part of the prow and then (ii) not part of the prow, with the potential result (iii), described below in *Figure 1.7*.

*Figure 1.7* – Volunteer functioning as not part of boat's prow.

Even without studying Newton's laws, an experienced sea-going Jute would foresee the *Figure 1.7* scenario long before the boat struck land. The crew should therefore have advised the volunteer to hang on tight, not climb too far up the prow, and most of all, concentrate on preparing for a jerky sequence of pushes and pulls.

This brings me to the field of psychology. Every person nurtures some potential for doing good, which we can represent like any other force. The Jutes' instinct to give *helpful* tips to a less able seaman could be the force *h*, for example. It would always be opposed by what Freud called the "destructive instinct," although his theories run deeper than needed here so I will label it simply the *asshole* instinct, or force *x*. This would have motivated a particular type of advice.

"That's right, Hengest."

"Up on the high, protruding prow is the best spot."

"Don't be a chicken, landlubber."

"Balance on the gunnel, mate. Then you can jump off the moment we stop."

"A bit further, attaboy . . . "

"Think about your first words on British soil."

And so on.

Given the aforementioned likelihood of resentments on board, based on the size of the boat, length of voyage, plus Hengest's trait of displaying stallion-like, alpha-male behaviour, I think we can safely sketch out the relative push of forces *h* and *x* on a typical Jute's mind as follows:

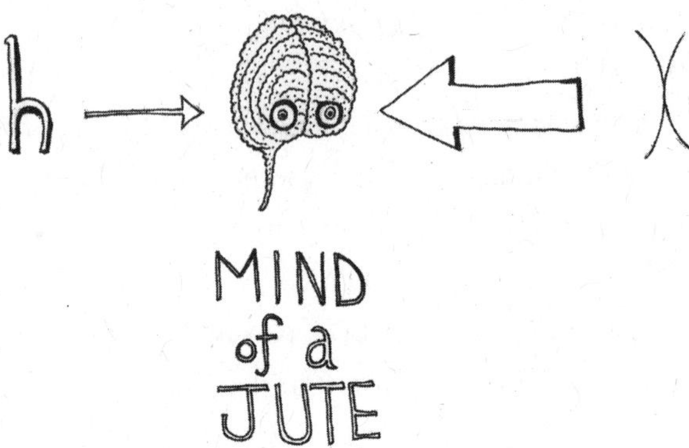


*Figure 1.8* – Instincts (helpful versus asshole) operating on the mind of a Jute, near Ebbsfleet, 449 AD

If I can assume that the Jutes were not mythical giants but Germanic pioneers of sail, and if Newton's basic laws of motion may be broadly trusted, it is a short leap from *Figure 1.8* to the conclusion that English's first word may be found in a speech bubble similar to the one shown in *Figure 1.9*.

*Figure 1.9* – The first word of English

So, where the science of linguistics asserts a permanent dead end, the art of asterisking has offered me hope or, at least, a temporary feeling of progress. The next step is to fill the bubble.

## 7. HOW TO SWEAR IN ANGLO-SAXON

When people fall off boats, a simple and near-universal brain operation occurs. It exploits a hotline from the amygdala to the speech motors, bypassing the ventral cortex, where politeness lives. It is a barbaric yawp. However, the sound of the yawp varies according to the time, place, and culture of the falling person.

Surveys have declared the most commonplace modern English yawp in the world to be "Shit!" Angles knew the word "shit" too, but probably didn't curse with it because the concept didn't tickle their deep fears. When people invite panic without actually being in danger, such as by watching a scary movie or poking a small cat, they trick the brain's inner apothecary into releasing a shot of pleasure-juice, roughly equal in power to a good laugh. This is why citizens of prudish countries exclaim things to do with sex and naked bodies, which are charged images even for individuals who consider themselves liberated (one's amygdala never really grows up). Similarly, in places recently ruled by Catholic priests, even atheists get a thrill from shouting "Jesus Christ" or "Damnation" or "Tabernacle!"

Of the roughly sixty thousand words of English surviving from the first millennium, none occurs in the context of an unbridled fuck-it fit. Language experts have blamed this absence on censorship, illiteracy, librarian-bias, monk-bias, poetic fashion, and bad luck. Finding the first word of English therefore takes some triangulation, tacking first toward a major taboo haunting Angle warrior culture, and then back toward Hengest's vocab. A logical formula lays out a plausible route:

As *fuck!* is to sex,
and *shit!* is to body products,
and *Jesus Christ!* is to blasphemy,
so **** is to the great Angle-warrior taboo.

According to a scholar named Geoffrey Hughes, ancient Angles didn't need gods or sexual repression to scare themselves. They believed in the magic power of plain words. Hughes looked at how warriors swore their vows, and he felt "the most striking and paradoxical feature of all is that oaths are uttered without appealing to any force above or beyond the speaker's own sense of honour."* This habit, based on a social prejudice that one's actions ought to match one's words, has largely died out today except in highly traditional enclaves such as the realm of bar pool where, according to the strictest practitioners, a player must call his or her shots in advance, no flukes. If I promise to bounce the red stripe off the back wall into the side pocket, and the shot succeeds, my name will enjoy instant renown and – in exceptional cases – earn itself a spot in future epic poems. However, if

* From his book, *Swearing: A Social History*.

the shot fails, even by potting three different balls, I lose my turn, or forfeit the game, or – in really egregious cases – pick up everybody's tab. A similar scheme apparently governed the warrior culture of Hengest's day.

It's possible that the epic poets handed Hughes and other scholars a bogus lead, and ancient warriors never really cared about oaths. The surviving parchments might be hiding the fact that Angle warriors threw fuck-it fits exactly as modern English-speakers do. But we can only work from what's been written down, even as we venture into unwritten spaces. Below is a list of English's ten oldest words with close ties to oath-taking, based on dates provided by the *Oxford English Dictionary*. In a purely literal sense, these might be called the language's first "swear words."

| **Old English** | **Modern English** |
|---|---|
| wreak | *avenge* |
| answear | *respond/swear against* |
| hate | *promise/call by name* |
| argh | *break oath/run away/coward/enemy* |
| yelp | *boast* |
| beot | *another boast* |
| wed | *pledge* |
| warlock | *oath-breaker* |
| oath | *oath* |
| truth | *oath (of fealty)* |

Any of the above might earn a grown-up warrior's frown if a kid spoke them flippantly. However, popular swear words like "fuck," "shit," and "Jesus Christ" usually share the common feature of naming a substance in particular need of control by the authorities. Regarding "fuck," if I am the sex police, some cunnilingus and heavy petting can escape notice without damage to my reputation, but when fucking goes unchecked, I will begin to look impotent. Babies will scream that society is beyond my command. "Shit" bothers the authorities where dirt and body-products have become a reigning taboo, perhaps due to a recent plague, or a power group's claim that humans are magical clean spirits rather than rude animals or machines. If I am the police force in such a place, I can let some piss and blood disappear into the carpet, but when the shit piles up everyone will see the failure of my pretense to ultimate control. And if I'm the church police in a Christian society, respect for the prophet on the cross is the bellwether of my power. If Jesus can be insulted without consequence, the whole congregation will wonder who's in charge.

Only three of the ten ancient swear words listed above meet the demands of naming the authorities' kryptonite. As mentioned, ancient Angle warriors depended on dinner invitations, and paid for their meals with loyalty to the host, which they guaranteed by means of their "truth," the oath of fealty. This vulnerable gesture needed to have the power to keep people close to a warlord or chief, even in the face of other interests, such as a desire to run away after dinner and skip out on defending the dinner-provider from other thugs, thereby dirtying up a system well-suited to the needs of rich people. A warrior who failed to treat the loyalty oath as a piece of precious magic was sticking dynamite into society's central bulwark. Therefore, the word "truth" might be more charged than a mere generic "oath" or "yelp."

Two other words, "argh" and "warlock," evoke the same spectre of a totem in peril, but from the other direction. Warlocks could later be magicians or wizards, but in Angle times the name meant a devil, an evil-doer, or most literally, a truth-denier – the syllable "war" is also the "ver" in "verify" and "verisimilitude," pronounced in a different accent, while "lock" is just a phlegmy way of voicing the word "lie" or "liar."

"Argh" began its life as an adjective ("vile, sinful, or likely to flee"), expanding over its career to serve as noun, verb, and occasionally an adverb meaning "in terror," as in, "Saint John quakèd argh."* When the word showed up in documents toward the end of the first millennium, it already seemed ho-hum, and weakened over the centuries into a mild term for feeling generally unsure. In 1728, "argh" made one of its final appearances before retiring to be a comical word for cartoon characters. "Dear Jenny," wrote the Scottish poet Ramsay, "I wad speak and yet I *argh*." If Jenny lived in a region where people had already stopped using the old word, she probably worried for a split second that Ramsay had been assassinated in the act of writing.†

Truths, warlocks, and arghs might all prick at Hengest's subconscious fears and motivate the first word of English.

* From a poem written in 1333 AD by William of Shoreham. "Quaked" means *trembled* (like an earthquake), not *quacked* (like a duck or charlatan).

† Perhaps Ramsay's attacker posted the letter for him, out of respect.

None are purely arbitrary answers to the riddle. However, we can do better than pick among them at random. After Geoffrey Hughes mapped out where swear words usually come from, he looked at their demises. It's a common story. The aged creatures, which are fearsome and awe-inspiring at the heights of their careers, descend through a stage of irrelevance into a final state of silliness. The falling action may have begun today for "fuck," "shit," and even "cunt," with "damn," "piss," and "bloody" having travelled further along the way, and "drat," "gosh," "golly," "gadzooks," and "zounds" safely through to the dumb zone.

The word "argh" turned silly, whereas "truth" grew to name today's most widely admired concept. "Warlock" took a special job in the fantasy role-playing community but did not become overtly ridiculous. "Argh," if it has retained any substance, is now a synonym for "fuck" or "drat" or sometimes "ouch," all of which fit neatly into Hengest's speech bubble. If I rewind the word's fall from power and extrapolate a dotted line past its debut in the written record, assuming a steady rate of momentum, its heyday should have occurred somewhere in the middle of the first millennium, squarely where I have been looking for our language's start-point. To echo Dr. Crystal's words: we'll never know for sure, but in my opinion *this* is as close as we can get to the origins of English.

"Argh!" said Hengest, his mouth full of sand. Despite all its cultural baggage, the word itself functioned as an empty sign, pointing nowhere. Hengest didn't think of cowardice, oath-breaking, or running away, any more than a modern person who yells "Fuck!" literally means, "Have sex!"

Next came more English words. I suppose some of them might be on the top-ten list of old swearing terms.

"Yelp!" Hengest might have muttered, flippantly. The sense of a sacred boast couldn't have been further from his mind.

A wave washed toward Britain. The now aimless asshole forces operating on the minds of the Jutes would, all things being equal, have transmuted into laughter. Even Horsey could have joined in. At some point, Hengest stood up and removed whatever had wrapped itself around his loins (a strand of sea-kelp, probably). Whether the word "truth" passed his lips is a matter for speculation, as are his next few actions, though one should always assume he behaved Hengestly, perhaps throwing aside the rope without pulling the boat ashore, then stomping up the beach of Ebbsfleet while muttering more curses, empty vows, vain oaths, and, you know, rfshft.

## 8. PUNS, 450 AD

A language is an accumulation, a nimbus, a gathering, a perfect storm. It is not just a dialect with an army and a navy. Yiddish, for example, is a language. However, the story of English contains militaries and, at times, tucks itself into their slipstream. If Hengest had hurt his wrist and lost his sword skills in 449 AD, perhaps the Celtic-speakers on the island could have stuck it out, at least until the Vikings came. We could all be speaking Swedish, and so on.

Once the belligerent jocks have opened a door and shoved a newborn culture through, they become ancillary, and the real opus of language-making begins. It usually relies on mothers and mild-mannered uncles who speak to the children. Other crucial parts, sung and unsung, pertinent or seemingly irrelevant, must be performed by all personality types, by the stoners and the slackers, the preps and skids, and most especially, the squares.

"Hengest, I've thought of something," said Horsey while giving his brother a piggyback on their brand-new island.

"Umph," the hero probably said.

"Back on the beach, if you'd sworn with that one about avenging, you know, the verb 'wreak.' It was first on the list. . . ."

"Hmm?"

Hengest was probably riding Horsey up a sand path from Ebbsfleet to meet an encampment of Britons. Following on foot, I presume, came the Saxons, Jutes, and other Angles, including Horsehair. It's possible that a British scout led the way, having been dispatched to check out the newcomers who were camping illegally on farmland beside the beach. These are roughly the circumstances as reported by the Vulnerable Bead.

"'Wreak' is more authentically spelled 'wrecan,'" Horsey persisted, I expect. He perhaps heaved his brother higher on his back for comfort. "So you could have made a pun because you're a wretch, spelled 'wrecca.' Remember, from that poem?"

"Gnrgnr," said Hengest, or something equally awake-sounding.

"Wretch meaning an epic hero, of course," Horsey added, quickly. "So you *could* have said – Hengest? – you could have said, 'ic wrecca me wrecan,' you know, 'I, the wretch, will avenge myself.'"

How Horsey learned about the use of "wrecca" in *Beowulf* is an insoluble mystery, or at least a complex one that would require an understanding of dark matter. It didn't bother Hengest, though. The hero's nose rested on his brother's helmet. He snored in two short bursts.

"I just think punning in Anglo-Saxon is sort of cool," said Horsey, though he must have realized he was talking to himself.

Puns come in two varieties: harmless and dangerous. Horsey just indulged in a harmless pun on the Angles' way toward an encounter with island residents. When the meeting took place later that day, the natives may have fallen victim to an example of the dangerous sort. Years of Roman colonial government brought civilization, begetting peace, begetting education, begetting Latin lessons, begetting mild cultural affectations and continental airs, begetting people who liked to pursue snobbish interests of unclear utility and thereby, you know, self-realize or whatever. All well and good until the barbarians come. The nickname "Welsh" didn't apply to people from the north, whom the Angles called Scots, Picts, or Dalriadans, among other names. From Hengest's point of view, a Welsh Briton was a pushover. As recorded by Geoffrey of Monmouth, the hero's opening remarks to the natives imply he also saw them as pathetically gullible. He tried the following speech on them:

> The reason of our coming is to offer our services unto thee or unto some other prince. For we have been banished from our country, and this for none other reason than for that

> the custom of our country did so demand. For such is the custom in our country that whensoever they that dwell therein do multiply too thick upon the ground, the princes of the divers provinces do . . . cast lots and make choice of the likeliest and strongest to go forth and seek a livelihood in other lands, so as that their native country may be disburdened of its overgrown multitudes . . . [and] they did appoint moreover us twain brethren, of whom I am named Hengest and this other Horsa, to be their captains, for that we were born of the family of the dukes. Wherefore, in obedience unto decrees ordained of yore, have we put to sea and under the guidance of Mercury have sought out this thy Kingdom.
>
> —from *The History of the Kings of Britain*

History's broad curve shows a *drip-drip* defeat of the Ancient Britons after they unwisely believed Hengest's story – a foreign prince! Here to serve us! Chief Vortigern instantly hired the hero to be their battle-beast and see off the northern bullies, who were always ruining everything.

An etymological tic may help explain the Britons' daft choice to welcome Hengest and his soldiers. In the local Welsh dialect known as Ancient Brythonic, the word "hen" meant "old," and "cest" meant "belly." The two words had probably never been combined before, but a Brythonic rule about consonants (obeyed in Welsh speech today) dictated that, if they did join up, the *c* of "cest" would need to become a *g*. Therefore, while "Hengest" flattered the hero as a stallion in his own language, it sounded like "Oldbelly" to the

British leaders. This surely amused them and, as proven by the world's most terrible politicians, nothing is more lethal than a thug who has been mistaken for a bit of fun.

"Chief Oldbelly is a dear, simple creature," announced Vortigern, king of the Britons. (He had no right to mock. His name meant "Supreme Leader," a supremely ridiculous thing to be called, especially during early childhood.)

"And so *honourable*, in a savage sort of way," agreed one of Vortigern's civilized colleagues. "How wonderful is his warrior's code!"

"Indeed," said Vortigern. "And now that he's sworn his little oath, he'll be as loyal to me as my own ass!"

Ironically, the word "ass," meaning a donkey, is one of very few Ancient Brythonic terms to have survived the Dark Ages and entered modern English. Things were looking good for it until the Americans absent-mindedly parked their slang term for "bum" right on top.

Welsh legends don't blame Vortigern's poor judgment on mere gullibility and arrogance. They suspect sex. A Danish scholar working in 1605 recorded a folk memory about what happened one night, soon after the Angles arrived, when Horsehair caught Vorty's eye.

> As this Lady was very beautiful, so was she of a very comely deportment, and Hengest having invited King Vortigern to supper, at his now builded Castle caused that after supper, she came forth of her Chamber into the King's presence, with a cup of gold filled with wine in her hand, and making in very seemly manner a low reverence unto the King, said with

> pleading grace and countenance, in our ancient language, *Waes heal hlaford Cyning.*"*
>
> — From *The Restitution of Decayed Intelligence*, by Richard Verstegan

Horsehair's reputation suffers from the one-track minds of male historians, who have generally paid attention to her only when she was shaved and looking her best. In the above scene, she was an angel, nice but dull. To be fair to Richard Verstegan, he did allow Horsehair to be a whore too.

> Of the beauty of this lady, the King [Vortigern] tooke so great liking that he became exceedingly inamoured of her, and desired to have her in marriage, which Hengest agreed to upon condition that the King should give unto him the whole Country of Kent.
>
> —*The Restitution of Decayed Intelligence*, a few lines later

As a result of this deal, Horsehair married the British leader, who already had two children from a previous hook-up, giving Hengest's sister-daughter the new role of step-mother to Ancient Britain's young princes, named Vortimer and Catigern. Hengest took the southeastern province of Kent as his kingdom, where he was supposed to settle down like a good father-brother-in-law, and only emerge to visit Vorty and Horsehair for supper once in a while, maybe fix things for them around the house, kill a few pesky Scots,

* "Wassail, Lord King." The word *wassail* was like saying, "What's up?"

then politely say his goodbyes and leave the Britons alone without overstaying his welcome. Vortigern ought to have looked up "Hengesty" in a dictionary. It did not mean what he wanted it to mean.

## 9. TIME AND PACE, 450 TO 470 AD

Swordfights, killings, arms cantilevering upward as their restraining tendons are sliced apart on one side only, these fine brushstrokes blur into mush on the canvas of English. To get the full picture, data must be crunched, images compressed, the operatic cycle of battles reduced to a tinny noise.

When Hengest had cut down every Pict in sight, his contract was complete, yet he carried on working. He tore apart anyone he met, including Britons, then demanded more roast chicken (or whatever) at the end of each day. If this was typical Hengest behaviour, it's a wonder the northern Europeans didn't boot him overseas sooner than they did. Vortigern tried to defend his father-in-law's actions, arguing that Chief Oldbelly couldn't be blamed for murderous thuggery because it came naturally to him. But in 455 AD, six years after Hengest's arrival, the poor Welsh folk finally lost patience. Oral histories recalled how the supreme leader's own sons, Vortimer and Catigern, led their people into war against the immigrants, fighting four significant battles. The graph below sums up what happened in terms of the volume of blood spilled between the Welsh and Angles during this period, which amounts to approximately the opening one per cent of English's existence as a language.

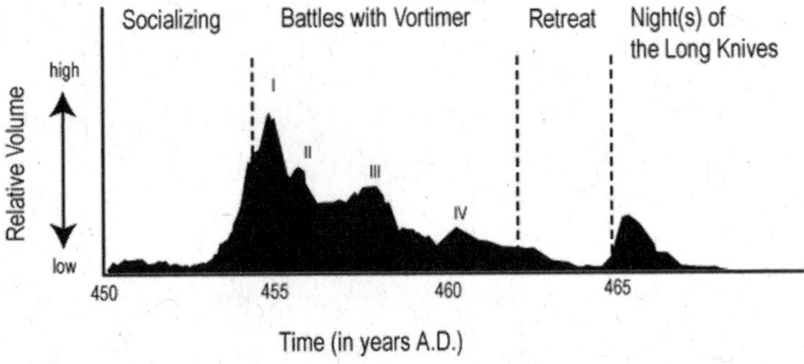


*Figure 1.10* – Anglo-Welsh relations (by spilled-blood volume)

The first battle wrung the most blood from both sides, and it contains the saddest pixel of all. Horsey took an arrow in the chest.

"Hengest!" he groaned, setting his brother gently down from their last piggyback together. "Alas, I am wreaked!"

"Argh!" Hengest roared, in all likelihood.

"If only I *could* run away," Horsey gasped (perhaps). "Oh no, wait. You meant the swear word. Ah, ugh, plug."

And then he was gone. He left only the lightest mark on history. The Vulnerable Bead wrote about a stone monument to Horsey that sat for a while on a hill near the battlefield. The *Anglo-Saxon Chronicle* gave the nerd's death a cursory mention in their entry for 455 AD, while focusing on the hero's actions. "His brother Horsa being there slain," said the *Chronicle*, "Hengest afterwards took to the kingdom with his son Oisc."

That's the first written mention of Oisc. He was probably a toddler but scholars have struggled over the dates and existences of Oisc and another child named Octa, since the histories of Kent have muddled up their relation to Hengest.

The *Chronicle* and the Bead both state that Oisc was Hengest's son, with Bede naming Octa as a grandson. A Welsh history and another local record of Kent's kings reverse this, recording Octa as the son, and Oisc the grandson. Modern experts tend to shrug their shoulders or flip a coin, but in doing so they overlook a third possibility – all of the ancient sources might be telling the truth, *if* the boys' mother was Horsehair. She was approximately fourteen years old when she left home in 449 AD, under Hengest's supervision. The only motives for refusing to believe Oisc and Octa were simultaneously the hero's sons, grandsons, and nephews would be our faith that Horsehair had no Electral perversions to match her father's Oedipal ones, and that Hengest was morally incapable of impregnating his own sister-daughter. This claim rests on no evidence. Rather, it contradicts the knowledge we already have. Assuming that Hengest persisted in his Hengestness (as I understand the word), Oisc and Octa ought to be asterisked as brothers. As well as each other's uncles.

The hero's next move caused less factual controversy but more lasting rancour, at least among the Welsh. He vowed to avenge his brother, and then, in a rare gesture of politeness, lived up to the oath. He clipped Prince Catigern's head off its shoulders, and the war against Vortimer then settled into a blood feud, chugging on for years. Welsh legend states that after the waves of violence crested four times, Vortimer finally succeeded in driving the Angles all the way back to the coast, where they scrambled into their boats. Few non-Welsh historians trust this version, but considering all that Wales has put up with in the story so far, I think we should grant its people the consolation of almost beating the English, once upon a time. What ruined the Welsh victory, the ancient Welsh poets alleged, was Horsehair. A historian named Wace, who was French but a Celtic sympathizer, wrote the story down in the twelfth century:

> Rowena, that evil stepmother, caused Vortimer, her husband's son, to be poisoned, by reason of the hatred she bore him.
>
> —*Roman de Brut*, by Wace

The Ancient Britons had mistaken Horsehair just as they had underestimated Hengest. She wasn't merely an angel and a whore – she was a wiley witch too. After Prince Vortimer puked and died in front of her, she sent word to the Angles on their boats, telling them to return to shore. Then, in her sneakiest move yet, Horsehair invited everybody who was still alive to dinner, including Vortigern, Hengest, all the British nobles, all the Angles, the Saxons, and if they existed, the Jutes. At dinner sometime between the main course and dessert, the English-speakers pulled out hidden weapons and stabbed the Britons dead.

These events have turned the whole male-voice choir of Wales against Horsehair. For centuries, Celtic storytellers idealized the murdered Vortimer as a hotshot who could have ruled the world if Horsehair hadn't spiked his drink. In poems, the English became "cyff Rhonwen," an insult meaning "Rhonwen's breed." As late as 1700, a Welsh nationalist writer named William Morris felt motivated to nickname Horsehair "y biswail," which means "the cowshit."

Many writers doubt that Horsehair's deadly dinner, the famous Night of the Long Knives, really happened. The number of victims sounds unrealistic. Three hundred British leaders died, old stories say, and although killing so many in one evening might be possible, the thought of *cooking* for them all, using Dark Age kitchen tools, tests even my suspension of disbelief. Surely the tale has undergone compression in the rumour mill, with the actual events filling several evenings – a fortnight of long knives at least, and more likely, months of them.

The chart of bloodshed that I showed earlier depicts a two-dimensional tranche from Hengest's triumph. To gain depth perception, we need another point of view. I have therefore asterisked the sound of the Anglo-Celtic relationship based on the dominant events that took place during the same period as before, using a standard spectrum graph to show high and low noises at various strengths. The resulting artwork tunes our attention to a note of poignancy that was missed by the first chart.

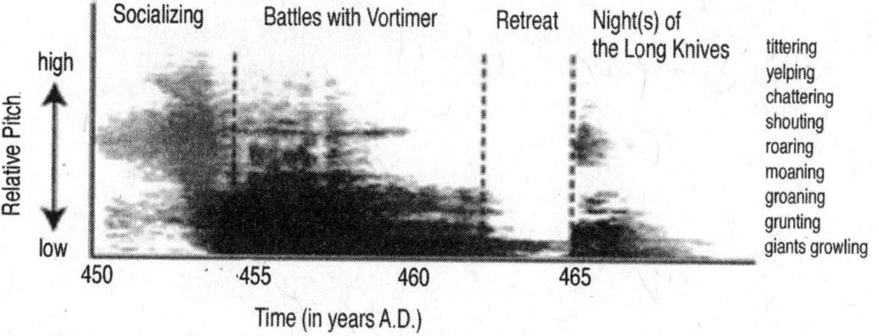


*Figure 1.11* – Anglo-Celtic relations (by sound)

The darker patches show where the sound of Angles and Britons interacting was probably most intense. A shocking coincidence, ignored by scholarship until now, will immediately catch the eye of those who have worked in the control booth of a talk-radio station. Placed one atop the other, the two charts precisely resemble a studio monitor set up to display volume and frequency readings at the moment when a radio host or guest utters a three-part noise ruled unacceptable for broadcast in America:

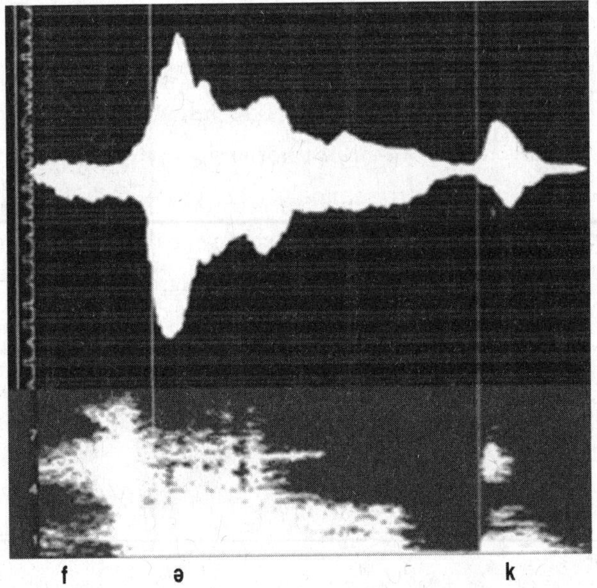


*Figure 1.12* – Studio-monitor capture, showing waveform and spectrum for /fək/

The initial /f/ sound is, on a larger scale, much like the noise of tittering and dinners. It sends higher frequencies to the engineer's spectrometer but less intense noise. When the word bursts into the vague, lazy vowel known as "schwa," marked by the symbol /ə/, the spectrometer becomes crowded around the low frequencies. By coincidence, the sound is roughly what a warrior will say as he comes to terms with his blood loss. The final /k/ sound consists of a small high hiss and a medium-sized, deeper vibration. The same could be said for a mixture of socializing and death groans (perhaps followed by giants tiptoeing away). Overall, the spectrograph pattern is how a customer-service robot can tell that you are swearing into your telephone.

For those many word-lovers and philologists who are frustrated by the lack of a proven origin for "fuck," the coincidence between these charts offers a strange new line of inquiry, which may also tantalize people curious about higher forms of intelligence. It looks as though, within a special frequency band measured over an extremely long timespan during the fifth century, the word "fuck" may somehow have been spoken by – what? The land itself? Father Time? The very historical period in which Ancient Brythonic gave way to the forces of English? It's a highly mysterious concept, far more disturbing than Horsey's brief bouts of clairvoyance, and I think it cries out for further study (studies *plural*, that is) with no expenses – including dinner expenses – to be spared.

## 10. HENGEST, CURSED, 473 AD

Something has been bothering me about my hero. The average life expectancy for a language is, ballpark, two thousand years. For a human, less. Now that I think of it, this might be another reason why stories of English usually lack a protagonist, quite apart from that stuff I said earlier about linguists ruining the plot with science envy and artlessness. If Hengest died peacefully in his mid-seventies, he leaves me with a substantial chunk of English to get through without him, specifically, everything between about 500 AD and 2020 AD, which contains some of the best moments.

Only *if* he died, though. He passed through pre-medieval history's trusted sources without chalking up a death scene, which is a strange omission for a founding figure. The ninth-century *Anglo-Saxon Chronicle* managed to confirm the 455 AD killing of Horsey, who otherwise didn't register. It found nothing about Hengest's end. Storytellers often conclude that Hengest must have died before his son and/or grandson Oisc took charge of Kent in the year 488, but this is just editorializing, shooting from the hip.

"Hengest's actual death is not recorded so it seems likely that it is a peaceful one," writes the historian Peter Kessler, for instance, in his comprehensive work, *The History Files*.

"Likely" is a fine word. One must, however, be vigilant for boring-bias. When police work leads to a body, the detectives always ask if anyone wanted to murder the person in question. In the same way, when I come upon the lack of a body, I wonder if some malicious party sought to prevent its corresponding death. Consider the following:

1. Hengest's final mention in the *Anglo-Saxon Chronicle* occurs at the year 473 AD. The Ancient Britons are reported to have "fled like fire" from him.

2. Like all Celtic cultures, the Britons knew two main forms of resistance – military and druidic.
3. I would asterisk that, in defeat, those Celts hated Hengest.
4. Military defeat plus hatred equals a good time to fall back on one's secondary form of resistance.
5. In druidry and shamanism, the most vindictive thing you could do was issue someone a binding curse, called a "tynged." The word literally meant "fate."

The only surviving fragments of Ancient Brythonic writing are personal names on curse tablets. For a curse to work, it needed to exploit a name's power and ideally tailor a cruel fate to suit the intended victim. In *The Lord of the Rings*, Tolkien's giant tree-man character scolds some hobbits for revealing their names to a stranger, alluding to a fear of Celtic cursing and the mechanism of turning a name against its bearer. Semi-literate amateur Welsh folk might cast their spells simply by sticking a pin through an enemy's name scratched onto a piece of wood, which they dropped into a magic well. Professional druids could do better by welding a stronger bond between the curse and cursee. For instance, in Hengest's case, they could graft their magic onto his name's components, "old" and "belly," then inscribe the bind-words as runes onto a small writing surface and tie it with special knots to his possessions, clothes, or better still, his body.

That the Welsh druids felt unmoved to curse Hengest, or that they would fail to exploit the vulnerabilities of his name – both appear ridiculous premises when exposed, yet they underlie the conclusion that the hero "seems likely" to have enjoyed a gentle, unnoticed death in his dotage. It is also likely, *more* likely, that the druids did indeed curse him before they fled into the hills, that Hengest woke up one morning amid the leftover dirty dishes and corpses from another long evening of long knives, yawned, scratched himself, and discovered on his wrist a bracelet consisting of braided twine and a roe-deer's knucklebone with funny writing on it. The hero probably assumed it came from a girl.

"To Hengest, the Stallion," he said, pretending to be able to read.

He would have chuckled, no doubt, and rifled through his mental logs to figure out which rape victim had taken a shine to him. Since we don't have this roe bone today, we obviously cannot read the engraving. However, extrapolating from what's known about druidery, I can sketch the outline of a temporary stand-in for the sake of progress.

In the myths of Christianity and Islam, everlasting life counts as the ultimate reward. You can either gain it metaphorically (by ascending to heaven) or literally (by drinking from the Holy Grail). The flip side is that everlasting life can also be the ultimate punishment, if you are sent to hell. The option is available to one's metaphorical spirit alone, not to the literal self with its knee problems, bunions, anxiety condition, smoker's cough, lactose intolerance, rfshft. But the druids weren't limited on this score. For them, sentencing Chief Oldbelly to an eternal life in the literal sense perfectly turned the hero's name against him, binding him to the horrible *tynged* of endless old age and an interminable belly that would continue to feel hungry after his body weakened, when he could no longer threaten people with a sword to get another dinner. Unlike in the legends of Sisyphus on his hill or Prometheus on his rock, the bringer of English wouldn't even have the comfort of a permanent home. He could hardly rule Kent, in this condition. He'd be condemned to wander in order to find income, flee from landlords, and overcome breaks in cash flow due to the cyclical nature of the national economy. All these punishments could be inflicted with a simple curse, a name bound to a fate.

If only Horsey had lived to acquire a nerdy interest in dying languages. He could have translated whatever words were on the knucklebone and warned Hengest to cut the knots, cast the cursed bracelet into the sea or bury it in an urn. Instead, Hengest was trapped, a wretch in every sense of the word, and as he grew older and older, he probably treasured the trinket as a souvenir of his days as a macho sexual predator. He would always keep it with him. Ingeniously cruel! If true, the asterisked curse would explain the lack of Hengest's death notice in the *Chronicle*. It would also require an update to the definition of "Hengesty":

(j) construed or contrived to be immortal
(k) geriatric and hungry (cf. Brythonic **hengest* "oldbelly")

Tolkien's warning haunts me anew. "In this peculiarly difficult line of enquiry, one has frequently to begin with a temporary theory." How prophetic, his pun on temporariness, meaning both that one's theories may not last forever and that they must pertain to time, just as a "necessary" theory pertains to need, a "voluntary" one to desire, a "mercenary" one to reward. Much depends on a double meaning, as Hengest very slowly found out.

PART TWO

# *Rise of the Poets*

## I. THE FIRST POEM, 660 AD

After 473 AD, Hengest's steps through history become what an etymologist would call "obscure." It's one thing to suspect that the hero's life continued past the point at which ancient records stop mentioning him. It's something apart to figure out where he went.

We can assume his body aged normally. Muscles stiffened like dry rubber, joints fused, and his sword-fighting prowess sapped away. English balladeers turned to celebrating younger bucks such as Wight, the legendary first Saxon chief of the Isle of Wight, and Stuff, who was Wight's brother. History does not remember what Stuff did. However, in the mid-sixth century he became some sort of big deal, and the attention paid to new heroes like this one surely bothered the Stallion's ego. The day Hengest said goodbye to his weapon would have been particularly hard, I imagine. *Beowulf*'s author called it "Hildeleoma, a sword famous among the Jutes," underlining Hengest's former status – a named sword was the warrior equivalent of a named chair at a university. Selling Hildeleoma for seed money to start a small business might make sense, but seems too cerebral-cortexy for the hero of English. It'd be more in character if he slammed the tool down, angered at some reminder of his weakness, or, even more pathetically, if he unleashed ex-alpha-male rage on an inanimate object, perhaps a large rock, only to provoke mockery from onlookers by losing his weapon in the duel.

Now, on that point, I have a lead. Stories abound of an unusual old man who haunted the woods during the Dark Ages, and he was indeed linked to an abandoned and uniquely desirable sword, wedged into a boulder. Time pinned the tale to a bricolage of adventures based on a wizard named Merlin, though folklorists wonder about the man's true identity. Some think "Merlin" was code for the Welsh king Ambrosius, a charismatic Che Guevara-like icon for Celtic diehards. Ambrosius's fans spread a rumour that he'd retired to a private home high on Mount Snowdon, where the pure air helped him far outlive the usual human expectancy. Many tales imply Merlin wasn't *Homo sapiens* at all, but a magical soul left over from the epoch of gods and giants (or Jutes). Like Hengest, he straddled the genres.

Whoever Merlin was, he behaved strangely. In popular treasuries, such as Geoffrey of Monmouth's *Life of Merlin*, the character shape-shifts, bursts out from behind trees to scare people, and shows up in two places at once. More poignantly, he keeps reintroducing himself to the same people, perhaps a symptom of chronic memory loss or the condition known as "prosopagnosia" (face blindness), although the confusion might not have been Merlin's alone. We don't know how many geriatrics wandered the British woodlands back then, talking to themselves and shouting nonsensical beliefs at bystanders. The wizard who led King Arthur to the sword in the stone could have been a different fellow from the so-called Merlin who, elsewhere in folk history, grew so hungry he ate moss and raw turnips and competed with wild boars for his food, or the Merlin who tried to blackmail the Welsh queen Ganieda when she cheated on King Rydderch. And so on. Dozens of these anecdotes survive, inspired by any number of elderly gentlemen in real life, all of them playing the angles and trying to score a handout, a payoff, or a dinner invitation. He may well have been Ambrosius in one scene, Hengest in another, and later on – who knows? – the Ancient Mariner, hopelessly lost in time and space.

The governments of mature societies slip help to homeless seniors via outreach workers, shelters, the public library system, etc., but in the Dark Ages, the wastrels could rely only on the mercy of churchgoers and the gullibility of wealthy strangers. Both resources were limited and suffered from the law of diminishing returns, exerting a kind of a capillary effect on an individual, drawing him or her away from the point of origin toward fresh faces and sources of charity. Since Hengest began in the southeast, the simplest hypothesis motions him generally northwest, aligning him with a large swath of *Life of Merlin*, which steers its composite hero up the island to western Caledonia. Notably, the English language found itself sucked in this direction too, growing from the bottom-right coast to top-left over many decades as alliances of jocks, caregivers, and punning uncles sought out new people to bully, nurture, and/or embarrass. Hengest needed to confine himself to the English-speaking world so he could voice his needs to nuns and monks or declare his bamboozling Merlinic prophecies to the rich. As his language stretched its territory, so could he.

These extrapolations draw from what I already know about Hengest's person and predicament while they also add bulk to the same pile – such is the bootstrapping nature of the asterisk reality. By moving toward lowland Scotland during this period, the hero would exhibit another trait that might count as "Hengesty," at least for awhile.

(1) coinciding in some respect with the spread of English

A sharp case of déjà vu would await the hero if he emerged from a forested area onto the coastal moors at the very limits of English speech in or around the year 660 AD. All footpaths in the area led to the "Fort of the Frisians," which ought to have caught Hengest's eye, considering his life-changing experience with Hnaef and King Finn at another Frisian fort. He might have wondered for a moment if he'd turned south accidentally and somehow crossed back over to the Netherlands. Today, people know the Scottish fort by its Gaelic name, Dumfries,* now a middling city blessed

* Competing tourist brochures dispute the origin of their town name. One interpretation, "Fort of the Frisians," rivals another plausible version, a "Hill (or pile) of Friars (or Fathers)." Strong evidence of Frisian sailing trips to the region

with a spirited, chronically out-funded soccer squad. But back in the mid-seventh century, if Hengest peered inside the fortress gates, he would have found a tightly run religious community set up by one of the first millennium's most notable activists and educators, Abbess Hilda.

Hilda stars in the opening pages of the *Norton Anthology of English Literature*, urging a young cowboy named Caedmon to study history and write poems on the topic. The Venomous Bede credited the abbess with kick-starting Caedmon's career, which took off after she heard his song, "Caedmon's Hymn," a poem praising the Christian God. It's often reckoned to be English's oldest piece of creative writing.

Hilda became a sainted figurehead, giving her name to schools and colleges around the world. The Catholic hagiographies focus on how she taught Rome's religion to illiterate pagans, but the abbess's sponsorship of Caedmon implies she cared about art for its own sake too. We don't know how many schools, abbeys, and/or poetry workshops she set up, or where they were, or even how many other artists she encouraged. Her diaries, letters, and teaching materials got chewed up by Vikings. All that remains of Hilda's original output is the stonework she commissioned, in particular a couple of northern abbeys and her giant-penis collection.

The latter might be the most puzzling thing she left behind. Her penises came in all shapes and sizes, naturally, but the largest is eighteen feet high and still stands today

gives weight to the former, but evangelical friars also frequented the west coast of Scotland. Fathers likely operated in the area too. At any given moment there were easily enough of either category to form a pile or even a small hill.

near Dumfries. (It collapsed at one point and lay untouched for two centuries before Victorian archaeologists carefully revived it.) The modern cultural motif of abbesses doesn't sit comfortably beside phallic imagery, so it's no wonder the Catholic Church underplays this side of Hilda's bequest. Perhaps she never understood the symbolism of her obelisks, seeing them as mere unsexed totem poles, but it's unlikely. She was an erudite, humane history buff. I think she deserves to be presumed canny until proven ignorant. Regardless, Hilda *found* rather than *made* the genre of the stone penis, which dated back to the cock-worshipping Picts, a pagan tribe of the island's north end.

In James Fergusson's seminal opus, *Rude Stone Monuments in All Countries – Their Age and Purposes* (written in 1872), the scholar argues that Scottish pagan rocks served as dancing sites, meeting points, waymarks, and, so to speak, teaching tools. Many bore carvings, usually a date with a picture of a battle or some animals, perhaps recording an extraordinary hunt. Fergusson guessed that a shaman or other theatrical type would host lectures beside the pole, to teach locals their own history.

Abbess Hilda and her team of trained monks hitched this Pictish tradition to their own, engraving the phalluses with cartoons of Christ's Passion or lines of pious verse. "On the front is a cross," wrote Dr. Fergusson about one early Christianized penis, "but like all in Scotland, without breaking the outline of the stone, which still retains a reminiscence of its rude form." Some of us might now fail to spot the "reminiscence," living as we do under a media soaker-hose of hyper-realistic pornography. Back in 1818, however, the archaeologists didn't miss it. Having hoisted the tumbled-down rock from its dormant position in a meadow at Roodwell,* near Dumfries, they tried to temper its visual lewdness by giving it an extension, with a stud inserted crosswise through the tip.

"Behold the Roodwell 'Cross'!" they announced.

Under this misnomer, the rude stone monument became a popular and educational tourist site where children could snigger and be taught to behave. Here is a photograph:

*Figure 2.1* – The Roodwell Cross

* This is the site's older spelling. A more common spelling today is "Ruthwell."

The not-really-a-cross is the best known of Hilda's old obelisks, mostly because it's engraved with "The Dream of the Rood," a rival claimant to the role of oldest English poem. The word "rood," previously spelled "rode" or "rude" (as in the medieval spiritual song, "On Rude, thow sched thy blude"), could mean a rod, pole, crucifix, or in this case, an eighteen-foot-tall dildo. Spoken in the first-person subjective voice, the rood poem tells the story of Christ's death from the point of view of the wooden crucifix. The physical object confesses to its mixed emotions. It's thrilled, on the one hand, to have such an intimate role in the life of Jesus, but it also feels nostalgia for its early days as a tree. The poem concludes with the prophet spread-eagled on top of the rood while a crowd gathers to watch.

The English words are carved in Germanic runes on the monument's north and south faces, crammed into narrow columns on either side of the space-hogging visual art. The rood's east and west faces feature Latin phrases in the Roman alphabet, apparently unconnected to the poem. Catholic historians such as Hannah Mary Wright have viewed this bilingual, biscriptal penis as a sign of smart evangelism, helping its message reach people no matter which form of writing they understood. "The rood was raised by a Saxon," Wright concluded, "in the early days of Christianity, to communicate to beholders the God-spell that tells of peace and pardon free-bought for whosoever will come and take thereof."

Such a strategy, however, relies on a nearby literate audience worth reaching, which Hilda lacked in the seventh century. It also assumes most people didn't already know the story of Christ on the cross, but in Dumfries, they did – friars had reputedly worked the neighbourhood for ages, and the evangelical St. Columbus converted most of the locals during the mid-500s. For the illiterate Angles, Saxons, and Frisians who now lived in this area, the far more revolutionary encounter was with the written word and, on a technical level, the lyric poetic form. Perhaps, rather than exploiting words as a means to the end of teaching religion, Hilda worked the other way round, enlisting rood and Passion tale into the service of teaching people their letters. Or, for advanced students, poetry appreciation.

I feel an asterisk coming on at the very thought.

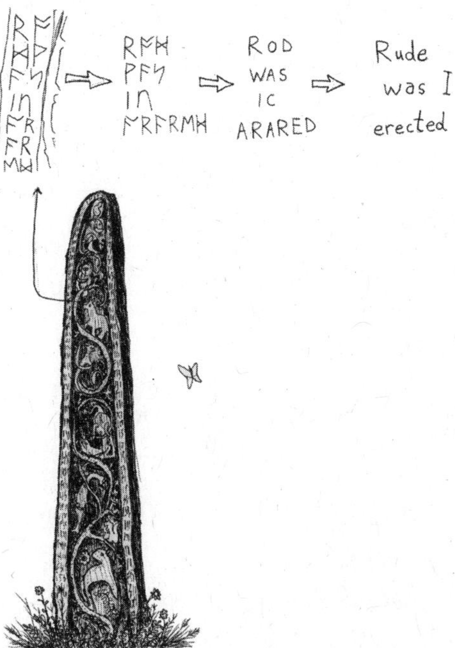


*Figure 2.2* – Poetry textbook, seventh-century Britain

## 2. THE MATURE STUDENT, 661 AD

"Today's lecture is on the poetic voice," Abbess Hilda might have said. "To warm up, as usual, we will sound out the runes. All together now."

Based on my own schooling, I expect she slapped a stick onto each rune, leading the chant from a flock of school-aged Jutes, Picts, and Frisians, plus a few nuns or friars looking to grow their skill-set, and, unless I'm very much mistaken, one extremely old man who attended mostly for the food and body warmth. I would guess his younger classmates avoided eye contact with him.

[*slap*], [*slap*], [*slap*], went Hilda's stick on the big rood.

"Arr, Ooo, Duh," came the chorus.

"Spells?"

"*Rood!*"

[*slap*], [*slap*], [*slap*], [*slap*].

"Ah, Huh, Ooo, Fuh!"

"Spells?"

"*Ahoof!*"

Before pushing this scenario further, I should mention that even if I could asterisk Hilda's whole lesson plan, it wouldn't make sense to most of us. Populated by words like "rood" and "ahoof," the English of those days barely evokes the modern version at all. A vexed issue with Old English poems is that although the words certainly need updating, a storyteller can do wrong by making them too modern, thus deceptively erasing real differences between the cultures of then and now. Often the best practice is to modernize over two stages, translating first closely then loosely, as I've done here with a verse from "The Dream of the Rood":

**Original**

*Rod* was ic arared*
*Ahof ic riicne kyningc*
*Heafunaes hlafard helda ic ni dorste*
*Bismeradu ungket men ba ergad*
*Ic was mith bloda bistimid*
*Bigoten of thaes guman.*

**Close**

Rood was I erected
A-hoofed I rightly king
Heavenly Lord, drop I daren't
Insulted us two men both conjoined

* *Rod*: pronounced "rude" in old-fashioned accents but spelled with a single *o* because English had not yet suffered a painful series of vowel movements, to be featured in Part Three: The Tongue that Ate Itself.

I was with blood besmattered
Begotten of this human.

**Loose**
I am the Rood, erect
Hoisting my true king
I dared not drop this Heavenly Lord
Men insulted us,* joined here together
I was spattered with the blood
That came out of this human.

The poem continues or begins on the reverse side of the rock. (Scholars dispute the page numbering.) As for what Hilda taught her students about the work, I dare pencil in only the broadest, most entry-level concepts in hopes of catching the mark.

"Rood was *I* erected," she might have repeated, pointing again to these runes.

Some tittering in the crowd, probably. Kids never change.

"'Rood' meaning 'a crucifix,' of course," continued Hilda. "But *this* penis is not Christ's cross, which rotted long ago. I should know because I hauled it up here myself, and any blood besmattered on it is mine or belongs to one of the Jutes who helped me. I 'hoofed' the king, says the rood. No, it didn't. Not this pole. So is it lying to us? Is it somehow telling the truth? Or perhaps we should be asking, can it tell us something *useful*? Well, what? To what purpose *might* we use it?"

* *helda ic ni dorste bismeradu*: An alternative translation is, "I wouldn't dare insult Hilda," though this has failed to gain much traction in the scholarly community.

And so on. Thanks to Hilda's tutelage, the Dumfrisians learned to tell a metaphor from a handsaw, or whatever, and most importantly, they learned to read. Events at a Frisian fort had already spun Hengest's life around. Now, if my asterisks are well placed, this second Fort of the Frisians did it again, giving the hero a new angle on what the instrument of his language could do. In a widely literate culture, knowing one's letters is just a token for entering the game, necessary but not sufficient. By contrast, in seventh-century Britain, if Hengest could interpret the mysteries of writing, he had a marketable asset, like web-dev skills, giving his Hengestiness a new flavour. He now owned something he could rent out in exchange for dinner.

> **Hengesty** *adj.* . . . (m) literate, educated, esp. in terms of having acquired some familiarity with poems

## 3. BOOKS, 850 AD

An asset only earns when there's a borrower. Hengest must have kept moving, pursuing the miniature word-rushes that sprang up around different monasteries and royal courts in the seven English-speaking kingdoms that occupied the flatter parts of the island. The hero may even have sold a few tall tales to the Venereal Bleed. But let me admit to you, who have followed me so far off the trodden path, that the old warrior could have gone anywhere in the eighth century. The period is an enigma, almost empty of historical dates, and with your indulgence I think we should skip it. My take on eighth-century Hengest is: he was often hungry, but he survived.

The ninth century is where the trail heats up, thanks to a curious anomaly and source of wonder for many English historians – "Why are we not Sexy? Or even Sex-ish?" The main kingdoms that glued themselves into England during this period were called West Sex, East Sex, South Sex, and Middle Sex, based on the word "Sexon," an old spelling of "Saxon," the label for people who claimed German ancestry but didn't self-identify as Angles, Jutes, Frisians, Half-Danes, Quarter-Danes, or giants. Since Hengest's disappearance into the woods, the Saxon brand had taken over much of southern Britain. The logical name for an amalgamated nation was therefore Sexland.

The first person caught on parchment calling the whole of southern Britain "the Angle kingdom" was King Alfred, which is mystifying because the man was a West Saxon king, not an Angle. Even the world's most exhaustively knowledgeable modern encyclopedia confesses to being stumped by Alfred's word choice. "How and why a term derived from the name of a tribe that was less significant than the others, such as the Saxons, came to be used for the entire country and its people is not known," declared the Wikipedia collective, last time I checked. King Alfred didn't even rule over the Angle-branded territories. They lay to the east of the island and, before Alfred was born, they had surrendered themselves to Norwegian Vikings. Alfred lived most of his days in the town of Winchester, West Sex, about halfway between Cornwall and Kent. He could have grown up without meeting any Angles at all.

King Alfred became so beloved by English historians that they named him "Alfred the Great." He earned the title by outgrowing the job of mere West Saxon king to achieve nationwide respect during his lifetime, and he did this in spite of his silly first name.

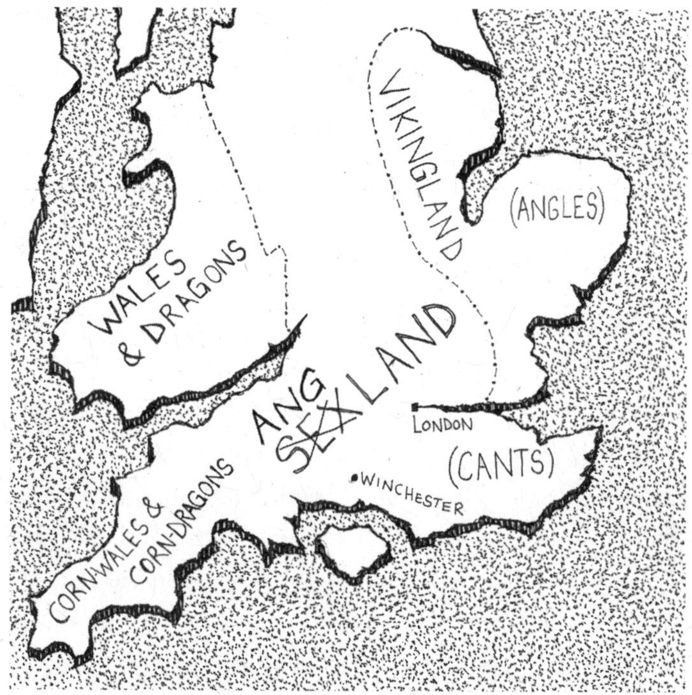


*Figure 2.3* – Angland in the late ninth century

"Alf" was the old spelling of "elf," and "red" was an English word meaning "advised." To the ears of his own people, therefore, Alfred was called "King Advised-by-an-Elf." This handicap, when placed alongside his nerdy hobbies of Latin translation, font collection, scrapbooking, and the operation of a small literary press, makes Alfred's success and popularity all the more inspiring. Winston Churchill felt moved to call him "the greatest Englishman that ever lived."

Our knowledge of Alfred comes from a biography written by a contemporary and close friend named Asser, who, albeit with hyperbole and a fawning attitude, composed the first full-length authoritative account of an English-speaking ruler's nature, upbringing, thoughts, and motivations. People rarely read the original text anymore because Asser wrote in Latin, partly to be cosmopolitan and mostly because his English wasn't very good. He grew up speaking Old Welsh, and never bothered to learn the Saxon tongue during childhood. From the vantage-point of South Wales, Angland's culture had seemed destined to die out under the weight of Celtic dominance. Asser therefore gave his book a Latin title too, *De Rebus Gestis Aelfredi*, which contains an ambiguity missing from the standard translation. In English, the word "rebus" means a kind of word puzzle but in Latin it meant "about or by things." The word "de" also means "about." (Asser probably added it for the sake of slower students in case they failed to spot that "rebus" was already in the ablative case.) So far, so good, but then comes "gestis," which may spell two different Latin words, one being a verb participle that meant "having achieved," while the other is an indicative verb in the second-person, "you passionately desire." This makes the whole title slippery. Most translators convert "rebus gestis" into a single noun with the sense of "things achieved" or simply "deeds." They gloss the book's name as *About the Deeds of Alfred* and hence, loosely, *The Life of Alfred.* However, given the tone of Asser's biography, the risqué alternative translation of *About Things You Passionately Desire of Alfred* may capture the author's intentions better.

Another problem with reading about Alfred in later editions of Asser's work is that the original was tampered with. Fake anecdotes appeared in the book, and these obscured Alfred's true greatness as a nerd. The culprits were usually people with an agenda that stood to benefit from Alfred's popularity somehow. English nationalists wanted to spread garbage about his supposedly huge military successes. Evangelicals claimed he cared deeply about God. In truth, like a studious kid giving his lunch money to bullies, King Alfred kept his enemies at bay by bribing them expensively until they left him alone for a while, and as for piety, although the king showed an early love for Christian verse, this reflected the parlous state of entertainment in those days more than any fundamental religious zeal on Alfred's part.

The best-known falsity about Alfred pushes a message that is vaguely sympathetic to the working class. It involves the man's attempt at baking. According to the legend, in the early years of Alfred's reign, the young king fled from Viking warlords who caught him unawares at one of his many houses. He wandered adrift in the marshes, sodden, shivering, and carrying the hopes and prayers of Angland in his knapsack. After several hours of this torture, Alfred stumbled into a peasant's hut where he met a woman called Peasantswife. She let the king sit in her kitchen and bake cookies while she headed out on some errands, but Alfred moped and gazed at his navel and let his cookies burn. Peasantswife returned too late to rescue things. She then found herself stuck talking the displaced ruler out of his depression. It's a tale of the mighty sunk low, which gives it pop value, and the event was once so widely taught in England that a standard textbook, Sellar and Yeatman's *1066 And All That*, renamed the king "Alfred the Cake" instead of "Alfred the Great."

The episode is pure supposition. It never appeared in Asser's writing, and while the original biography suffers from bias, its thoroughness cannot be doubted. If Alfred had ever baked anything, Asser would have lauded everything from the items' scent to their elegant poise when sitting on a plate and the dignified way in which they crumbled.

The anecdote crept into England's standard lore by way of the *Annal of Neot*, whose author had never met the king. Professional historians mistook the fiction for fact, an error usually blamed on the lax stance of one person, Matthew Parker, who was a Renaissance archbishop and scholarly jackdaw, and who produced many copies of Asser's book. He had a bad habit of copying and pasting diffuse sources into whatever format most pleased him, and this could cause problems for his readers. He carelessly inserted the *Annal* supposition into the Asser, where it remained for two hundred years, escaping notice through generations of editors, until finally, in 1848, a rigorous scholar named Dr. Petrie spotted the foreign object and removed it. By this late stage, to quote Asser's modern editors, "the damage had been done,"* and Alfred's historical reputation was forever scarred.

The best-known *genuine* story about Alfred, told in Asser's original text, lets the nerd-king's real colours shine, and it's a pity that the cake-or-cookies story has tended to eclipse it. One wet summer day, Alfred's mother sprung a competition to amuse her six children, among whom Alfred was the youngest. Holding up a small illuminated manuscript, the queen promised to award it to whichever child could memorize all the poetry written thereupon.

The older ones yawned and rolled their eyes, appropriately for their age. Alfred took the challenge head-on.

"Ooh, ooh," he gasped, touching the sky. "Please, please, let me try first!"

He had the thing down pat within the hour.

"Alfred is the winner!" said the queen, and handed him the prize to keep.

Meanwhile, the other kids had spent the time outside in the yard, setting fire to live hens using a straw fuse and hot tallow.

Asser wanted this anecdote to foreshadow Alfred's emergence as Angland's premier man of letters, and to demonstrate that the young prince always stood out among his mediocre siblings. The biographer didn't need to try so hard. Alfred's name already marked him as an exception. Apart from being advised by an elf, he was also the family's only child not to be called Ethel. His father, Ethelwulf (literally, "noble wolf"), named the first five offspring

* From *Asser's Life of King Alfred*, edited and footnoted by Drs. Keynes and Lapidge.

Ethelstan ("noble stone"), Ethelbald ("noble courage"), Ethelswith ("noble strength"), Ethelbert ("bright noble"), and Ethelred ("advised by a noble"). Hopefully, the kids were smart enough to nickname each other using the final syllables (Stan, Baldie, Swith, Bert, and Red), because the more common habit of clipping off a familiar person's name at the rear end would create chaos during team sports.

"Take the ball, Ethel."

"Thanks, Ethel."

"Pass it to Ethel!"

"Okay. Here you go, Ethel."

"Noooo! Not *that* Ethel!"

For me, though, reducing all Saxon names to their opening noises can help magically to disperse chaos by pruning down a notoriously complex family tree linking Alfred's family to the set of Danish kings and French conquerors who wrestled for control of the island during this era. By abbreviating all Ethelwotsits to two syllables, and all the Edmunds, Edwards, and Edgars to a simple "Ed," a two-hundred-year dynastic tangle can be made to fit into a single, sleek diagram that is no more convoluted than a typical organic molecule.

Regarding *Figure 2.4*, please note the presence of probable giants. I have visited and climbed Gorm the Old's grave in Jutland. It is more than forty metres high. As for King Rollo, the founder of Norman French people, he entered France from the direction of Jutland and was reputedly so large that no horse could carry him. The ground is said to have thundered under his feet.

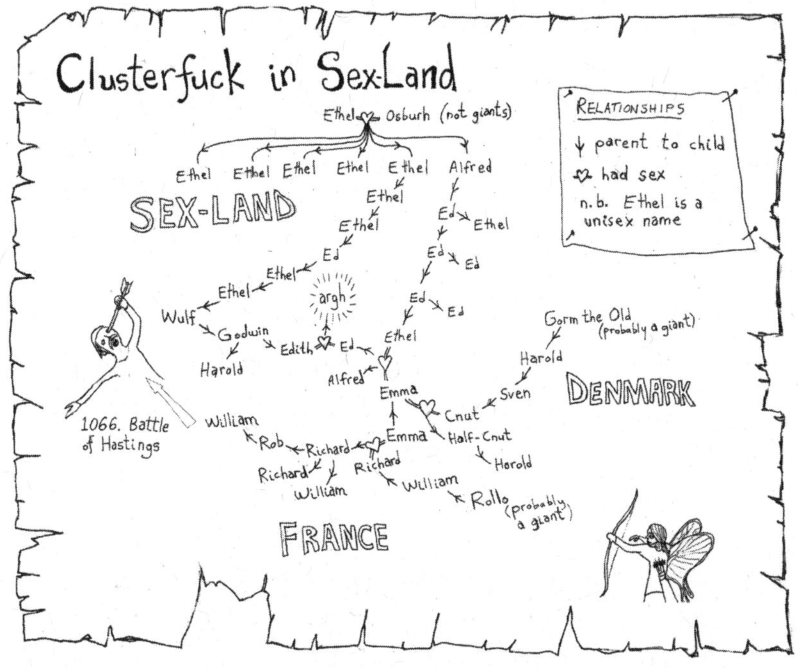


*Figure 2.4* – Clusterfuck in Sexland, 800–1066 AD

Please also note the second Emma, who was a child of the Norman French and also a mother to both Danes and Saxons. If it existed, Queen Emma's tell-all memoir, *I Married a Cnut*, would be a priceless historical document. Tragically, it doesn't. All we have is a piece of fan fiction named *The Encomium to Emma*, composed by a hack writer-for-hire, possibly a nearby monk in need of food. It is not approved for serious use by historians. As the scholar Simon Keynes put it, "the modern reader who expects the *Encomium* to provide a portrait of a great and distinguished queen at the height of her power will be disappointed, and might well despair of an author who could suppress, misrepresent, and garble what we know or think to have been the truth."

While various mediocre Ethels took turns being the West Saxon king and then dying horribly, Alfred spent his adolescence developing his inner spirit, backpacking alone through the hills between the Viking lands to the east and the Welsh lands to the west. Twice he ventured across Europe to Rome, where the young prince perked up like a cobra. He visited the Vatican, ate lunch with a real pope, and sprinted around the Coliseum pretending to be a gladiator.* When he returned home, Alfred suffered from the withdrawal symptoms that strike all travellers after they've been exposed to the world's hip zones. Boring old Sexland (West, East, or otherwise) didn't even have any dark Satanic mills yet to liven up its scenery.

After the youngest of the Ethels succumbed to acute nose-bleeding (cause: pike–in–face), Alfred took the throne. He barely got as far as drawing up a suggested reading list for his subjects before the nasty Viking army attacked the house, prompting him to flee into the woods and hide in local bakeries (or not) until the bullies rampaged on to France and left England unsupervised. When Alfred nervously returned to public view, the novice king took advantage of the climate of fear to give his kingdom a radical new set of priorities. It was a tactic straight out of what Naomi Klein calls the "shock doctrine," but with progressive aims.

"In all of Sexland there is barely one scholar who can read

* This is an asterisk-fact, but can we reasonably believe that he didn't?

Latin," declared Alfred to his people. This famous statement was his justification for spending tax money on a dream team of Latin scholars, some of whom were imported from monasteries in Belgium and Germany. The teachers came to educate the young men of West Sex.

Alfred left behind many memorable quotations, all recorded and embellished by the loyal Asser. Some stand up fairly well today.

"Even though we may reflect a good deal, we have little perfect understanding free from doubt," he said. And also: "One should understand everything according to one's intellectual capacity, given that we cannot understand everything as it really is."

Alfred's scholarly acquisitions included some of the best minds of his generation, and they bore many of the best names too. Werewulf (literally "man-wolf"), Grimbald ("fierce courage"), Plegmund ("play safe"), and John the Old Saxon. The scholars did more than teach. At a huge new royal building in Winchester, these men helped Alfred write translations, books of law, and essays on good behaviour. Individual monks had written documents before, but the new Winchester building housed the first multi-genre publishing program with a focus on English-language books. For anyone trying to make a living off the written word, Winchester was the boom town of its day.

Across the land, village priests acted the part of news magazines. They began their Sunday services with an editorial comment or sermon, followed by a calendar of upcoming market days and dances, messages from potential invaders, tips on how to get out of Hell using familiar kitchen implements, advice on gardening and life after gout, and all the usual departments. Toward the end (where some print magazines still place their dwindling classifieds sections), a priest would say something like, "Winchester House is looking for an ambitious, gung-ho, willing-to-do-anything sort of person who wants to gain experience in the thriving new media industry. Must be literate and bring his own pillow."

It only makes sense that the gossip found and attracted you-know-who.

"We can take you on, but don't expect to be compensated," King Alfred probably said to a gaunt old hero at the door one day.

"I am Hengest, the Stallion," said Hengest. "I am the founder of the English language (ignoring the rumoured presence of Frisian and Anglian forts centuries before my arrival). Surely this qualifies me for a staff job with hot dinners, dental care, massages, vacation time, and so on?"

"Yes, yes," Alfred replied (let's say). "In the ideal world, yes. But times are tight, what with paying off the Vikings and everything, and it is what it is, so all I can offer is an unpaid internship until the market picks up."

Hengest might have looked over his shoulder at the long line of malnourished warriors, monks, bards, etc., who were all ready to seize Alfred's offer if the hero refused.

"Very well," said Hengest (approximately). "I will volunteer to help you, King Alfred the Great, as we publish the first books in my language."

"Er, let's work up to that. You can start by making ten copies of this."

Even if their conversation sounded a bit different at the time, the thrust is predictable. A newbie scribe on the lowest rung of the hierarchy at Winchester would be led to a wooden desk in some alcove at the intersection of several long halls.* Possibly he shared his space with a chamber pot. On Hengest's desk would be space for three piles of parchment – (1) the foothill of scribbled notes that he was expected to copy, (2) a sheaf of blank pages, freshly tea-stained brown (as you will know if you have made parchment at home, the process involves stretching and drying a piece of goat skin, then staining it with tea to achieve the antique look), and lastly, (3) a gap waiting for the intern's output of neat manuscript pages ready for binding. The ninth-century equivalent of a modern book was a stack of cut parchment held between two thin, flat pieces of wood tied up with leather or twine. Hengest would have copied documents by hand for Winchester's prestigious scholars, working day after day, with rare breaks for gruel. At night, the homeless ex-warrior probably slept underneath his desk on the dirty oak or stone floor, propping his head on a woodblock.

Many important items might have crossed Hengest's desk for copying. One example could have been King Alfred's own translation of the classic *Consolations of Philosophy*, which included a preface written by the king himself. It featured the following sentence:

* Grand Anglo-Saxon architecture consisted mostly of halls with high ceilings propped up by the latest invention, the "leaping buttress."

> I ge-saw hoo tha chirchayn yonder all Sexking stooden mathma & booke ge-filled.
>
> —From the preface to *Consolations of Philosophy*, King Alfred, 890 AD

I like to dilute the ancient look of Old English by applying what I call the Gnu Rule. It involves pretending never to see the syllable *ge* at the beginning of a word. "Mathma" has nothing to do with mathematics, by the way. It meant "treasure." So, with a modern filter applied, Alfred's sentence would sound like this:

> I saw how the churches all over the Sex Kingdom stood treasure- and book-filled.

However, this wording does not quite match what's found in surviving copies of Alfred's *Consolations of Philosophy*, which all refer to "tha chirchayn yonder all Angleking." Lexicographers quote that phrase as the precursor to "England" becoming the accepted label for all combined Saxon domains. To encourage history to make more sense, I have penciled an asterisked word – "Sexking" – into the original, motivated by the knowledge that Alfred thought of himself as firstly a West Saxon, plus my suspicion that the truly unacknowledged legislators of the world have never been the poets so much as the copy-editors. What appear to be Alfred's own words have reached us by way of an invisible hand.

"Whoops," muttered Hengest, erstwhile Prince of the

Angles, as his pen slipped on "Sexking" and spelled "Angleking" instead.

The hero then respected the golden rule of copy-editing – be consistent – and repeated his pet error at every chance throughout Plegmund's translations of the Vulnerable Bead, as well as the interminable martyrologies and law records, Grimbald's issues of the *Anglo-Saxon Chronicle*, and at every opportunity thereafter, until a most influential piece of Winchester House Style hardened into concrete. After all, if Alfred the Great wanted to call his territory "the Angle kingdom," who had the right to correct him?

One mystery is hereby solved, and another born, because the question arises of why no one at Winchester caught and reversed Hengest's sabotage. It's a baffling proposition to think that a company would rely on free labour for vital clerical tasks without bothering to deliver proper supervision and training, or that senior editors would feel too occupied with their important roles to sweat over page proofs. Still, history demands empathy. I guess we need to remember it was a tough period for the book industry, and everyone had a lot on their plate.

## 4. MORE COCK JOKES, 885 AD

Alfred's efforts to fund a writing industry helped foster a nation's team spirit, a sense of cultural togetherness that began to glue the fragments of England into one solid piece, or so I was taught at school. Now I wonder how this worked. A few rich kids read the English version of *Consolations of*

*Philosophy*, and the most sycophantic ones might have ploughed halfway into Asser's *Things You Passionately Desire*, but that hardly amounts to nationhood. It's often true that high culture works like public radio, in that a person needn't listen to it to receive its salutary effect. But still, looking down the list of Winchester House publications, there's not much to inspire camaraderie. Except maybe one thing.

Late in the publishing house's life, long after the death of its beloved founder, Winchester House put out a book of poems, featuring most of the finest works written in the Old English language, and along with that, some penis jokes. The single surviving edition is now English's oldest physical book. It sleeps today in a glass box in the small West Saxon town of Exeter. The front cover is missing, as are the opening pages, which may once have included library catalogue information, preface, and the name of the editor(s). My tour guide in Exeter pointed out the book's triangular missing chunk, dating from when someone sliced bread on it. There are also stains and burn marks testifying to its use as a beermat and tinderbox, along with several other dents, unexplained. I heard a rumour that the Exeter rugby team lost their game ball one day and played with the Oldest Book instead. The point is, no respect.

Inside the book, beside the elegies, lyrics, liturgies, and works of avant-gardism,* are ninety-six riddles, written in the

* e.g., the "Rhyming Poem," a piece of experimentation in which the final words or syllables of each couplet correspond in terms of the vowel sounds and (if present) end-placed consonants. I imagine most readers found the technique alienating and pointlessly intellectual.

form of a "What am I?" or "What is it?" puzzle to which the answer is always "a cock." This makes them stick out in the otherwise well-behaved volume. One professor has argued they were added as bait for reluctant readers, helping to induce them to swallow the drier material. If that speculation is right then the riddles' insertion may be the most influential act ever performed by a poetry editor, since few others can claim to have used a trick of anthologizing to play midwife to a national consciousness. I have to wonder who this brave figure was. It's a pity about those missing pages.

Scholars call the poetry collection *The Exeter Book*, although this was certainly not the original title. When the Oxford World Classics series re-packaged the thing as *The Anglo-Saxon World: An Anthology*, they just wanted to sell books but may accidentally have arrived at a more authentic result. The date of first publication is also controversial. We only know that in 1050 AD, a bishop named Leofric (meaning either "boss *of* love" or "bossed *by* love") gave his copy of the book to a local church library in Exeter. The library archived Leofric's note on the gift card, which is unhelpfully vague:

| | |
|---|---|
| mycel englisc boc be<br>ge-wilcome. | *Big English book. You're*<br>*welcome.* |
| þingum* on leoðwisan<br>ge-workt. | *Work of poetry about*<br>*something.* |

**þingum:* A kinder translation is "many things," which makes Leofric seem less dumb, but is not necessarily more accurate.

This doesn't prove the book was new in 1050. From the sound of Leofric's level of poetry appreciation, he might well have re-gifted it. Experts in the art of handwriting say the anthology's scribe wrote in a square-edged minuscule style seen on other parchments from the 900s. But the editor gathered much of the poetry from the century before that, with extra space for Cyncwulf ("kin of/relative to a wolf"). He was an Angle man who fled the Vikings to seek refuge in West Sex around the time of King Alfred's childhood. Together, these clues offer a choice: (a) *The Anglo-Saxon Anthology* (or whatever they called it) was first published during King Alfred's reign and written out by a scribe with futuristic handwriting; (b) an editor who had old-fashioned poetic tastes as well as an enjoyment of penis jokes made the book in or around 950 AD, relying on other poetry collections assembled in the past; or (c) the anthology *was* fresh in 1050 AD when Leofric wrote his gift note, but the publishing process had taken two centuries from initial proposal to the book's launch party. Expanding the (c) scenario, it could be that (i) several generations of editors worked on the book, gathering poems, selecting, laying out pages, copying, adding, re-copying, or (ii) there was a single editor who ignored his deadlines and lived much longer than any normal human being.

Historians usually overlook (c) (ii). Their asterisks don't equip them with a plinth upon which it can naturally stand. For me, thanks to my prior construction of Winchester House's intern, it makes perfect sense. I've seen how internships tend to go. The poor creature toils away on garbage tasks, largely ignored, until one day an unwieldy project comes up that none of the senior editors wants to be responsible for, and, hey presto, opportunity knocks. Faced with a mountain of drivel from Cynewulf and other aspiring ninth-century poets, the likes of Grimbald and Werewulf found an excuse to dump the anthology on their lackey. But the hero went rogue. Perhaps he even started penning entries of his own. The riddles have a Hengesty flavour to them, in the sense of asserting Stallion-like attributes, disobediently crossing the line, making inappropriate expressions of sexuality, rfshft.

| | |
|---|---|
| Ic eom wunderlicu wiht | *I am a wonderful thing* |
| wifum on hyhte | *to women a thrill* |
| neahbuendum nyt | *handy in the neighbourhood* |
| Nængum sceþþe | *I harm no one,* |
| burgsittendra | *no upstanding citizens,* |
|     nymþe bonan anum |     *except my nemesis.* |
| Staþol min is steapheah | *My trunk is towering,* |
| stond ic on bedde | *standing up in bed,* |
| neoþen ruh nathwær | *my netherlands are shaggy.* |
| Nepeð hwilum | *Once in a while* |
| ful cyrtenu ceorles dohtor | *a really hot country daughter* |
| modwlonc meowle | *a really hot woman* |
|     þaet heo on |     *that wants me in her grip* |
| ræseð mec on reodne | *grabs me on the red bit,* |
| reafath min heafod | *pulls my head* |
| fegeð mec on faesten | *hides me in a tight spot.* |
| Feleþ sona | *As soon as he/she feels* |

| | |
|---|---|
| mines gemotes | *our coming-together* |
| seo þe mec neardwað | *she, my captor* |
| wif wundenlocc | *lady in ringlets,* |
| wæt bið þæt eage | *gets wet in the eyehole.* |

"Heh, heh," Hengest presumably chuckled as he finished the last line. Best one yet.

Whoever wrote them, the poems are gross. Believe it or not, the one reproduced above is among the more tasteful of *The Anglo-Saxon Anthology*'s ninety-six penis riddles. Below is possibly the rudest. You may want to cover one or both eyeholes while reading it.

| | |
|---|---|
| Ic þa wihte geseah | *I saw this thing,* |
| womb wæs on hindan | *a belly was behind it,* |
| þriþum aþrunten. | *(it was) a-throbbing and a-thrusting.* |
| Þegn folgade | *A champion held on* |
| mægenrofa man | *strapping man* |
| ond micel hæfde | *with a fat head* |
| gefered þæt hit felde | *he laboured till he laid it low* |
| fleah þurh his eage | *pale fluid burst from its eyehole.* |

Interestingly, in the Oxford World Classics version, Hengest's poems are chaperoned by comments from two professors bent on construing answers other than "cock." Hengest didn't bother to include answers in the back of the book (the riddles are obvious and all share the same solution), leaving his work vulnerable to scholars so perversely decorous that they can read the first poem quoted above and agree "an onion" would fit the puzzle nicely, while the latter poem, in their minds, evokes "hand-bellows," a tool for blowing air into a fireplace. It just shows that smart people can come to the wackiest of conclusions.

Hengest committed another major sin by leaving out the answers to his riddles. In doing so, he robbed us of written evidence for what late Anglo-Saxon men called their penises. There are hints but no confessions. For example, in one of his riddles the four letters *h, a, n,* and *a* appear in red ink running vertically through the middle of the lines. "Hana" meant "rooster" (the male partner to "hen"), which many cultures conflate with penises, so it's a plausible piece of Alfredian English slang. In another riddle, the speaker portrays his cock as a candlestick or "weax." In yet another, he compares it to a sword or "weapon." These might be fresh poetic alloys or hoary old double meanings so commonplace that, as with "cock" today, speakers didn't perceive them as metaphorical. Only lexicographers from the tenth century, if they survived today, could tell us how "weax" and "weapon" fared against "hana" in the cock-slang steeplechase. Of more urgency, these people could explain how they lived to be over a thousand years old, but that's the problem with lexicographers at parties. They fixate. By the time the ancient nerds had sewn up an account of their ranking methodology, digressing into the ambiguous "rood" as rod, penis, and/or crucifix, modern party-goers would feel the secret to eternal life was coming at too great a cost and escape to the bathroom lineup, snack table, out the nearest window, rfshft.

For those of us who want to know some ancient dirty talk, however, Hengest's riddles do yield one tidbit. He wrote "nathwaet" and "nathwaer" to mean a man's you-know-what or a woman's you-know-where (and vice versa). So if you are at a cocktail party and a thousand-year-old lexicographer raises talk of putting "nathwaet nathwaer," you may need to stall for time, pretend not to understand, excuse yourself, then swiftly choose among the escape routes mentioned above.

Meanwhile, in old England, Hengest had a surprise coming. As cocky as his riddles might have made him, he was surely brought down to earth when a genuinely good submission showed up in the Winchester slush pile, one that spoke to his heart in a way the dull efforts of Cynewulf, Caedmon, and Boethius never could. If the hero's penis jokes were the fluffers of *The Anglo-Saxon Anthology*, this new poem, the first good piece of creative writing in the English language, was its ready, shining star.

## 5. THE WANDERER, 890 AD

"The Wanderer," it was titled.

"Good title," Hengest may have said. "Wait, wait, don't tell me. *I am a wandering thing. / I explore dark passages / and when I fall down in a hole / I find myself covered with slime / and smelling of snails.*"

(Once a person starts making up penis riddles, I imagine it may be hard to stop.)

The poem admonished Hengest with a beautiful opening couplet:

"*Often the lonely bachelor / looks to himself for solace.*"

"No kidding," said Hengest, moodily.

The poem persisted, as below. If you are declaiming the Old English out loud or in your mind's ear, please remember that the *ð* and *þ* letters sound like "th." Beyond that, you can pretty much pronounce things however you want without fear of indisputable correction.

| | |
|---|---|
| metudes miltse | *It is destiny's pity* |
| þeah þe he modcearig | *though he, moody* |
| geond lagulade | *and far across the water* |
| longe sceolde | *must for ages* |
| hreran mid hondum | *ply hand to oar* |
| hrimcealde sæ | *amid a frigid sea* |
| wadan wraeclastas | *to walk the ~~wretch~~ hero's path.* |
| wyrd bið ful aræd | *Reality has been fully briefed.* |
| swa cwæð eardstapa | *So quoth the wanderer* |
| earfeþa gemyndig | *hard times on his mind* |
| wraþa wælsleahta | *the horrid slaughter* |
| winemæga hryre: | *a friend and brother dead:* |
| "Oft ic sceolde ana | *"Often, stuck on my own* |
| uhtnas gehwylce | *waiting for dawn* |
| mine ceore cwiþan" | *I whined to myself."* |

"Me too," Hengest might well have said.

| | |
|---|---|
| "Nis nu cwicra nan | *"Not, no, none now live* |
| þe ic him modsefan | *that I can be moody around* |
| minne durre | *who let me* |

| | |
|---|---|
| seotule asecgan | *openly speak* |
| Ic to soþe wat | *I know it's true* |
| þæt biþ in eorle | *that for a man* |
| indryhten þeaw | *it's orthodox* |
| þæt he his ferðlocan | *that he keep his real self* |
| fæste binde | *tightly locked* |
| healdc his hordcofan | *to guard it like treasure,* |
| hycge swa he wille | *whatever he actually thinks.* |
| Ne mæg werig mod | *Never may a weary mood* |
| wyrde wiðstondan | *defy/defeat reality* |
| ne se hreo hyge | *nor does the inner grump* |
| helpe gefremman | *offer help* |
| forðon domgeorne | *therefore the go-getters* |
| dreorigne oft | *usually hide depression* |
| in hyra breostcofan | *deep in their chest* |
| bindað faeste | *locked tightly* |
| swa ic modsefan | *so I, moody* |
| minne sceolde | *must do the same* |
| oft earmcearig | *often wretched (in the emotional sense of the word)* |
| eðle bidæled | *robbed of my home* |
| freomægun feor | *far from my own kind* |
| feterum sælan" | *all tied up in knots."* |

"Believe me, I've been there," Hengest probably mumbled. "Wow. What a great poem."

| | |
|---|---|
| "Wat se þe cunnað | *"Whoever's been there knows* |
| hu sliþen bið | *how vicious* |

| | |
|---|---|
| sorg to geferan | *a partner sorrow makes* |
| þam þe him lyt hafað | *to them that's got little* |
| leofra geholena | *solid friendship* |
| warað hine wræclast | *they know the ~~wretch's~~ hero's path* |
| nales wunden gold | *instead of woven gold* |
| ferðloca freorig | *(they know) the frozen inner world* |
| nalæs foldan blæd" | *instead of all that's good on earth."* |

"Oh, *I* do! *I* know the frozen inner world!" sobbed Hengest.*

| | |
|---|---|
| "Forþon wat se þe sceal | *"Lo, he must deal with knowing* |
| his winedryhtnes | *his favourite prince's* |
| leofes larcwidum | *good advice* |
| longe forþolian | *is long gone,* |
| ðonne sorg ond slæð | *then sorrow and sloth* |
| somod ætgædre | *team up together* |
| earmne anhogan | *against the poor loner* |
| oft gebindað. | *often tie him up in knots* |
| | *(as previously discussed).* |
| Þinceð him on mode | *He thinks, when in a certain mood* |
| þæt he his mondryhten | *that his best friend is right there* |
| clyppe ond cysse | *to hug and kiss* |
| ond on cneo lecge | *and he rests on his knee* |
| honda ond heafod | *his hands, and his head* |
| swa he hwilum ær | *just as once upon a time* |
| in geardagum | *in the old days* |

* I have asterisked a new sense of "Hengesty" to cope with this scenario: . . . (n) deeply moved by poems about ~~wretches~~ heroes

| | |
|---|---|
| giefstolas breac | *he enjoyed piggybacks** |
| ðonne onwæcneð eft | *then after snapping out of it* |
| wineleas guma | *the friendless man* |
| gesihð him biforan | *sees before him* |
| fealwe wegas | *the dusky waves* |
| baþian brimfuglas | *paddling shorebirds* |
| brædan feþra | *spreading their feathers* |
| hreosan hrim ond snaw | *in the pouring sleet and snow* |
| hagle gemenged." | *mingled with some hail."* |

I expect Hengest did not speak for a minute after reading this. Nor did he rub his temples, nor stare at the ceiling, nor pick his fingernails, nor eat a snack, nay, with his mind's eye, he watched his twin sibling and erstwhile piggyback provider, Horsey, as the kid died from Catigern's arrow, woke, commented on "argh," and died again in the hero's arms. Never had Horsey shown Hengest anything but loyalty. Well, loyalty and some envy. And surreal moments of clairvoyance. But it had mostly been loyalty.

"Oh, brother," Hengest might have finally said. "*That's* a poem."

If Hengest checked the name on the manuscript's cover letter, he would have learned that, as with so many other works now canonized by the *Norton Anthology of English Literature, Volume One*, the author was listed as "Anon." It's become a common joke to pretend that one man, calling himself Anonymous, created the stunning wealth of

* *giefstolas* — literally, a "*gift-seat.*"

historically important verse marked in this way. But I know several male poets. The idea that they would contribute anything of significance without pasting their real names (including, often as not, their middle names) all over the material strikes me as implausible. If Anon's true identity was lost to the ignorance and carelessness of time, I bet she was an Anonyma, a woman who chose the pseudonym to dodge the biases of critics.

Now, as to where she lived. Exploiting the science of forensic linguistics, which regularly helps the U.S. justice system to solve its murder cases, I can narrow down the author's location based on her word choices. For instance, early in the poem, she uses the phrase "hrimcealde sæ," meaning "amid the frigid sea." Any good forensic linguist would spot how "hrimcealde" never occurs in other Anglo-Saxon writing, only in the Norse language, and therefore the author must be guilty of consorting with Vikings. People are packed off to jail with less. I would like to see fingerprints and DNA too, but in their absence, the existing evidence places the poet in or near Viking-occupied territory.

Hengest surely wanted to see more from this talent. However, the inter-regional mail system between Vikingland and England was neither reliable nor quick. This problem, along with the desire of every office-bound worker to stretch his legs and take a field trip at the company's expense, surely motivated Hengest to visit the author in person. It's a good thing she (hopefully) included a self-addressed envelope.

## 6. HEALTHY VIKINGS, 891 TO 1049 AD

While "The Wanderer" might be the best work of lyric poetry written in Old English, the chief example of the longer epic genre is certainly *Beowulf*. The two pieces of creative writing seem to be signed by Anonyma, whoever she was, so the precise moment of their creation cannot easily be placed in time or space. Some years ago, a fellowship of prominent linguists, poetry critics, and historians lent their efforts to a book of heartbroken scholarship called *The Dating of Beowulf*, in a passionate attempt to "date" the famous epic. Their quest mattered deeply. As the book's editor put it, "If we cannot decide when, between the fifth and the eleventh centuries, the poem was composed, we cannot distinguish what elements in *Beowulf* belong properly to the history of material culture, to the history of myth and legend, to political history, or to the development of the English literary imagination." Disappointingly, all the men, women, and horses in *The Dating of Beowulf* couldn't pull it off, and the work's origin remains a mystery. *Beowulf* is nevertheless the best-known poem of its time (whatever that time was).

What makes dating Beowulf difficult, apart from his work schedule and general dickishness, is that the poetic voice appears to have first-hand experience of several different centuries at once. There is flattery or an in-joke for almost everyone, Viking or Angle, Dane or Norwegian, West Saxon or Mercian, eleventh century or tenth, or ninth, eighth, seventh, or sixth. The main characters are Vikings and the setting is Scandinavian but the language is English. The poet draws up a family tree for the hero Beowulf so that he shares ancestors with King Alfred. Forensic linguists have looked for patterns in the poetic metre, local spellings, and "datable anachronisms," such as a casual nod to, say, King Offa and Queen Cynethryth of Mercia, who reigned in the 700s, or a veiled dig at a forgotten Frankish king from the 600s. They have found all of these things, thus connecting the poem to all conceivable dates and regions. Lazy minds suggest the canonical poem must be a collage, a palimpsest drawn by many oral storytellers, but J.R.R. Tolkien long ago rallied the troops against that view. He persuasively asterisked a single genius author of phenomenal erudition and skill. The question is who. Toward the end of *The Dating of Beowulf*, Alexander Murray heckles his colleagues with the remark that their desires tend to influence their beliefs, and that scholars seem to choose whatever answer suits their own fantasies and purposes. The attempt to date *Beowulf*, Murray writes, has too often been dominated by "a conspiracy of romantic hopes."

Love is blind. Desire is the enemy of discernment. And still, what keeps us going, and thinking, and learning at all, if it isn't desire? Should it be obedience?

Several professors, including Murray and the editor of *The Dating of Beowulf* ask their readers to consider the scenario – though they don't claim to have proven its truth – that the poet was an Angle, living in Viking-occupied lands, financed by the Danish government in the tenth or eleventh century. The poem's purpose was to teach Vikings to speak English and teach the English not to hate the Vikings. It was a cultural knitting exercise, a vibrant toot from the peace train. The mixture of Mercian, West Saxon, Viking, and Angle words was no muddle caused by multiple retellings but an outcome of the writer's ecumenism. In other words, *Beowulf*'s style matched its function.

It may surprise some people to hear that a poet could have been funded by Vikings, who are notorious for burning libraries. In fact, archaeologists and Viking fans believe that eastern Britain enjoyed a creative uptick to mirror the English one engineered by King Alfred. Not all Vikings were hooligans. Parts of the occupied territories had even begun to resemble modern rural Denmark, with well-behaved Anglo-Norse citizens devoting themselves to responsible agriculture, tidiness, and a healthy arts scene that produced exquisite brooches and pottery. And although the Vikings did not sponsor any written anthologies, they liked spoken-word performances. In the words of a recent wall text at New York's Metropolitan Museum of Art, "The sophistication and delicacy of Viking art presents a striking contrast with the stereotype of the rude and restless barbarian."

Viking journalism, however, was lacking. We don't have anyone like a Viking Asser writing *Things You Passionately Desire of Chief Guthrum*. Instead, historians base their picture of life in the occupied territories on works such as the Norse sagas, which feature gratuitous asides on the topic of bathing. The sagas corroborate other evidence of body-care routines, such as the plethora of Viking hair combs unearthed in England, the ancient ruins found at natural hot springs wherever Vikings travelled, and a piece of West Saxon gossip in a medieval chronicle to the effect that Vikings groomed and washed too much, changed their clothes willy-nilly, and "drew attention to themselves by means of many such frivolous whims."* The rough portrait is that, while the jocks raided libraries and burned manuscripts, an opposing subculture of Anglo-Dane homebodies were living in a cross between an artisan retreat and a spa.

When Hengest arrived in Vikingland, he would have found it easy to communicate with many of the Mercians, Angles, and former Danes who lived there. After a century in each other's company, the people spoke an Old English barely different from Hengest's own West Sex dialect except for a few eccentricities of accent and diction. Anglo-Danes called their shirts "skirts," and their shrubs "scrubs," for instance. They called their crafts "skills," and their shules "schools." In summary, more or less all their words began with an *sk* sound. Otherwise, they sounded just like the people in Winchester.

Etymologists cannot answer how "skirt" came to mean a lower-body garment for women. Somebody, at some point, must have got confused, letting the meaning slip down from a woman's torso, an event that went unrecorded and which may have occurred anytime between the late 800s and the year 1325, when lower-body skirts get mentioned on paper. If Hengest saw a Viking road sign saying, "Skirts are scorned!" or "Skip that skirt!", he probably wouldn't have understood

* From *Wallingford's Chronicle*, compiled during the early 1200s from sources no longer available.

what it meant, and would have needed to ask the locals for help.

"Excuse me," the hero might have said, if he was feeling polite.

A more Hengesty approach, as I understand it, would be – "Hey, you!"

I want to know the details of Hengest's exchange with Anglo-Danes on his way to find the author of "The Wanderer." This requires some extreme asterisking, since I have only my knowledge of Hengestiness and a general depiction of Viking culture to work with. However, as Dr. Murray described, top scholars allow their desires free run when dealing with the place and time of *Beowulf*'s creation, so I suppose I needn't be holier-than-them about this.

"Yes?" replied two local women and one man, all of them tall, blond, and sitting together in an outdoor bath. They were combing each other's hair. None of them wore any clothes above the waist.

Hengest asked what a "skirt" is.

They explained.

"Ah," said Hengest. "See, I would call that a 'shirt.' With a *sh*. Like in 'shit.'"

"Shit?" inquired one of the women.

Let's say she was shorter than her friend, for distinctiveness's sake.

"What's a shit?"

"You know," said Hengest. "As in, 'you shit over the side of the boat, mate.'"

"Oh," said the taller woman, sliding deeper into the bath. "Like 'skit.' You say 'shit,' I say 'skit.'"

"Shit, skit," said the Viking man. "Shirt, skirt. Let's take the whole thing off."

The Vikings agreed that full-blown nudity would simplify matters and, exhibiting the frivolous whimsy typical of their culture, they disrobed.

"No need to be embarrassed," said the shorter woman. "We're all family here, as Anonyma would say."

Now that she was standing up in the bath, Hengest noticed she was taller than him.

"Who?" asked the hero.

"Anonyma."

"Oh. Is that person related to Anon, the author of 'The Wanderer'?"

The naked Vikings were incredulous, I expect.

"What? You don't know Anonyma?" asked the taller woman. She began combing her hair again, briskly.

"I thought *everybody* knew Anonyma," said the man.

The Vikings looked anywhere but Hengestward.

"It's getting late," said the shorter woman.

"Can you take me to her?" Hengest might have asked.

My desire would be that the Vikings agreed to do this because in education there is hope. And so, naked but for their boots, the characters headed down a gently degrading trail to the heart of the healthy Viking arts scene.

I sense the hero's adjective growing again.

**Hengesty** *adj.* . . . (o) directed by the desires or romantic conspiracies of later storytellers [cf. *Beowulfy*]

In *The Truth About Stories*, the writer Thomas King said: "In our cynical world, where suspicion is a necessity, insisting that something is true is not nearly so powerful as suggesting that something might be true." I'm not sure that *is* true, but it's a useful suggestion, and if Anglo-Vikings led Hengest toward the anonymous poet who wrote "The Wanderer" with such uncanny insight about heroes and/or wretches, and who, in her epic work, paused midway through the story of *Beowulf* to insert an episode about Hengest's fateful days at King Finn's fort in Frisia, then I suggest the hero immediately understood how she came by her knowledge of his past and his psyche.

"Horsehair?"

"Dad!"

I mentioned that Hengest's sister-daughter was viewed as an evil witch in British legend, a stigma caused by sexist and unfair prejudices. But while Horsehair's evilness was a figment of Welsh fantasy, we needn't toss away her witchiness in the same bathwater. As with Hengest, there is no record of her dying. One written tale claims she burned in a house fire that magically opened the earth's surface and swallowed her husband Vortigern into the ground, but this was another spurious insertion by a later translator with no direct access to the facts. The older version of the same story, written in Latin, reported only that the British chief died "cum uxori," meaning "with his wives," without mentioning Horsehair. Vortigern apparently had several wives, meaning that the set of fire victims could have amounted to some, rather than all, of the people who had ever married him.

"Could we really suppose that Rowena followed Vortigern to his death?" asks Robert Vermaat, the most widely read expert on the subject, before answering his own question: "Hardly."* She just wasn't that into poor Vorty. After all, she had poisoned his only surviving son, Vortimer. If Rowena/Horsehair played any role in the supernatural fire, it's more likely that she was the arsonist.

Descriptions of witches vary wildly. I think the most compelling comes from the movie *The Blair Witch Project*, which tells of a woman with unusual body hair who lives for hundreds of years. Horsehair certainly had the first quality, hairiness, in spades, and if she had the quality of long life too, it casts light on several other unsolved cases. The inscrutably timeless dialect of *Beowulf* suits Horsehair's own six hundred years of language use. The "anonymous" pseudonym also makes more sense because Horsehair's real name beckoned worse than routine neglect by poetry critics – she might reasonably have feared a witch hunt. Even the high literary craft of *Beowulf* fits the asterisked account of Horsehair's genetic stock, since her family also produced the word-nerd Horsey.

The more I think about it, the more I don't see how history hangs together at all without this pin in place: the Old English language arrived at *Beowulf*, its epic-poetic summit, when Horsehair, mother of English, was reunited with Hengest, father of English, after his heroic path had endowed him with powers of scripting and publishing. Author and editor worked in harmony at the Healthy Viking arts scene. Then, after

*From *Vortigern Studies*, Vermaat's online publication.

some time, they rode together back to Winchester House to finish the long-overdue anthology and plan its launch gala.

## 7. OLD ENGLISH CLIMAXES, 1050 AD

Bishop Leofric's description of the oldest book in the English language as "poetry about something" remains among the more dismissive reviews of all time. His personal copy visibly did not receive the care it deserved. It's an open question whether Leofric's book was a unique artifact, or if Hengest made others, but generally speaking, print runs (handwriting runs, really) were much smaller in the age of scribe and parchment. Readers were expected to come to the book, not the other way round.

How many people journeyed to Winchester or Exeter to read *The Anglo-Saxon World: An Anthology*, how many heard the penis riddles and felt a patriotic fervour, and whether anyone bothered to finish Boethius's *Consolations of Philosophy* – all of these questions point up the ladder of asterisks to desirable facts. We know that "The Wanderer" and *Beowulf* still foster romantic hopes today. Possibly they were even more powerful a millennium ago, advertising Old English's worthiness as a literary language, instilling pride, and so on.

By the time Hengest was going over his page proofs, Alfred and Werewulf were long dead. Winchester House fell under the control of two star scholars named Alfric (either "boss of an elf" or "bossed by an elf") and Wulfstan ("wolf-stone"). This pair of educated fuss-budgets muttered over the fine points of house style and proper manuscript mark-up.

Alfric, in particular, is famous for chewing out a particular scribe. "I beseech you in God's name to transcribe this *correctly*," he screamed. "You do great evil by writing carelessly unless you correct it." The scribe dutifully recorded these words on the page, which is how modern people know they were spoken. Some historians pick Alfric's comment to mark the Old English dialect's graduation to grown-up status as a written language, far from the oral muck of its early days.

Then the bad news came. Trouble was bubbling in Old England's royal seat. Aristocrats controlled English-language publishing, even if they didn't read books or know the pleasure of a good penis joke. Hengest had managed to place himself at the crest of a creative wave, despite his origins as a doltish sword-fighter, his mind-boggling old age, and his other Hengesty handicaps. After the launch of *The Anglo-Saxon World: An Anthology* in 1050 AD, he must have thought he was in the clear, having finally tugged himself up the hierarchy to a life of free dinners and editorial lunches. He might even have rented an apartment in Winchester for himself and his sister-daughter. The lull lasted a mere sixteen years. As mapped out earlier in *Figure 2.4*, the French-based children of Rollo came to the island of Britain, led by William the Conqueror, who killed a child of the West Saxon royal family, took charge of England, and chopped and downsized the old guard. The new king spoke no English. He certainly had no plans to fund a state-owned publisher staffed with anglophone scholars and a crusty old poetry editor. I can only assume Hengest's plum career tumbled and rolled steeply downhill, gathering no moss as it fell.

## 8. ENTER THE BASTARD, 1066 AD

In England, the regime change of 1066 AD is so famous that speakers often refer to it as "the Conquest," trusting their audiences to know which conquest they mean. The French invaders were "the Normans." This sounded funny to me as a child because I knew somebody called Norman. He was a pasty, milquetoasty person, a future accountant or deputy hospital administrator. To be "conquered by Normans" has never evoked for me the correct images of chain mail, horses, and post-ocular bloodspurts so much as a horde of dandruff-sufferers in brown cardigans. Perhaps this discomfort is widespread, a second reason why my English schoolteachers called the Anglo-Saxon invasions "the Anglo-Saxon invasions," but referred to the Norman Conquest as only "the . . . Conquest." It's like having had sex with someone called Melvyn. You might rather just say, "I had sex."

After the invasion, English played what looks to have been a magic trick, seen through the lens of leftover documents. It passed underneath the Romance tongue,* vanished, and then popped back on top, lively as a hummingbird. It also metamorphosed, shedding some old Angle vocabulary and gaining two gaudy wings made of French and Latin. At journalism college, my instructor drew a picture of this creature, with its Germanic flesh and Romantic attachments. He solemnly argued that punchy newspaper style draws on the robust Angle thorax while avoiding the scholarly,

* A Romance tongue is what the Romans spoke, plus the later languages based primarily on Latin (like Spanish, French).

upper-class, bureaucratic frippery spoken by Normans and Latin-loving monks after 1066 AD.

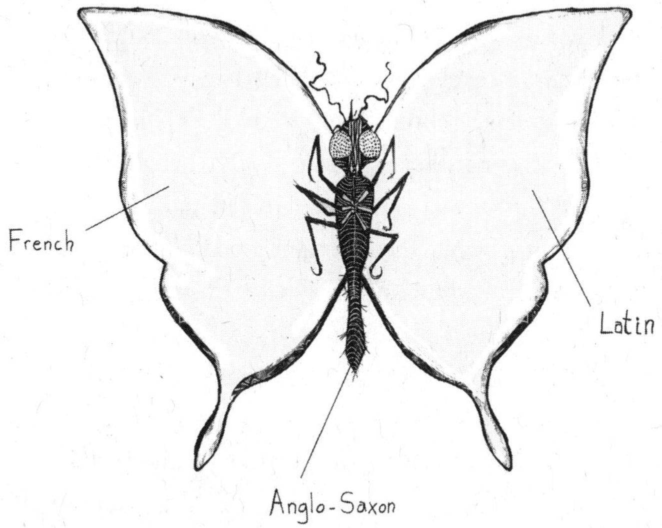


*Figure 2.5* – Middle-aged English, early second millennium AD

Though I am a fan of simple diagrams, this creature poses a threat to the carefully woven fabric of English's story. Many tellers have become charmed by mismatches between Romance and Angle words, leading them to draw solid, weighty conclusions – such as that leftover Angle words are by nature short, curt, and common. Saxon means meaty, in this account. A social split between the Germanic working class, French one-percenters, and a Latin-speaking intelligentsia has left behind a vocab to match: Anglo-Saxons "spoke" from the "gut." Normans "parleyed" using their "stomach." Monks "negotiated" based on their "intestines." And so on.

A seductive rift between old Anglo-Saxon English and middle-aged, Romance-infested English offers us a story about food. "Mutton," "beef," "pork," and "venison" are French words because the only people who could afford to order meat in restaurants were the Norman newcomers, whereas "sheep," "cow," "pig," and "deer" date back to Hengest's original hoard because Old English speakers farmed or husbanded or hunted the living animals. "The Saxons laboured while the Normans dined," quipped Melvyn Bragg, a British author and storyteller, phrasing this rule of thumb as neatly as anyone could. It implies that our lexicon recalls an old wage gap much as a tree trunk's inner rings may remember a wound.

Since English-speaking people today eat *oie* and *poule* only when following a recipe from Julia Child's *Mastering the Art of French Cooking*, the same logic would encourage me to asterisk that Normans turned up their noses at these foodstuffs, "goose" and "chicken," when offered by Anglo-Saxons. Otherwise, the modern English words should not have survived from the Hengesty period. They ought to have been supplanted by the conquerors' language. Perhaps the noble Normans thought the English cooks ruined bird meat by failing to add enough butter and lardons, or maybe the whole restaurant explanation is a canard. To define first-millenium English words as rough and rude, contrasted with polite second-millenium additions from the French and Latin, or to call one era's contributions "working-class" and the other's "bourgeois," serves a mildly useful role in asking journalists to think about their diction, but doesn't do much good for the story of English. For example, the rule fumbles over the very first word likely to have entered Hengest's speech by way of the Normans after 1066.

"Bastard!" the hero probably said, especially in reaction to *The Anglo-Saxon Chronicle*'s report on the Norman arrival.

If my journalism instructor saw this article, he'd approve of the solid Germanic word choices but he'd seriously bawl out the writer for burying the lead.

| | |
|---|---|
| 1066 ~ Harold cyng, his broþor, gegædrade swa micelne sciphere & eac landhere swa nan cyng her on lande ær ne dyde, forþam þe him wæs gecyðd þæt Wyllelm Bastard wolde hider & ðis land gewinnen, eallswa hit syððan aeode. | *King Harold, his [a just-mentioned earl's] brother, ge-gathered so mighty a ship force & eek a land force such that no king here on land ever never did, for he was ge-told that Wyllelm Bastard wanted to come hither & this land ge-conquer, also that did happen.* |

Wyllelm Bastard – i.e., William the Conqueror – became ge-saddled with the nickname "bastard" thanks to his Norman uncles, who envied the kid's power and hated his precociousness. William became the duke of Normandy soon after his seventh birthday. His father, a non-conformer, had journeyed to Jerusalem to atone for various sins but indulged in some more along the way, picking up a nasty disease, which killed him. William's mother worked in the stables, doing something with leather. (Gossipy French histories refer to her as a "tanner.") She and William's father never married due to silly local prejudices about dukes and tanners and income incompatibility, and besides, marriage – what a square institution! The conqueror's English enemies knew this story, so "bastard" quickly formed an unofficial part of the new English government's name.

In old-fashioned French, "bastard" literally meant the child born to a woman who got pregnant after having sex on, or beside or against, or over, an "ass saddle." This object resembled a regular horse saddle but was shaped specifically for an ass, in the sense of donkey or mule. The French word for an ass saddle was "un bast." Folk wisdom declared it the most comfortable spot for sex in a barn or stable, much less scratchy than taking a roll in the hay. Like "bast," the element *–ard* was a new piece of language to most English-speakers in 1066 AD. Hengest, however, should have found it distantly familiar.

In the Angle lands of northern Europe and other German-speaking places, people knew a word "hardt," which could mean "sturdy" or "brave." This was the meaning Hengest might remember from his childhood. Somewhere around the ninth century, roughly when Hengest was trying to get a job at King Alfred's publishing house, a new fashion flowered among German men on the continent. They began adding "hardt" to their names, for effect.

"This is my son, Rein," a mother might innocently say to another parent.

"Mom!" young Rein would protest. "I'm Rein-*the-brave*!"

These asterisk characters spoke old German, of course, so the kid's nickname sounded like "Rein*hardt*" in real life.

He was, let's imagine, an ancestor of guitar-picking legend Django Reinhardt.

It became so common for German men to put "hardt" on the end of their names that neighbouring cultures could make jokes about it.

"Ah, regard," a French wit might say as she pointed to a duck waddling past her. "There goes Quack-the-Brave!"

In French, Quack-the-Brave's nickname sounded like "Quan-ard" because France's ducks go "Quan" instead of "Quack," and francophones have a bias against harsh Germanic sounds, turning "hardt" into "arrd." The witticism caught on. Today, people spell the duck's nickname "canard."

"Very good," said the witty Frenchwoman's friend.

Next, an illegitimate child passed them by, for some reason, pursuing the duck at a casual pace.

"Now, what do we call this son of an ass-saddle?" asked the friend.

(The last part would be spelled *fils de bast*, in French.)

"But of course," replied the renowned wit. "He is Ass-Saddle *the Brave*!"

Bast-*hardt*.

In Britain, from the eleventh century onward, conquered Angles and/or Saxons learned this pattern for making words. They began calling their wise guys "wizards," putting two Germanic parts together by the mechanism of a copied French joke. Sluggy guys became "sluggards." Drunk guys, "drunkards." By this point, the scent of wit had long dispersed and the suffix –*ard* implied nothing more than "guy" means to us today.

To recap: English words ending in *–ard* reached Hengest's speech by way of Normans, most of whom claimed to be related somehow to King Rollo, who was either a giant, a Jute, a Norwegian, a Half-Dane, or all of the above. King Rollo's descendants in northern France grew up learning French, which included picking up *–ard* words, pinched mischievously from European Angles and Saxons living roughly where Hengest originally came from. "Bastard" is thus a beautiful case of form matching function, embodying a warp in the family tree. A less-publicized part of its function is to warn storytellers against patronizing that butterfly my journalism instructor tried to draw. It is not a simple creature, let alone an innocent or harmless one.

## 9. ORGIES, (ONGOING)

Immediately following the French invasion, the island became a place where fancy jobs went straight to applicants with French-language skills. Monolingual Angles and Vikings lived in the sloughs of despond, sitting ducks for the call of unhealthy pleasures. They huddled with time to kill. They grumbled together about the selfish Normans and, worse, any splitters who adopted French culture in order to get work. Many long evenings passed by the fireside, in a haze of homebrew, until those with fighting spirits forged pacts of solidarity and committed themselves to self-annihilating rebellions, while those with amorous spirits slunk off in pairs or, if open-minded and plastered enough, somewhat larger groupings. Next morning, the jocks set off to get themselves killed, while the lovers' meshing of tongues (the fleshly sort) gave way to another meshing of tongues (lexical). At a thousand awkward breakfasts, Angles and Vikings explored the seams of idiom, the divergences in grammar and moral stances, all of which helped chat up the next evening's drunken prospect. Thus, Anglish and Viking speech intertwined beneath the blanket of French oppression. No part was too private to receive the other's touch.

"I'd like your 'we,' 'he,' and 'it' in my mouth, if that's not too weird," said Viking.

"And in return, how about I, so to speak, 'nime' your 'they' and 'them'?" replied Anglish. (He licked his lips to get ready.)

"Have my 'take'. It's better than your 'nime.'"

"Okay," agreed Anglish. "Then I'll 'take' your 'they' and 'them.' What a sexy set of pronouns they 'be-en'!"

He wrapped his arms around Viking and nuzzled her neck. She smiled thinly.

"Um, we might have to do something about 'be-en' too," she said.

Anglish let go of her hand. He was quiet for a moment.

"What?" said Viking.

"Nothing. I've always liked my 'be-en,' you know."

"I find it ugly."

"Oh."

Anglish bit his lip and waited for a change of topic.

"Like, actually hideous," continued Viking. "When I see 'they be-en,' I want to spit or punch an animal. 'They are' looks more tasteful and sounds more sensible. You can't see that?"

Rather than respond, Anglish kicked a rock, hurt his foot, and pretended he hadn't just done that.

Viking touched him on the chest.

"Is there some reason why you . . . "

"Fine, they 'are,' not 'be-en,' they 'are.' Fuck, whatever."

And so on.

Somewhere else on this broad canvas, tiny amid all the foreground and background, must lay the dotty stars of Hengest's plotline. My only touchstone is that he lost his job at Winchester House, which ceased operating under the Normans. The logical next step for him would be a stab at freelancing, but so few pieces of written English survive from this period that I imagine it was a tough time to earn one's nickel as a monolingual scribe or a literary editor. Monks switched over entirely to Latin, seen as a ticket to global success in a post-national age. English poetry appreciation tanked. Even the penis jokes apparently dried up, or got lost, or became too rude to write down. Looking backward from the modern era, the first six editions of the *Norton Anthology of English Literature, Volume One* hiccupped past three centuries at this point, skipping from their samples of 1050's *The Anglo-Saxon Anthology* straight to Chaucer's "General Prologue" of 1386. Between those dates, literature-wise, it's bare pickings for the story of English.

However, there is one useful straw lying over the mid-point of the *Beowulf*-to-Chaucer gap, in the form of a poem attributed to Anon. If this piece is a genuine Anonyma, meaning that it was written by Hengest's sister-daughter, and if the pair became fellow travellers after Winchester, having attempted to bury the hatchets of their troubled relationship (the abandonment, the sibling rivalry, the editor-author tension), then the lonely verse offers the best (and only) clue to my hero's journey.

## 10. ART MEETS COMMERCE, 1205 AD

"The Owl and the Nightingale" – anonymous poem, eponymous birds. They who fight and squawk and squabble and sort of debate. Against the near radio silence of written English between 1050 and 1350 AD, the poem shines with the subtlety and grace of a golden literary talent. Such writers are rare. Apart from Horsehair, the nearest known capable author was Geoffrey Chaucer, but he wouldn't be born for another 150 years, leaving *Beowulf*'s creator as the only available genius we've heard of. Okay, that doesn't prove much. "The Owl and the Nightingale" could have been written by any unheard-of nobody, but wait, there's more, because the poem's scenario exactly matches the life situation of English's founding partners during those dark and evil days. As far as I can asterisk, the piece is Horsehair's disguised memoir.

Its two main characters are: (1) an owl with poor social skills and a bad odour; and (2) a nightingale who sings for the sake of beauty, even though this is an unaffordable hobby in a tight market, as the owl pointedly complains. That each "bird" objects so much to the other's lifestyle only makes sense if they feel bound together, such as by marriage or close blood tie (or both). Otherwise, they could ignore each other and go about their own business. If the owl and nightingale are symbols for Hengest and Horsehair, respectively, their interaction gives us a sense of how the travel partnership had been working out since the Bastard axed Hengest's job at Winchester House.

Horsehair rendered a typical conversation between them, in rhyming couplets, as follows:

| **Ule** | **Owl** |
|---|---|
| . . . Seie me nu, þu wrecche wiȝt | *. . . Say to me now, you ~~heroic~~ wretchy wotsit,* |
| is in þe eni oþer note | *is there, in you, any other point* |
| bute þu hauest schille þrote? | *beyond your vocal training?* |
| Þu nart noȝt to non oþer þinge, | *You're another nothingy no-name,* |
| bute þu canst of chateringe, | *except that you know how to chatter on,* |
| vor þu art lutel an unstrong, | *for you are little and wimpy,* |
| an nis þi regel noþing long. | *and nor is your dress long enough, by the way.* |
| Wat dostu godes among monne? | *What good do you do in a man's world?* |
| Na mo þe deþ a wrecche wranne. | *No more than does a ~~heroic~~ wretchy wren.* |
| Of þe ne cumeþ non oþer god, | *From you comes not-no-none other good,* |
| bute þu gredest suich þu bo wod. | *but that you sing like you're mad.* |
| an bo þi piping ouergo, | *And when your piping is over and done with,* |
| ne boþ on þe craftes namo. | *there ain't no more marketable skills in you.* |

| Middle English | Translation |
|---|---|
| Alured sede, þat was wis | *Alfred said – i.e., the wise Alfred –* |
| (he miȝte wel, for soþ hit is) | *(or he might as well have,* |
| | *anyway, it's probably true),* |
| "Nis no man for is bare songe | *"Ain't no man, for his bare song,* |
| lof ne wurþ noȝt suþe longe." | *Loved nor worth anything* |
| | *very long."* |
| **Niȝtingale** | **Nightingale** |
| Wi axestu of craftes mine? | *Why ask you about my* |
| | *marketable skills?* |
| Betere is min on þan alle þine | *My one is better than all of yours.* |
| betere is o song of mine muþe | *Better is one song from my mouth* |
| þan al þat eure þi kun kuþe | *than all that your type ever knows.* |
| an lust, ich telle þe wareuore. | *And listen, I'll tell you wherefore.* |
| Wostu to wan man was ibore? | *Do you know the whole reason* |
| | *humans were invented?* |
| To þare blisse of houene-riche | *For the bliss of that ol' magic* |
| | *kingdom.* |
| þar euer is song & murȝþe iliche | *Thereabouts it's all song and* |
| | *mirth, constantly,* |
| þider fundeþ eurich man | *and that's what drives every man* |
| þat eni þing of gode kan. | *that knows anything about* |
| | *what's good.* |
| Ac þu nost neuer wat þu menst, | *Ack, you never know what you* |
| | *mean,* |
| bute lese wordes þu me lenst: | *yet you lend me your garbage* |
| | *words.* |
| for ich kan craft & ich kan liste, | *Because I know crafts & I* |
| | *know arts* |

| | |
|---|---|
| an þareuore ich am þus þriste. | *therefore I am, as you see, spiritually sturdy.* |
| Ich kan wit & song mani eine, | *I know wit & song – many kinds,* |
| ne triste ich to non oþer maine: | *and I don't put my trust in no other form of strength,* |
| vor soþ hit is þat seide Alured: | *because it's true-ish, what Alfred said,* |
| "Ne mai no strengþe aȝen red." | *"The strong will never beat the well read."* |

When Hengest criticized Horsehair for singing, he might not have meant it literally. The nightingale's song could be a metaphor for Horsehair's poems, none of which had been selling because the only people with disposable income for the arts in those days were French-speaking. The gap in our written records proves a lack of demand for published product but not a lack of work made in private, so Horsehair's astounding voice (what the poem calls her "schille þrote") may have given the world thousands of exemplars, every bit as good as "The Wanderer," but now composted thanks to poor or non-existent critical attention, public libraries, etc. As she pumped out anonymous English literature to no avail, I expect Hengest let slip some untactful jabs, sparking the real-life squabbles that inspired "The Owl and the Nightingale."

We must remember that Horsehair could not be an unbiased narrator of these disputes. She might be caricaturing Hengest's real position. Also, her poetic licence let her add frills and owl-related riffs, adding murk to our lens, but through the cloudiness we can just make out that the pair had been fighting a classic dispute between prose and poetry, truth and beauty, commerce and art, line and curve. For instance, here is how the nightingale, Horsehair's poet avatar, attacks the owl's life choices:

| **Niȝtingale** | **Nightingale** |
|---|---|
| A wis word, þeȝ hit bo unclene, | *A wise comment, though it's a bit dirty,* |
| is fele manne a-muþe imene, | *is common to the mouths of many a man,* |
| for Alured King hit seide & wrot. | *because King Alfred said it. And wrote it.* |
| "He schunet þat hine wl wot." | *"He cowers, that knows he's shat himself."* |
| Ich wene þat þu dost also, | *I reckon that you do this too,* |
| vor þu fliȝst niȝtes euer mo. | *for you fly always by night.* |
| þu art lodlich to biholde, | *You are loathly to behold,* |
| & þu art loþ in monie volde. | *& you are gross in various senses of the word.* |
| þu starest so þu wille abiten | *You stare as if you plan on biting* |
| al þat þu miȝt mid cliure smiten: | *whatever you can stick your claws into.* |
| þi bile is stif & scharp & hoked, | *Your beak's stiff, sharp, hooked,* |
| riȝt so an owel þat is croked. | *just like a bent fork.* |
| eauereuch childe þe cleopeþ fule, | *Every child calls you foul,* |
| an euereuch man a wrecche, hule! | *and every man, a wretch, owl!* |
| Ac þu, ereming, þu wrecche gost, | *But you, O exile, wretchy spirit,* |
| þu ne canst finde, ne þu nost, | *you cannot find, nor do you know* |

| | |
|---|---|
| an holȝ stok þar þu þe miȝt hude, | *a hollow tree stump where you might hide,* |
| þat me ne twengeþ þine hude. | *where no one may zing your backside,* |
| Vor children, gromes, heme, & hine | *because children, grooms, he-men, and yokels,* |
| hi þencheþ alle of þire pine. | *they all think of how to torment you.* |
| Nis noþer noȝt, þi lif ne þi blod | *There's nothing worthwhile in your life or your character* |
| ac þu art sheueles suþe god. | *but you sure are quite a scarecrow.* |

The pop wisdom that "you always hurt the one you love" touches on the accidental hurt a person always inflicts, without malice, upon those who share his or her life. It's also widely accepted, I think, that the people closest to you are best placed to deliver pain *with* malice, because they know this art (and they know this craft) better than anybody, and are able to find your weakest, most sensitive points. The nightingale's insults sound arbitary to us, but to Hengest, they surely dug into old and festering wounds that only Horsehair knew about. His response shows the points on which he felt he needed to defend himself:

| **Ule** | **Owl** |
|---|---|
| hit is min hiȝte, hit is mi wunne, | *It is my wish, it is my want* |
| þat ich me draȝe to mine cunde. | *that I hew to my own stereotype.* |
| ne mai me no man þareuore schende. | *No one should shun me, therefore.* |

| | |
|---|---|
| on me hit is wel isene, | *Concerning me, it is obvious* |
| vor riȝte cunde ich am so kene. | *that my stereotype makes me so fierce.* |
| ȝet ich can do wel gode wike | *Yet I can do awesome work* |
| vor ich can loki manne wike | *for I can work in men's places* |
| an mine wike boþ wel gode | *and my work is awesome** |
| vor ich helpe to manne uode. | *because I help put food on the table.* |
| Ich can nimen mus at berne, | *I can nime – I mean, take – mice at the barn,* |
| an ek at chirche ine þe derne: | *and eek! at church in the dark.* |
| a uorbisne is of olde ivurne, | *An adage coming to us from olden times* |
| þat node makeþ old wif urne. | *is that "need makes the old woman run."* |
| Site nu stille, chaterestre! | *Sit still now, chattering woman!* |
| nere þu neuer ibunde uastre: | *Never were you ever tied up worse.* |
| alle þine wordes þu bileist | *All your words, you massage* |
| þat hit þincþ soþ al þat þu seist. | *so that everything you say seems true-ish.* |
| alle þine wordes boþ isliked | *All your words are slippery* |
| an so bisemed an biliked | *and so true-sounding and charming* |

* The lazy repetition of "wike"'(work) makes sudden sense if I can asterisk "wick" to be an old slang term for a penis (see earlier, "More Cock Jokes"), in which case these lines are playing to the galleries. Ditto with "cunde" (stereotype) and "cunt," a few lines earlier.

| | |
|---|---|
| þat alle þo þat hi auoþ | *that all those who hear them* |
| hi weneþ þat þu segge soþ. | *they get the idea that you say the truth (ish).* |

That answers how the pair survived. Hengest had been catching mice, presumably to feed them both, and he even claims to have taken some sort of job "in men's places," which could mean anything from being a bathroom attendant to an escort to a burglar. Either way, it sounds like the ancient Welsh curse was haunting him again, forever returning "Oldbelly" to hunger and wandering. If Hengest's life ever became a movie, I think the hardest part of making it would be the toll on the poor actor's body.

The nightingale never wins the fight. After sixteen hundred lines, neither side has proven itself superior, or even able to espouse an especially coherent point of view, nor do the pair seem sure how to divide one's yin from the other's yang in order to square off properly against each other. On these grounds a few professors called the poem a mess, wondering where the missing conclusion ended up. But the smart ones saw the poem's perfect voicing of anxieties on behalf of imaginative people confused about what to do with their lives.

Crucially for "The Owl and the Nightingale" and its place in the story of English, the poem found a buyer. He's named as Nicholas from Guildford (a town near London). Both owl and nightingale flatter him obscenely in the rhymes, a crafty sales trick of Horsehair's devising. "He is wise and careful with words, and awesome at making judgments," says the nightingale about Nicholas. "He's mature and very well read," agrees the owl, "and doesn't lust after bad advice." The birds tell Nicholas he must decide who won their debate, and even though smart readers are meant to see this as a hopeless task, Nicholas didn't need to. He just had to take the praise and hand over his money so that Hengest and Horsehair could eat a better meal than fried mice.

The successful sale probably seemed like good luck at the time, but could have had something to do with the goings-on among aristocrats, who had just lost most of Normandy to the French king in 1203. French-speaking Norman families still owned the bulk of the island's money and would fight for land in northern France for long afterward, but a few wealthy people might already have veered into islander separatism, and everyone – regardless of ethnicity or language – needed to commiserate about England's terrible new Norman king, John. He expected rich people to choose between their property in Normandy and what they owned in Britain. Plus, a generation of smart, rich teenagers had been forced to study at Oxford because John's father banned them from going to the University of Paris. Some medley of all these factors, along with many unknown ones, evidently created the conditions for selling an English-language poem in the early 1200s.

A single poem wouldn't buy anyone's ticket out of poverty, however, which is why I have another new theory. Near the final lines of the poem, the owl describes the wonderful Nicholas as living in Portesham, county of Dorset, which is nowhere near Guildford. Modern critics gloss over the point, asterisking that Nicholas must have moved to Dorset, having grown up in Guildford. I'm not a fan of this asterisk. It seems equally likely that Nicholas wasn't Horsehair's only customer for the poem. In a grand irony (and quasi-victory for her nightingale), Horsehair could have turned "The Owl and the Nightingale" into a marketable commodity by changing the name and details of the flattered human judge for each potential buyer. She could then sell the same "personalized" vanity poem over and over, a brilliant scheme and nice little earner, and yet vulnerable to typos such as forgetting to change a place name or two when making copies.

"Hey," Nicholas of Guildford might say upon noticing the mention of Portesham. "What's this about me living in Dorset?"

Horsehair would need to think on her feet. This would be her best move:

"Like the owl tells the nightingale, 'Ich am witi, ful iwis, and wod al þat to kumen is.'* You *shall* live in Portesham, someday. Five coppers, please."

Just so, after living on scrounged diets and mutual resentment, the father and mother of English could make it out of the woods, thanks in part to the return of a literary market. History's roller coaster delivered the hero safely through the French loop-de-loop. And, for the record, local county rolls in Dorset note that a "Nicholas of Guildford" indeed came to live in that region, several decades after "The Owl and the Nightingale" was written, so it seems he took the strange traveller's advice.

* "I am witty, really wise, and know all that is to come."

PART THREE

# The Tongue that Ate Itself

## 1. CHEAP GUIDEBOOKS, 1300 AD

Long ago, the Roman Church came up with a business idea: (1) persuade people to visit Rome; (2) sell souvenirs. This worked on a few zealous folks who risked their necks and spent their savings to ride, hitchhike, or foot-hike across deadly medieval Europe to reach the Vatican, where they bought badges. Some examples of these pilgrim badges survive or have been sketched by those who claimed to have seen originals, and while none specifically said, in Latin, "I saw the Pope *for realz*," or, "My buddy went to Rome and all I got was this lousy badge," the pragmatic intent was the same. The badges proved that their purchaser cared enough about Jesus to go on an expensive and impractical foreign trip, which was presumably one of the anti-poverty activist's unstated priorities. However, too many people stayed home.

Smart entrepreneurs within the church spotted a way to reach those customers who balked at higher levels of commitment. They began pushing the concept of a "minor pilgrimage," a product akin to "entry-level pro gear" or an "affordable luxury sedan," i.e., you can show off for a fraction of the financial injury. It caught on. By the start of the fourteenth century, the mini-pilgrimage market had grown into a vast sector, and it needed people who could write.

We have solid evidence for this in the form of pilgrimage guidebooks. A copy of Master Gregory's *Guide to Rome*, for example, was fortunately protected inside an elegant library in Oxford. Further afield, two copies of a large book called *The Pilgrim's Guide to Santiago* survive in European libraries. First published in the late 1100s, *The Pilgrim's Guide* offers vague and misleading suggestions for pilgrims crossing Western Europe, although the book is so unclear that modern interpreters cannot agree on the recommended route. Its only point of certainty is the destination, a Spanish cathedral called Compostela, which had risen to join Rome and Jerusalem at the top of the Catholic pilgrimage business.

Within the English-speaking world, smaller pilgrimages also left behind a few badges for scholars to inspect, along with plentiful mentions in later books, poems, stories, and financial accounts. We know that people in Britain visited the shrine of Reading to see the bony hand of St. James and a piece of St. Pancras's arm, or the shrine in Walsingham to see the Virgin Mary's congealed breast milk. However, history preserved zero examples from this period of a travel guide for such minor pilgrimages, to match the large European-focused books. This is in spite of the fact that lightweight guidebooks for local pilgrims almost certainly existed.

In the late 1200s, holy sites blanketed the English market such that, no matter where a customer lived, he or she could pick from a range of one-day, two-day, three-day pilgrimages, and on up, according to budget and inclination. Like any smart operator in a roaring trade, a shrine manager would fight for attention, aiming at niches, seeking a competitive edge. Top-of-line English shrines such as Canterbury Cathedral drew visitors by offering highly believable claims and a mainstream product – e.g., the body parts or bodily fluids of a major celebrity, blurbed by all the influential bishops. Lesser shrines might appeal to more offbeat or specific types of curiosity. At the very least, they could offer a convenient location, a well-groomed footpath for pilgrims, the promise of glimpsing the sea along the way, and a nearby pub.

Scholars know about this because of a few booklets discovered in churches that housed a holy relic or two. "Some shrines employed a notary or local monk to compile their miracle stories," write Drs. Bell and Dale in a recent essay on the English shrine business.* "These were bound together with songs and hagiographies to provide a kind of promotional brochure to be placed near the shrine."

These booklets do sound excitingly like "promotional brochures," but if that was their purpose, they had a distribution flaw. By the time a pilgrim found the booklet, he or she had already arrived at the shrine. It could serve only to upsell customers, encouraging them to pay extra for a more

* "The Medieval Pilgrimage Business," *Oxford Journal of Economics*.

intimate use of the holy relic, or maybe to buy two souvenir badges rather than one so they could spread word of the shrine to friends and acquaintances. A brochure of this sort could not directly fish for new pilgrims and reel them in.

Bell and Dale came to a general asterisk-conclusion: "Our medieval forebears were very much aware of what we describe today as 'brand management.'" This sounds true. Regardless of who we are and where our forebears lived, people all over the place generally know about brand management. Even dogs know about it, hence all the peeing. A society capable of inventing a business based on selling three-day hiking trips to lick an old bone, peruse a coffee-table book, and buy a pack of souvenir badges could surely spot the need for cheap advertising leaflets that drew customers onto the desired pilgrim trail. To keep costs low, these were probably of disposable quality, and have since rotted.

Unlike other jobs for thirteenth-century writers (such as scribbling out pardons to forgive sins, recording lists of valuable property and people), shrine advertising didn't require official monk status, church accreditation, or a nod from the French-speaking government, making it the perfect career for a Hengesty person. The hero's time as an overworked intern, copyist, and editor in Alfred's Winchester House had trained him in the mass production of text. Meanwhile, Horsehair's background as a poet set her up to invent heartwarming narratives and catchy, memorable slogans. This was exactly what the minor shrines needed.

"The link much missed from the evidence is the pamphlet literature," moaned the historian David Carson, writing about political propaganda during the fourteenth century rather than cheap shrine advertisements, but the problem's the same.* When dealing with objects that were prone to dissolving (especially when brought along on a rainy multi-day hike), it's hard to know what circulated when. Without Hengest and Horsehair's actual pamphlets, the closest I can get to the details of their work is by way of asterisking their business plan.

Packs of cheap paper didn't arrive in England until the 1400s, and animal-skin parchment cost serious money. Although no record states precisely the cost-per-sheet circa 1300, an English monk from around that time wrote a short book preface very much focused on the topic of money, as follows:

| | |
|---|---|
| Þeos Boc was geal ge-writen | *this book was all ge-written* |
| on feower | *in four* |
| Wyken and kostede þreo | *weeks and costed three* |
| and fifti syllinges | *and fifty shillings* |

Going off this book's page of contents (because the rest of the pages disappeared), a modern scholar figured it filled one hundred and fifty-two "folios," which were large sheets of parchment folded in half to create four book-sized pages. The monk's labour might be included in the price or not, and ditto for expenses such as ink, lunch, massages, etc. For simplicity, I assume these came out of a different budget.

*David Carson's book is called *John Gower, Poetry and Propaganda in Fourteenth-Century England.*

Since a shilling was twelve pence, the unit price therefore comes to roughly four pence per parchment folio, which was slightly more than the cost of a gallon of wine in those days. Even if Hengest and Horsehair made ultra-simple pamphlets of four to eight pages from a single folded sheet, the results would still have been too expensive to give away as junk mail.

Snag two: most people couldn't read.

A duplex problem needs a two-faced solution. Hengest and Horsehair must have illuminated the meaning of their brochures by adding rudimentary sketches and maps, catering to the illiterate *and* enhancing the documents' value. A potpourri of artwork, poems, trail tips, and other handy info could turn their pamphlet into a low-cost, rude version of those fancy books that no normal person could afford.

As the logic of modern marketing has shown us, a product's central weakness must become its strength. A mere four pennies – barely more than a jug of wine – could buy early medieval English-speakers an entry-level luxury book (perhaps folded into eight pages measuring 10½ by 15 centimetres) available for purchase at, say, a portable kiosk set up in a village market. These cheap guidebooks may not have been "built to last" but they *were* "conveniently disposable." And whereas the few surviving European pilgrimage manuals from the period were bound between thick wooden plates and clamped down with metal clasps to prevent buckling and breaking of the parchment, Hengest and Horsehair's travel booklets would soon resemble the old roadmap of Ontario I peeled yesterday from a damp corner of my garage.

*Figure 3.1* – Disposable guidebooks, circa 1300 AD

The four-penny cover price zapped away their material costs, so Hengest and Horsehair could pocket whatever fee they charged the shrine manager for their services – and what a bargain for that manager! He or she could recoup the investment from all the suckers who showed up to kiss the sacred sheep knuckle. The pilgrims paid, felt better, got the badge, headed to the pub. Everybody won.

With literacy slowly on the rise in England and paper on the way, there could hardly have been a better time to get a head start in the commercial writing trade. It would be like buying Apple shares circa 1994. I sure hope Hengest and Horsehair figured this all out for themselves.

## 2. THUGS, 1320 AD

Unless I wanted to sell a cut-price luxury guidebook, I would never recommend the early Middle Ages of England as a good spot for a hike. Heirloom wildflowers abounded, sure, along with a pre-industrial wealth of songbirds, footpaths free of barbed-wire interruptions, and fields free of suburbs, but all of this raised a sum of charm insufficient to balance against woodland bandits and dogs with "the rage" (rabies).

"It's remarkable," Horsehair probably said to Hengest one day, "that in all these years of foot travel as we pump out poems, pamphlets, etc., no thug has seriously injured either of us."

"Nor a raging dog," Hengest might have added. "It's a good thing I learned the hat trick."

As a full-time traveller, Hengest must have picked up medieval advice on dealing with rabid animals. One of the European pilgrimage guides suggested people should hold out a hat at arm's length for the raging dog to bite, teeing up the dog's head in just the right spot, such that the person could kick it unconscious with his or her boot heel. (Hengest's helmet, if we ever found it, might bear some telltale punctures.)

"Do you reckon that trick works on thugs too?" Horsehair asked.

Being a canny sort of person, she probably knew that snippets of wisdom apply to some circumstances but not all. (Failure to recognize this point is a major cause of terrible decisions, in my experience.)

The best-marketed bandits in English history are Robin Hood's Merry Men. I shrink from calling them the "best-known" because so little about them is known for sure, e.g., did they exist, and if so, when? Movies drawn from the Robin Hood tales usually set themselves in the fog of King John's reign, around 1200 AD. Scholars, however, have dug up clues linking a real-life Hood to every century from the eleventh to the fifteenth, which could mean he was a witch and/or had been cursed to extreme old age by an angry Welsh person, or else that most of the clues are duds. Robin's fellow travellers are easier quarry because their team name, the "merry men," entered the language at one point only, in the early 1300s. It falls neatly beside northern English references to "John le Littel" (mentioned as a deer thief in court records from 1318) and "William Scarlet" (pardoned by Yorkshire police in 1318), not to mention a "Robby Hood" who, in 1317, owned property ten miles down the road from the town of Barnsdale, the alleged birthplace of Robin Hood in some of the ballads. Around that time, someone coined the term "merry men" and applied it, bizarrely, to people who lived rough in the woods.

The name's oldest written-down example is in a story called *The Tale of Gamelyn*, produced by an anonymous pen in 1350 AD. It doesn't mention any Robins, but Gamelyn is a wronged nobleman who escaped into a forest and joined up with a gang of outlaws referred to as Gamelyn's "mery men," during the reign of King Edward (1307–27). Whether the Merry Men followed Gamelyn or Robin, or neither or both, they took on vaguely positive attributes in the public mind, even as various tales added up to a nonsense of opposing facts. What mattered to their English fans was the thugs' mirth, as well as their left-wing politics and Anglo-Saxon ethnocentrism. The latter quality doesn't sound good nowadays, but back in 1320, with a stubborn Norman aristocracy still owning much of England, the Anglo-Saxon cause counted as a civil rights movement. Downtrodden folk liked the thugs so much that, toward the end of the 1300s, the brand suffered from "genericization," as with kleenex, escalators, and heroin. Any no-name set of boisterous companions would declare themselves to be merry men.

Calling hoodlums "merry" implies the presence of a marketing talent, which is an unusual knack among illiterate bandits. That's a prejudice on my part, not a proof that the Merry Men hired a consultant. However, knowing Hengest and Horsehair to be on the road in the early 1300s, pioneering the genre of advertorial documents, only a churl would ignore the coincidence between the pair's momentum and the most famous feat of medieval brand management.

The network of shrines and hiking trails would, certainly, bring the hero to Nottinghamshire at some point. Once in the neighbourhood, he and Horsehair could hardly avoid the woods, where an encounter with the local bandits would be more than possible. It might rather be taken for granted. Knowing the Angles by their story so far, and relying on common sense for the thugs, I can asterisk what happened next.

"Why are you offering me your hat?" one thug probably asked Hengest. "I just asked for your money or your life.

I said nothing with regard to hats. There is no hat option. Let's try this again. Your *money*, or your *life*."

"She's a poet and I'm a freelance editor," Hengest might have responded. "We don't have much of either."

Although true, I strongly doubt this approach helped him much.

"What's in your bag?" a secondary thug wanted to know (I expect), pointing to Horsehair's satchel of pamphlets and valuable unused parchment. If this were a movie, the audio folks would need to underlay a tense soundtrack with heartbeats.

"Open it up, you harlot," a third thug surely said, appearing from nowhere.

*Thump, thump.*

With his warrior days long behind him, Hengest had no tools for exerting power apart from a moderate level of editorial expertise. I suppose he could have tried to use this as a kind of weapon.

"I don't have a bag," Hengest might retort, for example.

This would at least take the attackers by surprise.

"Yes, I see that," thug number three would say. "I was talking to *her*."

"Aha!" Hengest could exclaim. "Then you shouldn't use the word 'harlot.' It only applies to men. That is a very common mistake!"

He might emphasize his statement by jabbing a finger at each thug in turn, as one of my high-school teachers did when trying to unnerve lippy students.

In action flicks, an off-topic, pedantic style of banter may be the mark of a fighter blessed with extraordinary skill and luck, such as James Bond. I wonder if thugs knew about this trope in the Middle Ages, and instinctively adopted battle-ready warrior stances, with their front legs bent, rear feet at forty-five degrees, arms raised. It's hard to know for sure.

"What are you talking about?" the first thug might have asked Hengest, nervously, or not.

"You mean, '*hwat*' am I talking about?" Hengest could fire back. "*H* comes before *w*, thug. Look it up."

He was right, technically, in that most English-speakers still pronounced "what" the ancient Angle way, unaware that Old English was over. The lazy *w* thing was beginning to sweep the country, however, and the fact that it had apparently reached the northern region of Nottinghamshire in 1320 AD should interest dialect historians who believe the habit began in the south of the island around this time.

"*H* before *w*?" the thug probably replied. "Since when?"

(I assume he'd never learned proper Winchester Style at school.)

"Since '*hwen*'!" Hengest could reiterate, sensing he had the upper hand.

Thug number two might ask his buddies why they didn't just kill this strange old man and get on with the robbery.

"'*Hwy*'!" repeated the hero in triumph, or so I'd guess (though perhaps his bluster would wear thin as he spoke). "*Hwy* can't you just kill this strange old . . . "

"Here," Horsehair said. "Take the bag."

I suppose the thugs took it, opened it, and found the contents puzzling.

"What are these?"

"*Hwat* are these."

"Shut up, Hengest. They're our trail guides for minor pilgrimages."

"*Pil*grimages?" a thug might ask.

If this man was, for instance, the famous Little John, he'd probably have wondered many times about going on a pilgrimage to clean himself of various sins, such as poaching those deer.

"Pilgrim*ages*," said Hengest. (His warrior instincts told him to fight to the death.) "Thugs, the word is French, so the stress falls at the end. It's not like English that way. Duh."

"Hengest, stop trying to correct these low-lifes. They represent the future of our language!" said Horsehair, or whatever. And she was roughly correct. Unlettered, circumscribed cultures such as bands of thieves often do a good job of tossing out old rules and forming new ones, thereby keeping the fashions ticking along.

"Hwat are you saying?" Hengest might well ask. "I guess you people would accept '*nat*ure' in the place of 'nat*ure*,' would you?"

*Thump*, *thump*, went the soundtrack.

Horsehair and the three thuggish, morose men perhaps checked in with each other before confirming their agreement.

"Yep."

"I would."

"Yep, me too."

"Sounds fine."

(*Thump*, *thump*.)

"And *hom*age, not hom*age*?"

More nods.

"*Hos*tel, instead of hô*tel.* That's okay with you, is it?"

All the thugs felt fine about these bastardizations of French words borrowed into English.

"And even kil*om*etre, dare I ask, instead of *kil*ometre?"

"What's a 'kilometre'? I've never heard of that one."

"*Hwat*'s a kilometre!" Hengest shrieked, possibly. "*Hwo, hwat*, I told you, *hwere, hwy, hwen*, and *how*. All six question-words begin with *h*. Is that so hard to remember?"

"Enough small talk," one of the bandits must have said, at some point. "Have you got any money or not?"

I know from earlier adventures that Horsehair could think well on her feet, such as when she poisoned Vortimer, invited the Celts to her nights of long knives, argued with an owl, and so on.

"No," she probably said, therefore. "But we can give you something much better, a service that will render you more prosperous, secure, and successful in every way. All you need to do is tell me about your gang, and some of its aspirations."

And so, if I have this right, Horsehair offered marketing advice to the morose thugs of Sherwood Forest, helping them build a sympathetic image around a fuzzy but appealing concept – happiness – that could be harnessed to a reassuring storyline. "We rob people, yes," it said, "but in a good way, and we're on *your* side." This message was simple enough to be strung into punchy couplets or short ballads and distributed to common folk by means of biodegradable pamphlets, word-of-mouth, rfshft. An example of Horsehair's work may be the once-popular piece of anonymous doggerel, "A Gest of Robyn Hode."* Like many modern commercials, it praises the brand by means of testimony from fictional witnesses, such as a random wandering knight who claims to have met the Merry Men and received a handout from them.

Now is the knight
  gone on his way
This game hym
  thought full gode
Whanne he loked
  on Bernesdale
He blessyd Robyn Hode
And whanne he thought
  on Bernesdale
On Scarlok, Much,
  and Johnn,
He blyssyd them
  for the best company
That ever he in come†

*Now the trustworthy actor*
  *has tested our brand.*
*He found the experience*
  *completely satisfying.*
*Whenever he looked*
  *at the spot where it happened*
*He praised Robin Hood.*
*And whenever he thought*
  *about the spot (etc.)*
*Focusing on Messrs.*
  *Scarlett, Much, and John*
*He praised them*
  *as "the best bunch of guys*
*I have ever met!"*

Doubtless, Horsehair's public relations coup prolonged the lives of Little John, Will Scarlett, Much (the miller's son), and Robyn Hood. More broadly, she changed perceptions of outlaws across the land, for which many grateful

* Date and author unknown (Horsehair, ~1330 AD?). It was reprinted on broadsheets from the late 1400s on.

† My translation fails to capture the original writer's pun on "income," a key term for those closely involved.

thugs ought to have thanked her. This goes some way to explaining how Hengest and his sister-daughter could pass safely through the island's woodlands, growing their business during these decades and centuries, while the English language waited for Geoffrey Chaucer to arrive.

## 3. THE SEVEN WORDS YOU CAN'T SAY IN MIDDLE-AGED ENGLISH, 1340 AD

The production and sale of junky pieces of writing gave Hengest and Horsehair a regular source of cash for food and shelter. According to Abraham Maslow's hierarchy of needs, they would soon begin to want other, more luxurious goods and services. They grew tired of hiking all day, I assume. They perhaps spoke of staying put for a few months, or making a major purchase such as a horse, even a cart to go with it. It would occur to them to expand beyond petty, bread-and-butter shrines, and try for a bigger customer.

The richest and most tempting game was Canterbury Cathedral, the apex of Britain's shrine pyramid, where in 1170 AD assassins had carved open St. Thomas Becket in front of the altar. (He wasn't getting married. He was the archbishop.) Pilgrims arrived by the hundreds of thousands, bringing their silver coins, gold, and jewellery, to pay tribute. Some, caught up in the spirit of the place, handed over their life savings in exchange for tickets to heaven, sold locally. These tickets were known as "indulgences," I guess because they were expensive but not useful. If any shrine could afford a full-time marketing team, this was the place.

Canterbury buzzed with dutiful monk-librarians whose foresight (or hoarding tendencies) gave history some truly unimportant documents, preserved simply by virtue of being written in or near St. Augustine's Abbey, a grandiose building that used to be a rival to the cathedral itself, although today it's just a pile of stones and half-finished walls that any idiot could build. The fact that the abbey's libraries and archives didn't save any anonymous promo brochures from the 1300s suggests to me that the items never existed, because this was the one place where they should have survived long enough to enter the permanent written record. Therefore, I can asterisk that Hengest and Horsehair's pitch to the shrine manager failed this time. It's easy to spot why. The archbishop already had the best marketing gimmick in the country – vials of blood taken from Thomas Becket's body when the revered saint lay dying on the cathedral floor, all those years ago, gasping final words for the faithful while underlings started tapping him like a maple syrup tree. Every priest in England owned some of Thomas's blood, and doubtless these influential men waved their gewgaws from the pulpit. You couldn't buy publicity like that. No matter how artful the handwriting, maps, and poems in Hengest and Horsehair's portfolio, Canterbury didn't need them.

After receiving a setback to one's ambitions, the usual step is to hit the taverns for a post-mortem drink (or six). If Hengest and Horsehair did so, and timed their visit correctly in 1340 AD, they would probably have run into another man doing exactly the same thing. His name was Michael, and he wrote the least successful book of the fourteenth century, entitled *The Backwards Bite of Inner Wit.** It is a work of translation from the original French, a language Michael couldn't speak.

Hundreds of years after the fact, critics still heap abuse on *The Backwards Bite* and its author.

"Unfortunately, Master Michael was a very incompetent translator," howled a founding editor of the *Cambridge History of English Literature* in 1908. She'd managed to find something nice to say about every other tiresome text from the 1300s. But not this one. "Michael often quite fails to grasp the sense of his original," she added, "and his version is frequently unintelligible without recourse to the French work."

"It appears not to have gained any popularity," snipes Wikipedia today. (The volunteer editors rank their stubby article on *The Backwards Bite* as "of low importance" to each of its four pertinent contexts: "The Middle Ages," "Christianity," "Literature," and, pathetically, "Kent.") "Only one copy has survived and that is almost certainly the original," the entry continues. "No demonstrable influence on later works has been found."†

The existence of a non-trilingual monk who felt entitled to wing a French translation from his office at the country's top abbey indicates that the English language's career prospects were looking up. Ignorance of foreign languages has often

*In medieval southern English, Michael spelled out this title as *Ayenbyt of Inwyt*. The prefix *ayen-* meant "against" in the sense of "opposite," "in reverse direction," "counter-wise," or "backwards."

† A much later work, James Joyce's *Ulysses*, did borrow the words of Michael's title to refer to pangs of guilt, which perhaps doesn't count as a "demonstrable influence" but is slightly better than nothing.

been a sign of strength, even a source of pride, for the English-speaking world. Michael's own job arc didn't look so good, however. He was near retirement age. Young, ambitious monks presumably snapped for his juicy post in Canterbury. *The Prick of Conscience*, a competing book on a similar topic, survives from Michael's day in 120 copies, denying Geoffrey Chaucer's *Canterbury Tales* first-place in the pop charts of Middle English verse (Chaucer's book came second, with 83 medieval copies). The full-length *Prick* even gave rise to a spin-off pocket edition called *The Shorter Prick of Conscience.* People generally loved books that explained why they should feel bad about things, as both the *Prick* and Michael's *Backwards Bite* aimed to do. In fact, these titles were synonymous. Michael's "backwards bite" referred to a self-gnawing, bothersome feeling. His "inner wit" meant the wisdom of the soul, precisely the same as a "conscience." Side by side, the pair of books proved beyond doubt that although the market hungered for the genre, it hated Michael's work in particular. An author could hardly meet a ruder response than this.

His source text, Brother Laurent's *La somme le roi*, found many readers in its home country of France, where it benefited from two factors – first, it was not a clumsy work of translation, and second, Laurent was the French king's personal priest. Michael found Laurent's book deeply impressive (to the extent that he understood it), and felt guided by a passion that he perceived as the Holy Spirit visiting him, calling upon him to ensure all English-speaking people heard *La somme le roi*'s message. As Michael wrote in *The Backwards Bite*'s opening apology, he had done all this not-very-good work for the sake of "lewd men, women, and children," so that they too would learn, for instance, to stay away from pubs.

"The taverne is a ditch to thieves," he wrote in *The Backwards Bite*, misrendering the French for "den of thieves." "There arise eludings, strifes, and manslaughters. And those that sustain the tavernes are the sharers in the sins."

I'm sure Michael agreed wholeheartedly with Laurent at the moment of translating these sentences. But that was before *The Backwards Bite* bombed. After hearing the public reaction, he surely did as any writer would, in his place.

"To hell with it," he might have said. "To hell with critics, to hell with consciences and pricks. Tonight, I'm getting trottered."

"By God's bones," Hengest could be saying to Horsehair at whichever Canterbury tavern best suited miserable people. "How am I going to buy myself a horse now?"

"Oy," Michael perhaps called out from across the room. He was, let's say, halfway through the second beer ever to pass his lips. "Stop swearing, thief! And don't even think about *eluding*. I know your kind."

"Who the God's-fingernails are you?" the hero growled, maybe, if he'd mistaken a recent trend of swearing by the nails that once pinned Jesus Christ's wrists to a crucifix, thinking instead that "Christ's nails" referred to a body part. Youth slang tends to confuse old people, and given how ancient Hengest had become, I expect he made errors like this all the time.

The monk would have muttered an offensive epithet into

his mug, judging by the attitudes evinced in his ex-favourite book. Even in disappointment, one doesn't shed all one's previous convictions at once.

"You what?" Hengest asked.

"You're worse than the Jews."

Then Michael probably ungulped a mixture of beer and lunch onto the world's only copy of *The Backwards Bite*. If he had never drunk alcohol before, then I guess he might even have passed out and hit his head on the stone floor, under the circumstances.

Michael held the belief that people of Jewish faith once "rode" the prophet Jesus to his death, in the old sense of the verb "rode" that meant to hang someone's body on a large rod, pole, penis, or crucifix. However, *The Backwards Bite* argued that, compared to uttering rude words, the lynching of Jesus wasn't so bad. (Warning: Michael's pronouns call for some reading-between-the-words.)

| | |
|---|---|
| Hi byeþ more worse | *They [swearers] are worse* |
| þanne þe Gyewes, | *than the Jews,* |
| þet hine dede | *that did stick him [Jesus]* |
| a-rode. | *on the rode [rude/rood].* |
| Hy ne breken | *They [some Jews] break not* |
| non of his buones. | *none of his bones.* |
| Ac þise | *But these ones [Hengest, etc.]* |
| him to-brekeþ | *break him [Jesus] up* |
| smalle þanne me deþ | *smaller than folks do* |
| þet zuyn | *to that pig* |
| ine bocherie. | *in the butcher shop.* |

I have checked, and the smallest cut from a pig is a slice of bacon, or if that doesn't count, then it would be a rib tip.

Casually naming slices of the prophet's body, such as "God's nails" or "Christ's arms," was strictly against the rules. His cross-bound parts might only be mentioned in solemn ways, ideally while standing in a sanctified location. The art of oathing hadn't changed much since Hengest's youth, except that now a warrior's own honour mattered less than that of Christ on the cross. And as before, most normal people got a kick out of defying the rules. "Some are so evil taught that they can say nothing without swearing," the *Backwards Bite* reported. "It is dreadful and horrible to hear and listen."

According to the modern scholar Geoffrey Hughes, the rudest phrase recorded in Middle English seems to be, "Harrow! By nailes and by blood," which is what the bartender Harry Bailey yells at an annoying pilgrim in Geoffrey Chaucer's *The Canterbury Tales*. "That shows us what Chaucer considered outrageous swearing to be," wrote Hughes in his *Swearing: A Social History*, although to be precise, it shows us only what the great poet saw as outrageous-but-publishable swearing. Chaucer's work never mentioned the word "goddamn," for instance, even though English soldiers were shouting it so often on the fields of France in the early 1420s that Joan of Arc nicknamed them *les goddems*. No English-language manuscripts mention "goddamn" until a Shakespeare script from 1591. "This clearly shows us how much older are many oaths than the date of their first written or printed appearance," said Ashley Montagu, anthropologist and author of *The Anatomy of Swearing*.* If Joan of Arc's French ears pricked up at "goddamn" in 1420 AD, it's a short leap onto the asterisk-fact that rude Londoners spoke and heard it on their streets thirty-odd years earlier, when Chaucer was writing. Perhaps the poet had a no-go zone (in public, at least) and "goddamn" was in it.

Taking Ashley Montagu's point about "goddamn," any swear word written down in the late sixteenth century falls under suspicion of existing in the oral slang of the late fourteenth. Some popular suspects are in column B, below:

| COLUMN A<br>**What Chaucer's characters said**<br>*(published in fourteenth century)* | COLUMN B<br>**What they didn't say**<br>*(published in fifteenth and sixteenth centuries)* |
|---|---|
| Christ's passion! | God's toes! |
| God forbid! | God's rood! |
| Benedict! | God's flesh! |
| Harrow! | Goddamn! |
| By saint so-and-so! | God's sides! |
| God's dignity! | God's hooks! |
| God's arms! | God's wounds! |
| Cock's bones! | God's 'lids! |
| By God's heart! | God's guts! |
| By blood! | God's nicks! |
| By nayles! | God's niggers! |

* Published in 1967. The scholar's full name was Montague Francis Ashley-Montagu. His birth name, however, was Israel.

Although English-speakers in the northern hemisphere referred to anyone with a skin colour browner than light tawny as "negars" from the 1600s on, the practice of swearing on "niggers" probably had nothing to do with this. More likely, people were trying to be polite by fiddling with the older word "nigs" or "nicks," which referred to cuts, slits, or wounds. Perhaps "niggers" sounded gentler to their ears, just as "fuddle" sounds softer than "fuck." In the 1340s, the Canterbury bartender who had to deal with Michael's drunken slip into unconsciousness would have reached instead for harsher, more guttural terms.

"Wake up, by God's guts," he might have said as he poured grey water over his customer.

These swear words could be streamlined by omitting the "God" particle, leaving just the letter *s*, as in "swounds" or "slids." Although the missing particle doesn't exist in a normal sense, we know it used to be there because the resulting words couldn't have taken shape without it.

"Snicks, g'dzhooks!" wheezed Hengest, perhaps, covering his mouth. "What a stink!"

A puddle of grunky material spread over the flagstones from around Michael's middle.

"Jesus's ribtips!" cursed the bartender, or something like that. "God's giblets! Christ's lardons!"

"Christ's *what*?" Horsehair asked, probably, because a poet must be alert for new slang.

"Godscock, I don't know what it means," the bartender might have admitted. "Something my goddamn kids say. Help me get rid of this turbulent monk, will you?"

I expect Michael woke up the next day, in a ditch, feeling as low in body as he had previously felt in spirit.

### 4. SCENIC WALKS IN PLAGUE COUNTRY, 1348 AD

If the English language of 1348 AD were sitting here in my office, shaking a little in its chair, I would tell it two things: (1) please calm down, and (2) I've got good news and I've got bad news.

The Black Death currently scouring Europe will more or less see the French away from Britain. That's the good news. It's not because speaking French leads directly to contracting *Yersinia pestis* (as far as doctors know), but in a numbers game where one in three people will spit blood and croak, whoever starts off with more players wins. Just like chess. Even Deep Blue, if already two pawns down when the piece-swapping begins, is in deep you-know-what. The French failed to breed fast enough in time for the plague. Their team contained too many jocks, bosses, and generals, but too few babysitters, house-trained uncles, young lovers, and nerds.

Dear English language of 1348, let this be a lesson to you. For now, enjoy the fact that as necks and armpits swell up across that little prison of an island, there will be vacancies in the civil service, at the church pulpits too, and at all the best restaurants. English-speakers will find they can get by perfectly well without learning a foreign language.

"Hallelujah," the English language would probably reply, in my office. "What's the bad news?"

"You're going to lose your nascent guidebook industry," I would tell it. "Don't worry. It's only temporary. It'll grow back, and you'll hardly feel a thing."

However, for the two human beings whose livelihoods depended on the public appetite for multi-day hikes, the Black Death raised a serious threat. It probably seemed okay at first, when the mortalities numbered in the mere thousands, and several pilgrimage guides needed updating. Hengest and Horsehair could hit up their old customers for a second-edition gig. After all, what is more frustrating than to obey a paragraph in a cheap guidebook that advises you to follow a side-trail down into the hamlet of Bottompiddle for a delicious lunch at the charming pub whose prices are so reasonable, only to find that the "signifier" no longer mirrors the "signified," so to speak – the pub is shuttered, the hamlet abandoned, the trail blocked by a smoking pile of charred, disease-ridden human flesh? During the early phase of the plague, owning the latest edition of a guidebook could make the difference between a pleasurable stroll and certain death, since the illness tended to strike village by village. Contagion could wipe out a whole community on the lee-side of a hill, while a bare mile over the hill crest, another township was thriving and its tavern offering a not-to-be-missed brunch with a view of the famous local waterwheel. But somewhere between the autumn of 1348 and the summer of 1349, a tipping-point occurred, as the death toll approached fifty per cent of the country's population. Then, if you were a sensible person living among healthy folk, not even the Catholic propaganda machine could persuade you to go for a long walk. People who were silly enough to leave their homes, such as priests, inevitably met the plague and succumbed. This inflicted a double-whammy on Hengest and Horsehair's business, diluting customer demand for their products while killing off the group of clients they most counted on for commissions.

It spelled trouble. A dire financial pressure would have pushed the two Hs, as it did so many footloose wanderers who survived the scourge, toward the capital city, which suddenly hungered for their skills.

## 5. THE SCRIBE RUSH, 1385 AD

Next to the Merry Men, the second-most-brilliant act of rebranding in the entire Middle Age of English came when somebody persuaded the rest of the country that London, in the wake of the Black Death, might be a good place to visit and even stay awhile. Thanks to this hoax, the city sucked in folks by the thousands. Some arrived with specific goals and a list of contacts. Others aimlessly followed the others. And just as a molecule may generate bizarre behaviour when it rapidly gains mass, so the city of London fired off curiosities, such as a fashion for wide, frilly hats, an elite social club based on silly handshakes, and the powerful "Chancery" style of writing, named after a fiefdom ruled by a curious man with a frilly hat and a long wig. His name was the Lord Chancellor. The style of writing developed by the Chancellor's employees morphed, with subtle changes, into the bureaucratic tongue now used in credit card agreements, legislative bills, and other mind-bogglingly dull strings of sentences throughout the English-speaking world.

Of all London's strange new fireworks, however, the best was its "scribe rush." Unlike a gold rush, which encourages the robbery, murder, and rape of local residents by mining company employees, a scribe rush tends to generate nice handwriting and that's about it. At worst, there may be cases of hand cramps, poor posture, and/or furrowed brows. And whereas a gold rush attracts riff-raff, scullions, and harlots, London's Scribe Rush of the late 1300s brought only, as one historian put it, "reasonably educated men who came from the provinces seeking their fortune, Dick Whittington-style."*

To be strict – as I sometimes am – Dick Whittington isn't the best example because he *was* a gold-digger. He starred in a folk tale, taught to me when I was young, that begins with rural Dick hearing the words, "London's streets are paved with gold." He fails to recognize this as false advertising. Having joined the first wave of suckers headed to the capital, Dick discovers his mistake, gets a low-level job, mistreats a cat, sells the cat, earns a fortune, and buys himself a political career.† The only connection between Dick and a typical London scribe is that their stories have glittered in the eyes of reasonably educated men ever since, for different reasons. Dick enacts the entrepreneurial dream, beloved by money-grubbers and the power-hungry. The

* Kathryn Kerby-Fulton wrote this in her book, *Written Work: Langland, Labour, and Authorship*.

† In the folk tale, Dick ultimately became the mayor of London. The cat deserves most of the credit for this, having laboured overseas in the rat-catching business for the sake of Dick's profits. The story is usually anthologized as "Dick Whittington and His Cat."

scribes play out the more literary dream of getting paid to hang around in pubs with notebooks, quill pens, and similar fetish toys.

Who invented the deceptive meme of London's gold-paved streets, no one knows, but this person was responsible for turning the city into a hotbed of economic activity. A *fool's* gold rush may do the same job as a real one, juicing up the market with migrants who pour in from the countryside. London's ingenious viral campaign took place straight after Hengest and Horsehair's guidebook business suffered its blow from the plague, a time when London's bigwigs would have felt motivated to hire the best public relations experts in the business, so the wretched freelancers may have found their new role here.

"You're a good liar, kiddo," Hengest likely told Horsehair, as her latest marketing brainwave vibrated out across the country.

"It's not lying, Dad," she protested. "The 'streets paved with gold' thing is a metaphor. People aren't supposed to take it literally."

I expect she was weighing the sack of coins handed to her by an ecstatic Chamber of Commerce. Her brother-father probably shrugged and patted his daughter-sister's head.

From what I can tell, the scribe rush arrived last in a series of even hastier rushes provoked by Horsehair in the late 1300s. First was the fool's gold rush, during which London's core rang with gullible yokels chipping at the paving stones, sluicing their pans of muck and gravel in the sodden streets, sleeping rough at night, and dreaming of that untouched alleyway where they'd finally strike it rich. (For most, this occurred metaphorically or, in regard to getting rich, not at all.) The wannabe Dick Whittingtons fuelled a secondary economy of taverns, gambling, brothels, and soon enough, litigation. A lawyer rush was spawned, with the founding of London's historic Inns of Court. They served no alcohol, despite the name. Rather, plaintiffs visited the Inns to tell a lawyer their stories of woe and damage. The lawyer then chastised them for having acted without a written contract, and then, having fought the case in the Court of Common Law, deliberately lost, and appealed it to the Court of Chancery, all the while tut-tutting at the regrettable nature of this drawn-out process and its great expense, the lawyer would up-sell his poor client on some safeguard documents – a will-and-testament, a proper gold-mining claim – all to be signed and copied in triplicate, for which the customer needed to hire the lawyer's expensive clerk or a slightly cheaper freelance scribe down on Paternoster Row. Eventually, all unhappy or angry people in London were persuaded to put the complex details of their lives into written form. And, just as today, the city's rich seams of anger and unhappiness ran deep and long, hence the London Scribe Rush.

It took place during the coming-of-age moment when, no longer a pipsqueak beside French and Latin, English assumed the form of a full-sized tongue able to govern a bona fide nation, emit literature of broad renown, and start invading other countries. One auspicious afternoon in the autumn of the fourteenth century, old Latin patted English on the head and handed it the keys to parliament.

"Your turn to drive, kid," said Latin.

And lo, English shunted the gas pedal like a nervous lover, first with Latin and French observing from the back seat, but eventually, heavens be praised, all by itself. Entire bills were written, half-read, voted on, and passed into law in English. Scribes can't take full credit, though. Their lot was not to be top-level language makers, composing the great idioms, choosing the ribbons of French, Latin, and more exotic vocab to colour the weave. Scribes did their labour in tiny places, putting the *–ed* in "groped," or the *–cion* in "discrecion."

"If you are stuck," wrote a modern advisor named David Crystal, imagining a newbie scribe, "you can always ask other scribes over a late-night pot of ale, and do what they do." This image of scribes in pubs recurs in many historical accounts, enhancing the period's appeal while also explaining a lot. The standard spellings and practices we have inherited from these people were largely concocted while drunk, or distracted. "The busy streets and taverns of central London mixed everyone together," continued Crystal, writing *The Stories of English*. "Then as now, professionals would have looked at each other's work to admire it, to rubbish it, to copy it." And to spill beer over it and throw darts at it, probably. The point being that once the daylight dimmed in official London, the scribes crept out to rule over a humble nighttime microcosmos, like the hosts of karaoke bars, with their mild but pervasive authority.

Full-time detectives from the loftiest institutions – Oxford, Cambridge, the University of Maine – have teamed up to conjecture a few of these medieval heroes back into existence, despite the problem that a scribe rarely signed his or her own work, and never included a bio. Scribes are generally assumed to have been men, or at least to have dressed as men, but even this is speculation. Undaunted, modern scholars turn to the murky science of scriptology,* in which a person's penmanship unlocks a hidden psyche and a life story. As with palmistry and tarot reading, it helps to know a few details about one's subject in advance, which is why the most successful effort so far depicts a man named Adam who worked as personal assistant to Geoffrey Chaucer, and who was named and cursed by the author himself. Chaucer portrayed Adam as long-haired, absent-minded, and skittish.

| | |
|---|---|
| Adam scrivener,<br>    if ever thee befall<br>Boece or Troilus<br>    for to write new,<br>Under thy longe locks<br>    thow maist have the scall, | *Adam the Scribe,*<br>    *if ever it falls to you*<br>*To write new editions of my*<br>    *books* Boece *or* Troilus,<br>*Under your long hair,*<br>    *may you get a notorious*<br>    *scabby skin condition,*<br>    *like really bad psoriasis,* |
| But after my makinge<br>    thou write mor trew.<br>So oft a day I mot<br>    thy werke renewe | *Unless, copying my poems,*<br>    *you write more accurately.*<br>*So often every day I must*<br>    *fix and redo your work* |

* Also called "graphology" or "handwriting analysis."

| | |
|---|---|
| It to correct, and eke | *To correct it, and – eek!* |
| to rubbe and scrape, | *to rub and scratch myself,* |
| And all is thorowe | *And it's all because of* |
| thy necligence and rape. | *your negligence and rape.* |

Scriptologists know Adam by the details of his S-curves, ampersands, and capital *G*s in manuscripts attributed to him. They observe that his handwriting sung with a fluid style, bearing an "agile duct" (which means that the line of ink dances all over the place) and a "vertical impetus" (i.e., the pen kept jumping upwards like a nervous jack-rabbit). From this, the scholars draw their psychic conclusions.

He was "conscientious and experienced," according to one expert. He liked his work, and fixed most of his own mistakes, though sometimes he rushed a job, or didn't understand his client's instructions. Strangely, professional scriptologists make little of Adam's most unique habit, which was to doodle barbed-wire onto his capital letters. Investigators see it simply as light-hearted decoration. I suspect darker things haunting the man's mind, but scriptology is a dangerous art to dabble with, so I'll withhold my asterisks on that topic. Copying from scripts believed to be Adam Pinkhurst's, *Figure 3.2* offers a safer extrapolation – a London street sign as the man might have enscribed it.

Adam belonged to a group of five particularly good London scribes, known to later scholars by their codenames, A through E, although there's no proof that the scribes used the code themselves, or even knew any special handshakes. Adam was Scribe B. Scribe E, a man named Thomas, dabbled in poetry and also worked as a legal clerk until he went mad. Scribes A, C, and D are anonymous, but giants of their field nonetheless, especially in D's case.

*Figure 3.2* – A London street name as Adam Pinkhurst would have rendered it.*

"Despite the fact that his real name remains, as yet, unknown, Scribe D has been described as so well known to students of Late Middle English that he hardly needs any introduction," says my favourite encyclopedia. Modern scholars have called the scribe's style "Anglicana at its best." A scriptologist called Jane Roberts collaged the thoughts of her colleagues to form an asterisk-portrait of Scribe D's life in "an entrepreneurial role, busy about the supply of reading matter for a coterie audience of civil servants and

* This road in downtown London has since been demolished to make way for a shopping centre. If it hadn't been, the roadsign might be a mecca for prurient word-nerds the world over, being the language's oldest example of "cunt" as listed in the *Oxford English Dictionary*. The shopping centre draws precisely no international tourists at all, but there you go, property developers and the ruining of things.

literary-minded gentry." Scribe D's letters are more regular than Adam's, resembling (slightly) a Microsoft ye-olde-blackletter font.

*Figure 3.3* – A London street name as Scribe D would have rendered it.

As Adam Pinkhurst proved, a scribe needn't have shown the delicacy and finesse of the above road sign to score high-profile work during the scribe rush. In Chaucer's lifetime, the literacy rate in London sauntered past the 40-per-cent mark and demand billowed for anybody with a lick of scribing and copy-editing ability. Eager whiz kids entered the legal trade, gasped at their new salaries, bought up charming but unfurnished downtown apartments, built aspirational book shelving into all the nooks and crannies, and then suddenly needed to fill the shelves. Satisfying and even lucrative calligraphy jobs were suddenly low-hanging fruit, even for, say, a washed-up former warrior who cared more about the immediate needs of his belly than the art of duct and serif. Since the days of Alfred, it had become Hengesty to know the rudiments of penmanship, a point captured best by splitting an aspect of the hero's definition, with regard to his acquired skills:

**Hengesty . . .** (m) (i) literate, educated, esp. in terms of having acquired some familiarity with poems
(ii) endowed with centuries of experience in scribing and copy-editing

Hengest might never have been a natural artisan, but his headstart as a working scribe ought to have vaulted him ahead of the weakest competition. And Horsehair surely found her way into the London poetry community. By piggybacking on her social network, the hero probably managed to avoid joining the grunts who scratched out endless rolls of bureaucratic or legal material for the Lord Chancellor. I hope he took part in the better-paid end of the scribe rush, copying literary manuscripts for rich buyers, working in most cases directly with a popular creator such as Geoffrey Chaucer, John Gower, or William Langland, who kept lists of registered fans and subscribers. In all of the English-speaking world's history, there was never a better time to work for a poet. In fact, these three decades at the end of the fourteenth century were probably the only time in recorded history when one *could* work "for a poet." That profession is not regularly found among the job creators. For this reason, many scholars give their lives over to marvelling at this rare blip in English's timeline. One modern expert, Janet Coleman, has called it, "England's literary golden age."

Some of the great names from the contents page of the *Norton Anthology, Volume One* worked in the late 1300s, with Chaucer, Gower, and Langland leading the pack. Many less great names wrote too – there was Thomas Usk, for instance, whose "Testament of Love" I have always ignored. As with the scribes, mediocrity didn't matter, and a merely half-smart writer could earn a comfortable middle-class professional income. Not from poetry itself, of course – *that's* never happened – but from dipping a cup into the law trade's rushing waters. The vital characteristic of this golden time is that all the poets were lawyers, and almost all the lawyers, poets.

With their pet scribes embroidering the tiny end of a prestigious new London Style of English, the lawyer-poets chalked out the fashions and cut the cloth. By day, they worked as trial attorneys, legal secretaries, arbiters, notaries, and inspectors. Then, unlike today's law-school graduates, they enjoyed plenty of free evenings and weekends and days off in which to exercise their minds on delight, performing tricks of metre, rhyme, wordplay, and metaphor. The lawyer-poet scenario appeals strongly to scholars, so they don't mind bending a few details to fit it. For instance, despite a total lack of biography for William Langland, who wrote "The Pilgrim's Progress," professors of literature have rallied to place him among "the community of letters that sprang up around the law courts," as Emily Steiner has put it. Since no one can prove Langland was any sort of lawyer, Steiner offers her colleagues a way out. "It is perhaps sufficient to say," she writes, "that a fourteenth-century Londoner with enough literate skills to compose a poem would likely have had some familiarity with the composition of legal instruments." Here, she pulls off a virtuoso rendition of the academic "likely," a special use of the word, meaning, "This is what I'd *like* to be true."

When poets and lawyers (likely) merge, the literary output of each profession naturally follows suit. Legal documents start to fool around. Meanwhile, poems cater to lawyer-ish tastes or get bogged down in the depressive, self-pitying complaints of a trapped professional. For example, the stories of Christ's death written during the scribe rush explain how the tale properly hinges on a binding contract, under which Jesus sold real estate in heaven conditional upon repentance. A Latin text named *Fasciculus morum** clarified the issue for its lawyer audience by printing the verbatim text of the prophet's contract with Christians. According to this source, Jesus concluded his time on Earth with an alien-like legalese sign-off: "Written, read, confirmed, and conveyed to humans on Good Friday, on the summit of Mount Calvary, publicly and openly, to last forever, in the year 5232 after the Creation of the world."

In another example of law's influence on art, John Gower's most popular poem, "The Lover's Confession," begins as all poems were supposed to, with an author's apology or "humility topos." But instead of claiming generally to be a meagre and ever-so-humble sinner, Gower gunned for sympathy from a specific group, people with similar lifestyles, nostalgia, and medical complaints:

* Literally, "a bundle of behaviour."

| | |
|---|---|
| Þus I, | *Thus I,* |
| which am a burel clerk | *a coarse and ignorant legal secretary,* |
| purpose forto wryte a bok | *plan to write a book* |
| after the world | *about the world that,* |
| þat whilom tok | *for a while, spent* |
| longtyme in olde daies passed | *a long time in the Olden Days (now gone),* |
| but for men sein | *and even though people say* |
| it is now lassed | *it is now mired* |
| in worse plit | *in a worse situation* |
| þan it was þo | *than it was back then,* |
| I þenke forto touche also | *I'm scheming to also touch upon* |
| þe world which neweth every dai. | *the "world" as renewable entity.* |
| So as I can, so as I mai | *I'll do my best with what I know,* |
| þogh I seknesse have upon honde, | *although I have terrible wrist cramps, tendonitis, etc.,* |
| and longe have had, | *and have done for a long time,* |
| yit woll I fonde | *yet will I attempt* |
| to wryte, | *to write in a creative sense,* |
| and do my businesse. | *while keeping my day job.* |

The poet proceeds to the "Tale of Three Questions," a story whose happy ending seems at risk because the heroine, who wants to marry a king, belongs to the wrong class of citizen so the marriage would be illegal according to the constitution. The drama resolves when the king signs royal property over to the woman's father, thus altering her status and creating a loophole through which the lovers can wed. Medieval lawyers must have found this breathlessly romantic.

Scribes and lawyer-poets back then belonged to the same "community of letters" that props up the brewery industries today. Geoffrey Chaucer and John Gower, the Eng-Lit icons, mention and praise each other familiarly in their work, and presumably joined Adam Pinkhurst and his peers at the archetypal scribes' tavern from time to time, so it's possible – *likely*, one might say – that Gower, Chaucer, Hengest, Horsehair, and Pinkhurst shared at least one lubricated chat together in a pub. I can even asterisk some of what they might have talked about.

It's not hard to figure out what John Gower, for instance, would say when he was drunk. Anxieties haunt his work. In particular, the sin of forgetfulness bothered him so much that he wrote rhyming verses to chastise himself into remembering how terrible it was not to remember everything. He didn't mind small stuff, like walking out on a bar tab or not locking a door, so much as the big, holistic type of mind-freeze, when he lost his sense of how the world worked, or succumbed (stealing a phrase from my critical edition of Gower's "A Lover's Confession") to "the mind's wilful divergence from the ordained order of things." To forget in this way was to invite chaos, John told himself, and chaos was the devil's lair, the opposite of godliness, the true soul of evil. He liked history only when he could remember what it was.

"Without history, there can be no memory," Gower said, in the pub. "And without memory, there can be no history."

He didn't write these words. I'm quoting again from the intro to my critical edition, which crystallizes the thoughts that most concerned him.

"Without a server, there can be no beer," Hengest probably replied, trying to catch the wait staff's attention. "And without beer . . . never mind. I don't want to picture that."

A highly likely location for their gathering was the Tabard Inn in the neighbourhood of Southwark, around the corner from John Gower's rented apartment in the Priory of St. Mary's Ovaries. The area was then cheap and dirty, across the bridge from the main scribing and lawyering district. If Gower's colleagues cared about his safety, they would often walk him home after work. (A rough map may help those unfamiliar with London.)

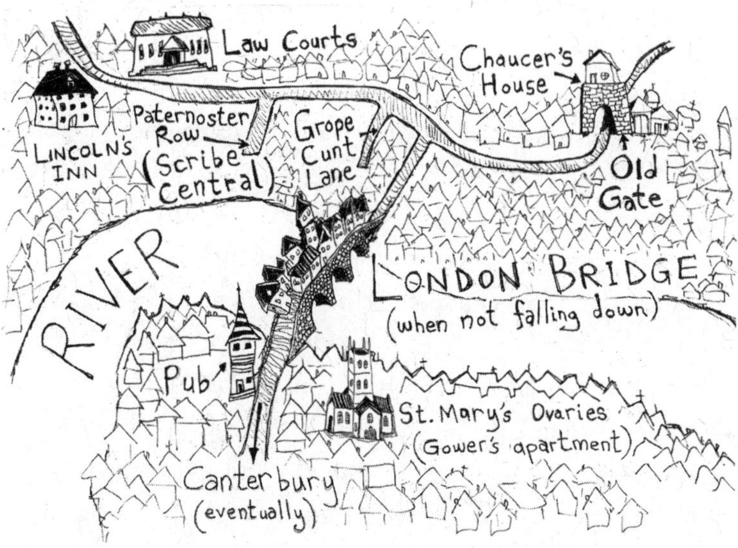


*Figure 3.4* – Downtown London during the Scribe Rush

"No, this is important," John insisted, if he cared about the point as much as my critical edition believes. "Listen. The poet is society's rememberer, who sees with a unified vision to charm people out of their melancholy and division."

"What'll it be?" a server might ask them, finally taking pity on Hengest's agitated hand movements. Perhaps this person was the daughter of Harry Bailey, who was the Tabard's alleged proprietor in *The Canterbury Tales*.

"Five pints of Rotten Rat," Hengest ordered, roughly. "And put it on my tab."

"What name, dearling?"

"Hengest."

"That's a funny name."

"It means, the Stallion."

"Cool. I love nicknames."

"So do I."

"Mine's the Wife of Bath." She smiled a gap-toothed smile. "Okay then, five pints of Rotten Rat for the Stallion. And what about the rest of you?"

Even if this brief mundane exchange was all that Bailey-the-Younger added to their evening (apart from the beer), her words would earn her a place in language history, especially if Adam Pinkhurst snorted as she left.

"Nickname! Did you hear that, Geoffrey?"

Chaucer probably ignored him. But I expect John Gower, with his fetish for order and memory, laughed too. He and Adam knew the correct noun was "an eekname," and that Ms. Bailey had misplaced the letter *n*.

"It's '*eek*name,' from the Latin prefix *ac*, meaning 'and,'" Gower may have mansplained to Horsehair.

"Are you sure it's not from 'aug,' as in 'augment'?" Horsehair asked. She remembered facts pretty well for her age.

"Absolutely sure," replied John, though I suspect he suddenly wasn't. The blood likely drained from his face and he felt that sickness he knew so well – the devil's prickling claw, the backward bite of inner error.

"I thought it was 'eekname' because it attracts attention," piped the hasty Adam Pinkhurst. "You know, *eek!* From the Latin 'ecce,' meaning 'Look at that!'"

If the dynamic between Geoffrey Chaucer and his scribe was roughly as implied by the poem, then Chaucer glowered.

"Goddammit, Adam."

"Gulp," the scribe whispered.

"*Eek*? May fungus rot your earlobes."

Without a dictionary to hand (or in existence), none of the drinkers could check the factual record and conclude that Horsehair knew her stuff. They needed to settle for smaller conclusions.

"What we know is," Adam said, pointing Chaucer's attention toward the server, "*she* was totally wrong."

"But God's guts, I like her," Hengest declared, maybe. He'd had some time since meeting the Merry Men to develop a trust for style over substance. "She has good taste. A 'nickname,' yes. I'll use that from now on."

"It's wrong," Gower protested. "And it goes against history."

"Ah. But haven't you forgotten something?" Horsehair might have asked him, if she was feeling cruel.

Gower would have blanched again. "Have I? I mean, Christ's bollocks, of course I have. I always have! But what, what, *what* . . . " Perhaps he started hitting himself.

By taking the inexpert side of this argument, Hengest showed some business savvy. The scribe game didn't call for square obedience to rules. It took derring-do, panache, and a wet finger in the wind. In a world where "a naperon" was fast becoming "an apron," but "narses" and "nedges" would ultimately fail to oust "arses" and "hedges," Hengest needed to be part talent scout, part style consultant, to keep his work up to date. Authority on language style has always come from the same place that cool does, a mystical sense of when to lead and whom to follow, a splice of independent spirit with shameless conformism. That is the first rule of lexicography – stay hip.

Hengest needed all his wits in this regard to make it out of the Middle Ages without losing his income stream. Even Scribe D's high-quality handwriting would be no match for the iron scribe, scheduled to arrive any decade now from the Gutenberg printing factory in Europe. As usual, the hero couldn't park himself for long.

Being a poet, Horsehair was entitled to a more stable paycheque, since she would of course have picked up work as a lawyer during this period. A sharp decline of high-quality anonymous English literature occurred after Chaucer's time, strongly implying that Horsehair put her poetry on the back burner. I wouldn't judge her if she did. After so many centuries of hunger, the financial rewards of a legal career would tempt a saint.

Nameless lit didn't go away after Horsehair's sell-out, though. If anything, its influence swelled to match the growth of lawyering in England. Horsehair's pen might have sped up in her new trade, where she surely became a high flyer. Judging from the many lawyers I have met, smart ones are like rare heartbeats against a long flatline of dolts and morons. The mother of English rose fast, I'm certain of it, up to the heights where constitutions and royal charters were written, not to mention the drafts of parliamentary acts, the advice and memoranda that spoon-fed ideas into the mouths of power. Horsehair probably had to grow her beard and wear men's clothes, due to sexism, but we must all make accommodations. On the plus side, maybe she hit pay dirt, and at any rate, she is likely to have been responsible for more than we know.

## 6. MACHINATIONS, 1480 AD

In 1480, shortly before pressing out the first nine hundred copies of what would be his hottest non-fiction title, William Caxton had to make a decision. He held in his hands the moveable metal type that would form the printed sentences of *The Chronicles of England*, a history book in which the authors blamed young women for the Black Plague. The women created the disease by wearing clothes that hugged their bodies tightly from top to bottom, almost giving visible definition to their ass-cracks, except that they sewed the tails of foxes into their shirts, letting the fur hang down on the inside to cover their bums. How this precisely looked, let alone how it caused plague, the book's authors didn't explain, but their gaps of logic weren't Caxton's problem. He needed to choose the correct letters to fill in the following blank:

> The women passed, so straitly clothed that they let hang fox tailles, sewed beneath their shirts, for to heal and hyde their _____.

("Heal" meant to conceal, in Caxton's day, not to heal a wound.)

Caxton's style of talking was "broad and rude," as he called it, a southern accent forged in the rural lands below London, where many plurals still ended in *–en*, as in "children," and arses usually began with an *e*–, as in, "ears" or "ers." Back in the old days, when William's father boiled him two eggs for lunch, the old man had called out something like, "Willie, get off your ears and come eat your eggren." (Or "eat your *eyren*," because southerners hated speaking with the back of their mouths.) Now, living as a grown-up in west London amid the grandchildren of gold-panners and scribes from all parts, Caxton knew that his speech could sound odd to the city audience, and might entirely bamboozle customers further north.

"Certaynly our langage now used varyeth from whan I was borne," Caxton once wrote in a preface, guessing wildly at how to spell things. "Therfor in a meane bytwene rude and curyous I have translated this booke."

(By "curyous" he meant highbrow, not curious. I guess "rude" meant "uncivilized," in this case.)

William Caxton had lucked out by scoring a head start in the London printing scene. Until shortly before 1480, he'd operated the world's only English-language press, and he dominated the scene even as competitors began to appear. For all the hype about the strange new technology, Caxton secretly knew that operating a printing press was dead easy, a matter of lining up the metal pieces in the mirror, rubbing some ink over them with a roller, tightening some screws, and shmooshing the type onto some paper, using a lever. Simple. He wasn't any kind of technical wizard. He'd stumbled into the printing industry one day on a trip to Belgium, where he wheeler-dealed for a living. Always alert for a nice little earner, he tested out the intriguing machine and, within minutes, accidentally became a craftsman. Back in Britain, he spread word that moveable type was costly and difficult to obtain, that the assembly and maintenance of wooden presses took years of training, and to this day some storytellers believe his line. It wasn't true. Caxton saw rival companies getting wise, threatening to steal the market away if his books didn't set a high bar for user-friendliness and design. He bribed politicians to pass laws that restricted printing licences, but couldn't trust (or afford) this tactic long term. For Caxton, finding the "mean between rude and curious" seemed all-important for his own commercial survival.

Lacking a dictionary or online corpus to steal from, the printer's quickest source for advice on spellings would be the small staff of typesetters, a group of ex-scribes and eager shop-boys. Each had their own biases, of unequal value. A younger employee might pick up new styles from his social life, a snapshot of his own time and place. A longer-lived worker, especially one who had travelled far and wide, had more data to draw from, more ability to see trends. If William Caxton looked up from his desk one day and spied, for example, an ancient wanderer who was peeking into the printing office to see what all the techno-fuss was about, the boss ought to have invited the wretch inside. And, upon discovering the man's unearthly wealth of experience, his familiarity with the literary canon, etc., Caxton must have glanced skyward and thanked whichever golden goose he prayed to. The printing boss would also be thrilled to learn that this old chap was short of work, being over-skilled in the old-tech world of handwriting and thus glad to offer consultancy at a bargain price.

"I've always spelled it 'ears,'" William Caxton would announce to his team around the boardroom table, to get things started. "That's how old-timers do it. My copy of Oldhelm's *On Virginity* has 'earses' in it. And these two things on my head are my 'eren.'"

"Eggs? On your head?" said a wag, destined to be fired if he wasn't careful.

"*Ee*-ren on my head," repeated Caxton to clarify. "*Eh*-yeren go on my plate. *Eh*-rs goes on my chair."

Clear enough.

"Oldhelm is old hat," a novice typesetter might have piped up. "The grand old Duke of York sits on his 'erys,' in his own words, which gives us a prestige example. He put it in his guidebook, where he explains what to do with a constipated hound-dog."

"What *do* you do with a constipated hound-dog?" someone probably asked.

In his book, *Master of the Game*, the Duke of York advised people to mix a paste of salt, almond oil, and an egg white, then "all this together put in his erys and he shal scumber." The word "scumber" was an abbreviation of "disencumber." It meant to defecate vigorously.

"Yuck," someone probably said.

Another sharp-minded typesetter might have told everyone that "erys" didn't work as a new standard spelling for Caxton's press because they had already printed Geoffrey Chaucer's *Canterbury Tales*, in which a character said, "Mine erys ache of thy drasty speech," referring to ear-ache, not rear-ache. Galled at his own oversight, the first typesetter probably fired back with bluster, emphasizing that the Duke of York spoke the King's English, which mattered more than the dialect of a dead poet.

"Just last year, Prince Edward wrote that the best way to bring a gall-stone out of a hawk is to 'anoynt its erys' with olive oil and then blow salt up through a hollow straw," the young journeyman might add, if he had really done his homework. "I found it in his *Manuals of Falconry*, cotton MS, British Library. There's even a picture, and it's not of the hawk's ears, let me tell you."

"Don't think much of how the royal family spends its time," said a sensible adult, if one was present.

Perhaps the second typesetter stood up on his chair and glowered at the novice. (I base this on my memory of office meetings at a publishing company where I worked, briefly.)

"Chaucer's got more sway than your scumbering toffs!" declared typesetter two. "Normal people read *Troilus and Cressida*, not *Secrets from My Hawk's Rectum.* When the famous lover listened to Cressida 'with his heart and *erys* spread,' book four, line 1422, Troilus wasn't bent over, holding his buttocks open."

"Oh yeah?" yelled his colleague, fists cocked. "How do you know?"

It is true that little certainty exists when one is dealing with Middle English.

"I am 90 per cent sure," the older typesetter could have replied, to be circumspect.

The debate raged on, I imagine, to and fro. It's likely that somebody mentioned John Wycliffe's *The Bible*, in which the main character, God, "afflicts the young men of Goth, causing the ars-ropes of them going out stonken." (The word "stonken" meant either "in an offensive manner" or "bad-smelling.") A typesetter who enjoyed William Langland's poetry could well have held up the "bare ers," from Scribe D's copy of *Piers Plowman.* And so the team had "ears," "erys," "ars," and "ers" to choose among. With the options multiplying in front of them, William Caxton surely called on his wisest consultant, the ancient wanderer, to settle the dispute.

"Scribe D is yesterday's man," Hengest probably said. For example, in those days, young women called my penis a 'tears.' Now I hear 'tarse' more and more. 'Get out your *tarse*,' 'Let us see your *tarse*, old Stallion!' Once upon a time, they lay with me under the 'sters.' Now half the time I make them see 'stars,' or so they tell me."

"How do you do it, at your age?"

"Don't answer that," said Caxton, I expect. "What's your point, ancient wanderer?"

"The writing's on the bathroom wall, gents. The vowels are moving. It's 'arses' for us."

Reading only from the pages of the *Oxford English Dictionary*, William Caxton appears to have invented the spelling "arse" in 1480's edition of his *Chronicles of England*, a doughty feat undermined by its setting amid misogynist propaganda. Caxton's name on the quotation doesn't mean he literally coined "arse," though. He was responding to the advice and habits of those around him, and above all, I guess he did whatever Hengest told him to. After Caxton printed the line about foxtail-wearing women who "heal and hide their arses," copycat editions of *Chronicles* followed his lead. Thirteen rival versions appeared within fifty years of the first printing. In total, the book outsold printed copies of *The Canterbury Tales*, *The Prick of Conscience*, and even Ranulf Higden's sci-fi blockbuster, *Polychronicon* (a history of all times and all places, especially England). From 1480 on, "arse" planted itself all over the place, which probably earned Hengest a pat on the bony shoulders from Caxton for his trend-watching prowess. But who wagged whom – that is the question. If Hengest's choices drove Caxton, and Caxton was a trend-setter, and the trends directed what Hengest chose, then the result, our modern standards of English spelling, would look to be off-gas from a perpetual motion machine, made from cogs of logic as circular as Ferris wheels. As pictures go, this image isn't so far from true, except that, as our best speculative blueprints show, the language-making machine was never a closed system, nor a very logical one.

## 7. READER'S DIGEST, 1490 AD

"The language is in a constant state of multidimensional flux," an old sage once wrote.* On a macro scale, he may have been right. Our global sum of flux *may* be constant – I can't find a sensible website that confirms or denies it – but in local zones, flux fluctuates in quantity, nature, and texture. English's Great Vowel Shift was a case of galactically rare flux behaviour.

As with the time machine in the classic science fiction film *Back to the Future*, one must admire the mechanism without asking too much about its workings. Somehow, the Great Vowel Shift achieved a hyper-concentration of flux, heating it to a point at which English began performing all possible or probable vowel movements at the same time. People's accents changed throughout the tiny English-speaking world, some faster and more noticeably than others. For many, the shift messed up links between how they talked and how they were taught to spell. It also altered what rhymed with what, creating havoc for songwriters.

Intense energy and chaos-generating ability made this beast special. After all, songwriters have always suffered. It's endemic to the profession. And people always mess with their own accents. I grew up pronouncing "balls" to rhyme

* From David Crystal's introduction to the book *Australian Language Matters*.

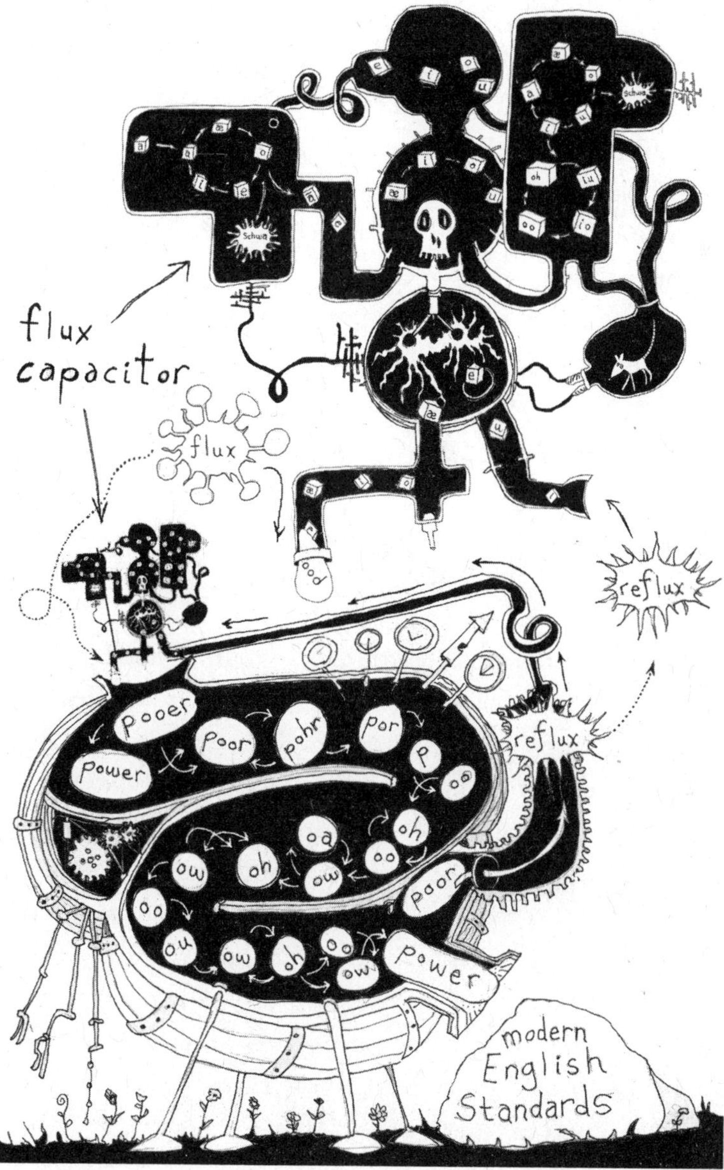


*Figure 3.5* – The Great Vowel Shift mechanism (artist's impression)

with "jaws" and now I rhyme it with "dolls," but that's because I moved west across the Atlantic. Under the influence of the Great Vowel Shift mechanism, however, a person began to utter wildly different noises while standing in one spot, especially if he or she stood there from the time of the Scribe Rush through to the late 1600s. Since Hengest and Horsehair were the only two people capable of doing this, and since I'm sure both of them found better ways to spend their time, it's safe to say that no individual tried out all of the mechanism's possible functions. I should add that nobody has seen the machine with their own eyes. All we have are artists' impressions based on rumours.

The coolest thing to do with the Great Vowel Shift, once one gives up trying to learn how it works, is to run the machine in reverse, feeding modern song lyrics into its rear end and listening to what might come out its mouth, so to speak. For instance, if Paul McCartney's most overlooked song, "Waterfalls," rode back through the vowel machine to the pre-shift Middle Ages, its chorus, which compares McCartney's need for love to a second's need for an hour, or a raindrop's need for a shower, becomes a song of nayding loov, leek a secoond nayds a hoo-er. Of course, due to habit, trends, and commercial pressures, McCartney sang most of his 1980 version in a southern Californian accent despite his origins in the northern English town of Liverpool, where the sound of "nayding loov leek a castle nayds a too-er" could derive from a person born an hour's drive down the M62 highway, rather than a time-traveller from the fifteenth century. Another good song to send back to the Middle Ages, in my experience, is "Sex Over the Phone" by the Village People, particularly the chorus, the final line of which sustains an *o* vowel for several beats during the word "phone." Rewound through the Great Vowel Shift, the line still concerns sex, but now the act takes place "awver tha faw-aw-aw-aw-awn." With the original evoking the so-called "Big O," this sound shift asks us to decide whether English-speakers typically screamed an "aw" when orgasming during the early Middle Ages, or whether this noise lies among the exceptions, governed (or not) by a deeper layer of sub-rules for vowels in peculiar contexts. These finer points explain, to those able to comprehend, why "swear" doesn't rhyme with "sweat" or "cheat," or perhaps it *does*, but only when you stand on a certain spot at a certain time, with particular people making particular noises nearby.

I have decided that sweating and swearing over the details is for the people whose jobs depend on it. The rest of us can just plug another song into the Great Vowel Shift's rear end, and proceed, with the help of a rough blueprint. (See *Figure 3.6.*)

The reasons for the Great Vowel Shift's arrival are as mysterious as its workings. Popular asterisks include the rush to London, the rush to imitate reasonably educated men from East Anglia, the rise of college culture, the demise of the British-French upper class, or else the Black Death, or the tight clothes worn by young women, or the misuse of fox fur, or the misdeeds of Coyote. What troubles me about the Great Vowel Shift is not how it worked or where it came from but why the English printers didn't behave as their

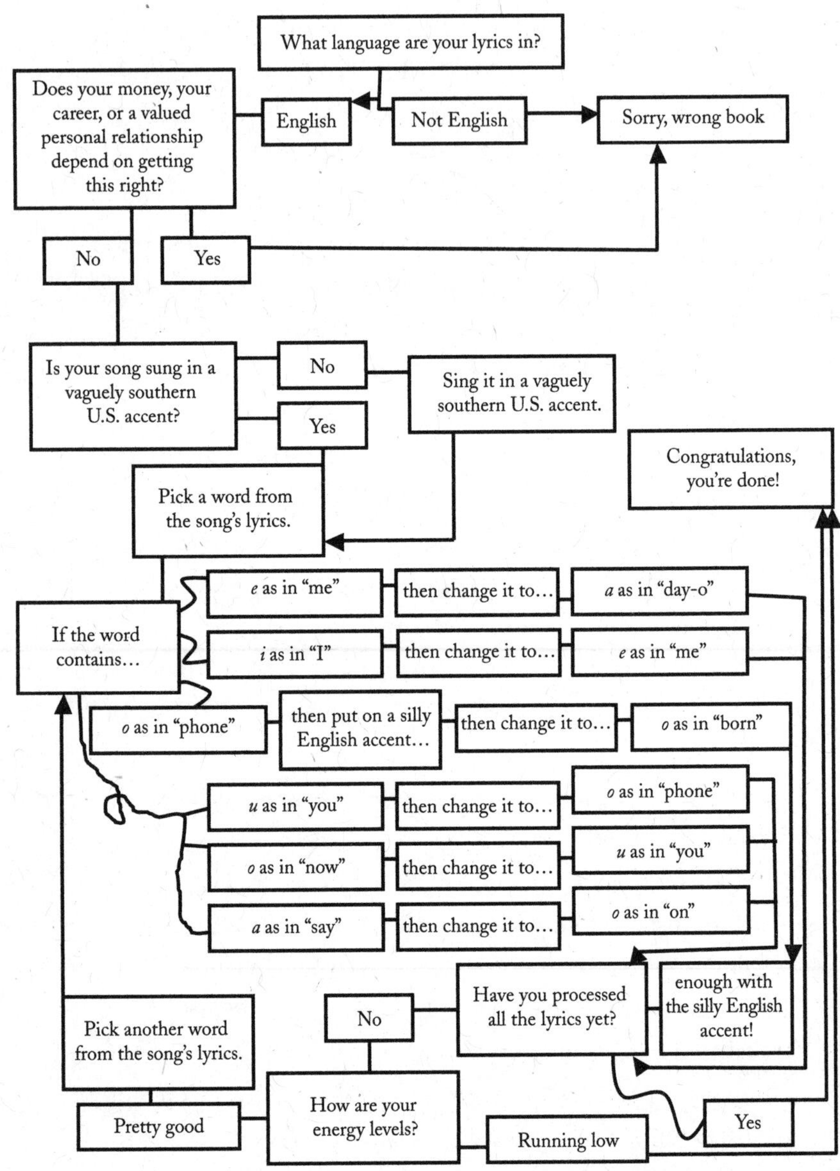


*Figure 3.6* – A rude mechanism for sending songs back to the Middle Ages

German and Dutch counterparts did after similar vowel movements in those lands. On the continent, printers moulded their spelling habits to fit their speech habits. While they didn't flush out all oddities in Dutch and German, their policy spared them some of the glaring clashes found in English. Caxton and his successors decided on spellings seemingly at random, pandering to particular local accents, then showing loyalty to Chaucer's old ways, then meddling completely by adding silent letters, such as when they injected an *h* into "ghost," "ghest," and "ghoose." (The second and third failed to sway the majority but the first one stuck.) Far from striving for order, English commercial printers seemed bent on stirring things up, all the while claiming to give people what they wanted.

Every action has its opposite. With one hand, Caxton and company made a mess. With the other, they unleashed "standardizing forces," which prevented the public from banding together to sort out the famously weird character of English spelling through democracy and teamwork. These forces, too, are a vexed topic. Nobody is sure what they looked like or what form they took. Maybe they were spiritual, emanating silently from the pages of documents like a ghost-letter *h*. Maybe they piggybacked on the psychological forces inflicted by cane-wielding schoolteachers (kinetic forces too, then), powered by a hodgepodge of textbooks and guides to grammar, rhetoric, and logic. Perhaps standardizing forces were *real* forces, like soldiers on horseback, which would be more romantic. Such people would work as mercenaries, probably, visiting country manors to gain access to rich children, showing up at key institutions – monasteries, private schools, local courtrooms – with offers of training sessions to professionals, supposedly to help folks stay up-to-date with industry standards set by the London printing cartel. It'd be one way to establish authority.

If horse-riding personnel drove English spelling standards in the fifteenth century, the presses carefully kept them off-book. The mercenaries either didn't exist, or did but operated like a secret police, officially unacknowledged. I would call this whole suggestion preposterous if stories of more callous and destructive corporate malfeasance didn't reach me daily. As it is, the main reason to assume the chaos of English spelling arose by accident is the lack of a plausible motive. What reason could London's presses have to sabotage and confuse an entire language community – their own customers – with an illogical system of orthography?

Perhaps it served the printers' interests, not to mention their egos, to put the consumers of written English into a disoriented state, softening up the poor folk to accept a powerful minority as society's trusted arbiters. But people wanted books anyway. Widespread perplexity wouldn't boost the printers' incomes much. The only profit here would go straight to the standardizing mercenary, if he or she managed to swing a commission from the printing cartel, and add that to whatever fees and dinners could be obtained on the road by charging suckers to hear the gospel of English's bizarre and always updating spelling rules.

The truth may simply be that one such mercenary gave a good pitch to the likes of Caxton & Co., who, having learned to trust his judgment in the past, gave him a budget to ride out on his horse and convince others to trust their brand. I've seen managers drop money on sillier proposals. The only real losers were (and are) the people who forgot how to spell "cough" or "dough," or rhymed "cheat," "steak," and "dead," thereby looking stupid and losing a job opportunity, or a date, a friend, a pet, rfshft.

Oh, Hengest.

## 8. THE DUNBAR AND KENNEDY SCHOOL OF ABUSE, 1510 AD

Sense (1) of the hero's adjective needs an update to account for his latest deeds.

> **Hengesty** *adj.* . . . (1) (i) coinciding in some respect with the spread of English
> (ii) responsible in some way for the chaos of English

He would have run into trouble eventually. As the hero rode north, clients and potential trainees became more challenging and mistrustful, less pliable, and certainly less keen to offer dinner to a Londoner who claimed to bestow tickets to prestige. The most dramatic clash between southern standardizers and the northern forces of resistance took place in lowland Scotland, particularly in the cultural centre of Edinburgh. This city, I suspect, would have been where Hengest met his match.

For instance, he probably saw this sort of thing:

| | |
|---|---|
| Quod he: "My claver and my curldodie, | *Said he: "My clover and my ribwort,** |
| My huny soppis, my sweit possodie | *My honey toast, my sweet hot toddy* |
| Be not oure bosteous to your billie, | *Be not too boisterous – i.e., rude – to your dude.* |
| Be warme hairtit and not evill wille | *Be warm-hearted and not evil-willed* |
| Your heylis, quhyt as quhalis bane, | *Your heels, white as whale's bone,* |
| Garris ryis on loft my quhillelille. | *Get a rise out of my willilillie.* |
| Ye brek my hart, my bone ane. | *You break my heart, my bonnie one."* |
| | |
| Quod scho: "My clype, my unspaynit gyane, | *Said she: "My clod, my un-housetrained giant,* |
| With moderis mylk yit in your mychane, | *With mother's milk still in your machine,* |
| My belly huddrun, my swete hurle bawsy, | *My slow-poke, my sweet hasty bullock* |
| My huny gukkis, my slawsy gawsy, | *My honey-gucks, my slozzy-gozzy,* |
| Your musing waild perse ane harte of stane. | *Your self-talk would pierce a heart of stone.* |
| Tak gud confort, my grit-heidit slawsy. | *Take good comfort, my great-headed sloz.* |
| Full leif is me your graceless gane. | *Entirely lovely is your graceless face to me."* |

* An edible plantain. The line loses some romance in translation from the Scots dialect.

"Be warme hairtit?" Hengest would react, upon reading the left-hand column. "That's what I call 'non-standard.'"

The author, William Dunbar, worked as a scribe for the government of King James of Scotland, where he had devised a different set of language rules with his Edinburgh colleagues. Some familiar rules applied here, too, though. Scribes, for example, still spent most of their time in pubs. In 1510 AD, William released a book of his own poetry with a small Edinburgh press and also won a promotion from the king that tripled his salary, so it was a great year, giving him every reason to feel patriotic and cocksure. No reviews of his book survive from the time, but modern critics call it the "culmination of medieval poetic practice," implying it's even better than *The Canterbury Tales*. True, several of those critics are the sort of men who could be biased toward Dunbar's onanistic fantasies about hot women putting out for medium-looking guys, but others are women, so the claim is fairly balanced.

Upon hearing news of the first Scottish printing press, founded in 1508, Hengest couldn't avoid travelling to Scotland, despite the country's uninviting attitude to Angle standards. The hero did not consider himself a coward. He had to pay Edinburgh a visit and try to impose his own ridiculous rules on the city's literati before somebody else did.

Having found William Dunbar in a pub, Hengest would probably be introduced to Dunbar's colleague and sometime collaborator, Walter Kennedy. The two had co-written one of the most verbally abusive poems ever composed, "The Flyting of Dunbar and Kennedy," in which they played the part of friends insulting each other for the joy of it, experiencing an endorphin rush from swearing and raging in a safe environment. (This was still the era before video games, so people had to try harder to stay amused.) Since Walter also worked at King James's Scottish court, the only reason for him not to socialize with William and Hengest in 1510 is the date of Walter's death, usually listed as 1508. However, the number is pure speculation, spun from a poem William wrote in 1505 that mentions Walter looking seriously ill. Callously, Scottish literature historians added a couple of years – to allow for a slow decline, I guess – and then declared the man dead. A kinder anthologist recently gave Walter another ten years, making him die in 1518, and I consider this more likely for my purposes.

Faced by the haughty William and the alarmingly sick-looking Walter, Hengest possibly told the Scots to get with the program and stop spelling the words "white" and "whale" with a "qu," for instance. Switching to the "wh" style of London's publishing industry could help these poets reach a mainstream audience. Secondly, Hengest might have pointed out that William's use of *–is* to mark plurals and possessives, as in "heylis" and "moderis," screamed rusticity. The latest London trend was to trim to a sleek letter *s*, as in "heels," or "mothers milk."

"I know what you're thinking," Hengest probably told the Scots. "You don't want to go avant-garde. But trust me. This will majorly improve your word power."

"Weird pooer?" the not-quite-dead Walter coughed out, I expect.

William could have joked to his friend, "An Erse would make a better noise!" This was an inside joke, quoting their flyting poem. It had originally been aimed at Walter himself. If Hengest caught the comment, he would have certainly misunderstood it, thinking he had spotted an opening for more fashion advice.

"Actually, it's 'arse' now," he'd have said. "We changed that one."

"Erse!" William would then fire back. "Not 'arse.' An Erse is a Gaelic-speaker, *dowbart*. I could wipe off your wisdom with an arse-wisp, which – as I probably need to explain to you – is the straw we use in the 1500s instead of toilet paper."

It has been Hengesty behaviour to find nobody impressive, except poets. I doubt he would have yielded to the authority of King James himself (although the royal chief tried writing a poem once). William and Walter, however, were genuine "makers," to use William's preferred word (which takes the Greek *poietes* back to its root meaning). The hero just might have realized they could teach him a thing or two, even at his advanced age. I hope, for his sake, that he did. The pair can teach modern people plenty too, especially on the topic of how to be rude with style, and I would keenly sign up for an "Improve Your Word Power" course if it were instructed according to the Dunbar and Kennedy school. As far as I know, no program of this sort has been offered. Nevertheless, I would like to help any prospective teachers of this course by asterisking part of the textbook, extracting useful material from "The Flyting of

Dunbar and Kennedy." The result, excerpted here, is a mini-Bescherelle of medieval Scots abuse, such as Hengest himself would have learned from, if he wisely grabbed his golden chance for some Continuing Ed (as we call it in Canada) at the feet of two master makers.

## DUNBAR AND KENNEDY PRIMER *for Ritual Scottish Insults*

### Module 1A: Preparatory Exercises

Practise the following insults in front of a mirror. Concentrate on articulating your consonants while keeping the eyes bulged.

| | |
|---|---|
| loun lyk Mahoun | *a crazy person, like the prophet Mohammed* |
| forflitten, cunt-bitten, be-shitten | *out-insulted, bitten by a vagina, and covered in shit* |
| yadswyver | *a person who often has sex with a donkey* |
| erss backwart | *ass-backward* |
| peilet gled | *a plucked hawk* |
| tykis face | *a dog's face* |
| byle button | *a tit biter* |
| baird rehator | *a terrible poet* |
| carlingis pet | *an old woman's fart* |

* Tip: When insulting people who live in the hills, you may eschew words altogether, and simply baa or bleat.

### Module 1B: Attacking the Family

Combine "begotten" or its short form, "gett," with any of the following. Please strive for metricality.

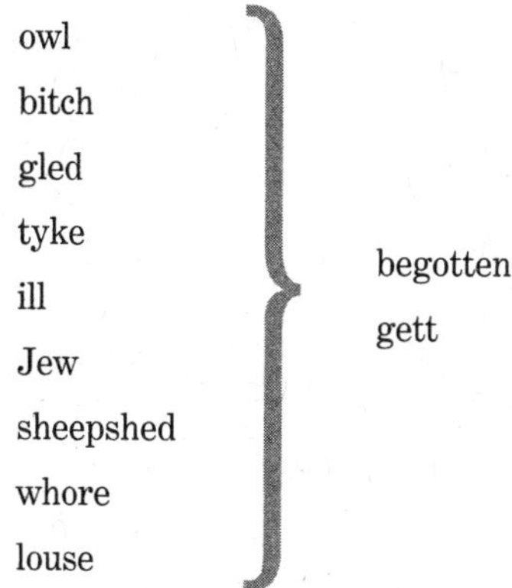


* Tip: For poetic purposes, you may replace "begotten" or "gett" with the phrase "heir to a . . . " before a noun.

### Module 1C: Painting a Picture

In the following phrases, Dunbar and Kennedy combine terms of insult with a vivid story or image. Be enthusiastic, but do not over-emphasize the alliteration.

"To tume thy tone it has tyrit carlingis ten."

*"To wipe your arse tired out ten old women."*

"Suier swappit swanky swine-keeper ay for swattis."

*"Sewer-stinking drunken lazy pig-farmer, condemned to drink light lager instead of real ale."*

"Thy gulsoch game dois on thy back it bind, thy hostand hippis lattis nevir thy hoss go dry."

*"Your sickly face does pin the charge on your back: your diarrhea-spewing buttocks never let your horse stay dry."*

Congratulations! You have now completed Module 1.

Hengest took to this subject feverishly, I expect, and like any mature student who finds a new topic close to his or her old heart, the hero felt curiously young again. Examples in my own social network show that, once sucked into a deep vein of scholarship, a student may be lost to the world for years. But how many years? It varies so widely, and the lives of Hengest's two Scottish teachers leave me clueless. As mentioned, Walter's last appearance in history is the description of his illness in 1505, and William's career after 1510 is a cipher. "The truth is that we possess very little information about William Dunbar that can be verified by external documentation," writes an editor of the poet's collected works. "Most scholars incline to the view that he survived on [past King James's death in 1513] . . . although there is no documentary evidence to prove that this was so." The island's greatest poet since Chaucer vanished from modern view until 1530, when another writer dropped William Dunbar's name into a list of favourite dead poets. As asterisked by most scholars, the poet spent the 1510s and 1520s being alive, doing *something*, but out of the public eye.

William's most famous quality was that he had "mastered the fine art of name-calling" (as his modern editor puts it), and since he disappeared from the royal payroll after a new King James took power, the simplest conclusion is that James II didn't value his caustic insults as highly as the first James had. William's rude mouth got him exiled. Now, Hengest had arrived in Edinburgh with moneybags full from thirty years of "standardizing" down south. These two asterisk facts line up neatly. The hero's profits from messing up English spelling funded Dunbar during the latter's missing decades. They presumably led an ascetic lifestyle together, teacher and student, to stretch Hengest's money. Perhaps they withdrew to a cheap dojo away from the town centre, high up on Arthur's Seat, or another mountain, where the hero might devote himself to Dunbar much as Luke Skywalker once did to Yoda.

## 9. ON THE BOAT AGAIN, 1530 AD

When Hengest emerged from the Dunbar and Kennedy School of Verbal Abuse, sometime before 1530, he found himself hoisted by his own petard. The momentum of English's chaos had rollicked on, but now the hero's version of London Style was decades out of date. His old task of travelling salesmanship called for persuasion and an air of trustworthiness, not a black belt in the art of vulgar put-downs. Like anyone today who pours a decade into sixteenth-century Scottish literature, Hengest had driven himself down a cul-de-sac, emerging extraordinarily qualified to do nothing most people will pay for.

Some graduates land up at their parents' house again. The hero couldn't do so, and although he'd never shown any reluctance to become a nuisance to others, the prospect of going back to London and living with his sister-daughter – while she won the bread at her fancy law job and he stayed at home cleaning her pots and doing her laundry – would probably have hurt what remained of his Stallion self-image. He would have cast his eye around for other options.

When a man feels trapped in a dead end, he may pick an escape route over-hastily. No doubt Hengest heard talk of a major trend in the 1500s known as "roaring," "ruffling," or "roistering." This was the practice of "a type of vagabond or parasite, of a military or pseudo-military kind, who made a living out of verbal aggression, extorting money by practised cursing and threats" (quoting *An Encyclopedia of Swearing* by Geoffrey Hughes). Hengest's ears pricked up at this news, I expect. A career in verbal aggression should have been perfect for a Dunbar and Kennedy alumnus. But there was a snag. Roaring, ruffling, and roistering, though they were rife countrywide and so culturally important that a stage play called *Ralph Roister-Doister* became the century's most popular show, did not count as, per se, a job. A roarer earned income by harrying victims until they handed over their lunch money. Some psychological abuse or deceptive storytelling might also be required. It was an outlaw gig. Wealthy business owners did not advertise for a "staff roarer" or "executive ruffler."

Hengest might not have realized this. If he didn't, and if one day in 1531 AD he wandered down by the docks at the mouth of Edinburgh's river Leith, cursing his useless field of study, he could well have spotted a sign placed near the gangplank for a large fishing boat.

"Rorer wanted," the sign said.

Hengest's first response would surely be: "Typical sailors. They spelled 'roarer' wrong."

This was a landlubber's mistake. The English language of the sea needed different words than the dialect of downtown Edinburgh. On dry ground, the Old English term "rore," meaning "to stir," had died out. However, it thrived aboard the buss-boats where rorers stirred and salted herring to preserve the catch during long ocean voyages. There's no way the Angle prince could be expected to know that.

Under the illusion that being a ship's rorer meant insulting the other sailors while they did all the hard work, Hengest must have imagined it to be a route back to the good old days of crossing over from Europe. He probably marched up that gangplank and took the job, with his hopes higher than they'd been in decades. He'd be miles from Scotland's coast before he learned the truth. Until the crew caught its first haul of fish, I suppose the hero roared, roistered, and ruffled obscenely, and then stomped below deck for his dinner, without anyone questioning his behaviour or alerting him to its false premise. The hero was accidentally speaking fluent Herringboat Standard, as all the crew did, having learned to "swear and show a manly bearing," in the words of folksinger Ewan MacColl's anthem for the herring fishery.*

Smaller herring boats returned to land in order to dry-cure their catch. A captain who needed an on-board rorer must have had other plans. He likely commanded one of the larger, decked ships that ploughed the waves for weeks at a time, subsidized by the Scottish king so that Edinburgh's industry might compete against the dominant Dutch. To avoid a head-on conflict with enemy fleets, the Scots would steer around their island's north horn toward the Faroe Isles, and on past Iceland if the herring shoals led them west. Like

* "The Shoals of Herring," from the album *Freeborn Man*, Ewan MacColl and Peggy Seeger.

a kid bumper-shining a city bus, the fishermen let themselves be dragged far from home, scooping thousands of silver jewels into their nets. When the fish came aboard, the time for roring was nigh, at which point Hengest would learn that he had signed up for a month of shovelling, turning, and salting stinky herring down in the dark belly of the boat.

I suppose he reacted by testing the limits of his expertise.

"Bugrists abhominable!" he might yell. Or, "Spink, sink, and stink to Hell!" It's hard to tell when "bugger" switched from "Bulgarian person" to "practitioner of bum sex," because both fit the same spot in a sentence, and we can't ask dead people what they meant. My big dictionary suspects a writer in 1555 implied sex when he described Saracens as "rancke bouguers with mankinde, and with beastes." But it is also possible to be a rank Bulgarian with both mankind and beasts, so I'm not sure.

"Nice naggy nipcakes!" Hengest could have shrieked, in which case he was using "nice" in its older sense of "stupid." Nobody knows quite how or when this one changed either. My dictionary complains: "In many examples from the 16$^{th}$ and 17$^{th}$ centuries it is difficult to say in what particular sense the writer intended it to be taken."

A nipcake is much simpler, however. It was a person who hid in the cupboard, secretly eating your cake.

"Wanfucked owls irregular! He-whores!"

After twenty years in the dojo, Hengest had plenty of insults to choose from. He certainly knew the trick of making coarse words sound dirtier by mixing them with Latin to leaven the soil. Horsehair's old "owl" pun (double-entendre with "wl," shit-covered) would be lost on the fishermen, so Hengest probably added the classical word "irregular" to point out he didn't mean owls in a wise or elegant sense. Meanwhile, the less Latinate "wanfucked" was built with a medieval word-part, "wan," which added a flavour of "bad or wrong or screwed-up" to any verb. The hero meant that his shipmates came into the world through some kind of weird sex that never should have happened.

"Cum-twang windfuckers," Hengest added, maybe. What sixteenth-century people meant by "cum-twang" is anyone's guess, including yours. It belongs to the library of sounds that refused to settle down and get married to an image. If "cum" meant semen in 1530 AD, no written evidence proves the point. And if "twang" suggested a state of being covered in stuff flung by others, again, the world's documents have chosen to forget it. A "windfucker" was a swift bird. From its name, some scholars asterisked that "fuck" once had a bland sense of penetrating or passing through. If they're right, the innocent f-word's skill at slipping the net of written English would astound the most talented herring. Maybe "fuck" never sounded polite, and what changed was ornithologists, who perhaps used to be a cruder class of people.

"Ingles!" was another option for Hengest. In the sixteenth and seventeenth centuries, people hurled it at those friends and family members who liked anal sex, part of a blooming homophobic strain in England, derived perhaps from national self-doubt and insecurity about how other cultures viewed the island people. While the term had nothing to do with Angles, the distinction escaped Spanish-speakers, who called their British enemies the "Ingles" of "Ingleterra," and still do. The true story of "ingle," however, is lost. All my big dictionary can say is that the same mindset that called rear ends "narses," or oranges "noranges," would call ingles "ningles," as in, "Begin, find your tongue, Ningle," a line from Ben Jonson's earliest known play, directed at an effeminate male character.

All of these asterisked insults would be a mere warm-up for the raucous display of which Hengest was capable, drawing from his era's full palette. He knew a hundred colourful slurs based on the Pope, I'm sure, plus the so-called "inkhorn" range, which offered gaudy plumes of fake-Latin multi-syllables. "You fatigated asininal excrescences," he could splash out, or, "You papistical, popestant, popely Pope's turds!" The hero didn't have much incentive to cease. The longer he swore, the longer he spent not scooping fish.

While cursing isn't outlawed in ocean-fishing culture, work avoidance certainly is. Scottish anglers were ordinary, god-fearing folk, not murderers likely to throw a fellow overboard, but they had another punishment available to them. By veering into the bountiful waters of the western Atlantic (perhaps dangling a few herring on their lines as bait for cod), the boat would pass near the fishing cabins of Newfoundland. These sites pre-dated the first permanent English settlements in North America, and served various needs for long-range fishing vessels from Europe. It is impossible now to tell whether the people who stayed in these cabins generally constituted whole boat crews, using the land as a base for fish-curing, repairs, etc., or if selected crew members were simply dumped there. It probably varied case by case. When Hengest's shipmates saw a chance to deposit their un-co-operative colleague onto a dry spot where he might catch red squirrels and shorebirds for food, they could spare themselves the moral complications of homicide and focus on a simple balance of forces, much as the ancient Jutes once did. This time, the equation weighed Hengest's attractiveness as a potential *help* on the way back (force *h*, keep him on the boat) versus his repulsiveness as a lazy *asshole* who had complained the whole way over (force *x*, push him off).

I'm just guessing here. The forces worked roughly like this:

*Figure 3.7* – Scottish fisherman's mind under opposing forces, 1530 AD

And lo, due to his rudeness, Hengest the Stallion landed in America.

PART FOUR

# Company

## I. WHATEVER THEY SAID, 1531 AD

Some Mi'kmaw elders have reported that Beothuk and Mi'kmaq got along just dandy in Newfoundland, five hundred years ago.* There is disagreement. Others heard that the two nations fought horribly. Perhaps both accounts are true – Mi'kmaq and Beothuk lived as seasonal or permanent neighbours for hundreds of years, maybe thousands, and at any rate, neither story can be disproved now. What's known for sure is that people from each culture scoped out the boat-folk who appeared on their shores from time to time, allegedly from the east. Sometimes these campers had items to trade. Sometimes they were dead.

The landing site of the Angle prince lies outside history, oral or written. However, non-murderous herring fishermen would find it morally comforting to dump the hero at a known European camping spot, where he might live in

* "Mi'kmaw" is the adjective. "Mi'kmaq" is the noun.

greater hope of a pick-up. A typical choice was the location of modern St. John's, now capital of Newfoundland and Labrador. In 1531 AD, a person could shelter there in leaky driftwood huts built by previous visitors. Another option lay around the point in the inlet of Quidi Vidi, a name that might be Portuguese, Spanish, or Latin, depending on how one splits the syllables. As "qui dividi" it would refer to a dividing line, literally "what divides" (in Portuguese or Spanish). The Latin phrase "quidi vidi" would occur only to a hard-core Classics nerd who knew that Cicero wrote "quidi" for "quicquid," meaning "whatever" or "something-or-other," hence the translation, "whatever I saw." As people now explain Quidi Vidi's name both ways, I suppose it may be said to house both senses, and I find it very likely that Hengest would land at such a poetic location.

The hero's previous arrival on a new island led to him severely overstaying his welcome. In Britain, he ate too much, taxed the Welshfolk's patience, and then drove the locals from their land and nearly silenced their language. He was a young buck in those days, an arrogant stallion at the height of his physical power. Eleven hundred years later, one might hope he'd show a bit more maturity. That hope would be in vain.

No doubt the hero of English was pleased when a gregarious Mi'kmaw or Beothuk passerby took pity on him, offered dinner, perhaps let him inside a proper tent, out of the rain, and even calmed the Angle down with sweet-grass smoke, as happened often when Europeans first contacted this island's residents. But a single meal would not suffice. Hengest must have become hungry again, asking for dinner-the-second, then dinner-the-third, and so on. Even a highly forebearing host would start to wonder how and when to get rid of him. The old man couldn't help much with a hunt, at his age. Unlike the rude warrior who sold his skills to the Britons and charged off to chop up the Picts, this wretch was frail, apparently powerless. A charity case.

It's unlikely that Hengest's hosts spoke English. A hundred years later and further south, when the Pilgrim Fathers arrived, those Angles were soon visited by Samoset, a man who strode into their camp, greeted them in their own language, and began to make small talk about the weather. Even more bizarrely, Samoset was not the most fluent English-speaker in the neighbourhood. He fetched Tisquantum, who had once fallen into the hands of Spanish traders and later escaped to London, where he became immersed in the local scene for years, crossing the Atlantic four times before the pilgrims showed up. A chance exists, then, that Hengest ran into someone he could talk to. But the tale of English-speaking locals at Plymouth is rightly told as a miracle for the invaders, worshipped in the feast of Thanksgiving. Similar events can't just be taken for granted. (A drawback of asterisked plotlines is that, unlike in the real world, they must obey semi-plausible odds.)

It's even more improbable that the hero of English conquered his nature, did the polite thing, and learned his host's language. This is sad because Mi'kmaq, for instance, offers an eye-opener for people who have previously spoken only a tongue like English, whose grammar largely deals with questions of time, as in who-did-what-when. Mi'kmaw grammar works differently, asking questions about knowledge and evidence. "In the Mi'kmaw language," wrote a teacher named Stephanie Inglis, "the positioning of events within time frames is not a relevant piece of information and is not coded by verb endings." She doesn't mean that when you speak Mi'kmaq, all events must take place at exactly the same time. But when referring to historical or distant events, a Mi'kmaw storyteller has the option of space-saving verb tenses such as the "long past," which avoids the need for phrases like "so I'm told," "probably," "allegedly," or "various scholars say," and so on.

"The long past is referring to long ago evidentiality or inaccessible evidentiality," Inglis reported. "That is, evidence sources that cannot be verified or checked but which may be taken as oral history." A *p* or an *s* at the end of a word is enough for Mi'kmaq to mark certain kinds of information as first-hand or second-hand, in that order. "Meski'kp" refers to something that looked big according to the person speaking. "Meski'ks" means the thing looked big, as testified by another source.* A "nek" sound following the *s* or *p* warns the audience that this bigness can no longer be confirmed because the source has gone missing for some reason.

A couple of letters that allude to how a person claims to know what he or she is talking about would make a huge improvement to English. Many languages around the world do it. Even the most literally Anglocentric person, who feels moved to cheer for a global organism growing on a tiny

* Examples taken from Dr. Inglis's 2004 essay, "400 Years of Linguistic Contact Between the Mi'kmaq and the English and the Interchange of Two World Views."

Angle core, should regret English's thinness on this point. The language had a chance to learn vastly in sixteenth-century America, and so did Hengest himself. If the hero had found a way to do something useful – like the dishes, at least – and copied those other Old World wretches who became bilingual and gained citizenship with one of the American nations, "going native" (as Rudyard Kipling would sneer), then the story of English would give off a different odour. The language had followed its founding warrior in the past. I guess it might again, sharing grammars with Mi'kmaq just as it once traded pronouns with Viking and mixed meats with French. But it didn't do this, implying that Hengest instead stuck close to Newfoundland's shoreline, facing outward, gobbling up the locals' handouts without giving much of anything in return, and certainly turning a deaf ear to the wisdom of evidential markers. Rather than feeling any guilt about the burden he was becoming to this land's people, he probably felt sorry for himself, somehow convinced he was alone in the world with no one to talk to, forever cursed to be the Wanderer. I expect he recited those old lines for comfort: "The friendless man / sees before him / the dusky waves / paddling shorebirds / spreading their feathers –"

Birds don't tend to obey commands. Nearby cormorants (or whatever they were) might just have bobbed, motionless, with a stunned look in their eyes. Perhaps Hengest threw a rock at them, for the sake of his romantic moment.

"Spreading their feathers," he continued, as the birds took flight, "in the pouring sleet and snow, mingled with some hail. Christ's gonads, there's a ship!"

A boat was bound to pass by at some point. This one's arrival may have been sped up by Hengest's hosts, whose coastal trade routes allowed messages to travel many miles. If nearby Mi'kmaw hunters felt unable to let the hero of English starve where he sat, one solution was to spread word to the effect that anyone who conversed with European boat-people should tell the foreigners to go to Quidi Vidi and pick up their garbage, pronto.

## 2. THE STORY OF ENGLISH, WITH PIRATES, 1532 AD

At the moment when its language broke over the Atlantic, England's royal machine ran on a motor fuel made of 66 per cent pirates. Like hyenas of the sea, well-armed English ships watched other European predators exhaust themselves with the rape-and-pillage work, then encircled the laden boats, cackling, and seized the booty. They pinched French beaver, Spanish gold, Dutch tobacco, Portuguese slaves, and so on. By the century's close, piracy was feeding Queen Elizabeth's coffers with twice the cash she received from all other income streams combined, although the line item in the royal accounts was labelled "trading and prizes." Presumably the government trotted out its experts to make sure everyone understood prizes were a routine element of trade, rather like the "bonuses" now given to deserving business executives when they return from their hard work on the high seas. This use of "prize" to mean "swag" or "ill-gotten gains" marks the English language's step into modern times, as seen from a European point of view, i.e., the recent period in which most states on the continent hired spin doctors.

My Quidi Vidi tourist brochures say the inlet's sixteenth-century European visitors were innocent fishermen, but the categories of "fisherman" and "pirate" needn't be thought of as mutually exclusive. A pirate captain hoping to plunder French fur-trading ships, for example, would be well-advised to dress his boat in a fishing-related disguise, and even drop a line in the water from time to time. He might strew some tackle and nets across the deck, and make his gang wear woolen beanies instead of pirate hats. Up above the crow's nest, he might hang the blue-and-white flag of St. Andrew, since this would scare no one. And if this pirate captain were profoundly devious, he could command the ship's boys to garb themselves in frilly frocks and cavort on deck in the manner of young fishwives.

The gullible French sailors, leaving the Canadian coast with a boat-belly full of beaver pelts, would spot this pirate ship in their telescope and, rather than run away, sail straight into danger. A few musically talented ones probably pulled out their squeezeboxes and started to play, while others fetched their best pantaloons and called out to the Scottish fishermen to come aboard – the thought being, we'll party with these guys, eat their fish, then seduce their wives. French men have historically held an inflated view of their own charm. This can only go well for us, figured the fur traders, I expect.

As soon as the beaver-carrier sidled close enough to be scooped up in a keep-net, the giggling pirate captain would tell (1) his ship's boys to tear their dresses off, (2) his crew to throw their beanies in the air, and (3) the harmless Scottish flag to slip down the mainmast and be replaced by that symbol known the world over as a signifier of death and ruin – the Red Cross.

"We're actually English pirates," the pirate captain would explain to the French, unnecessarily at this point because his gang would already be tying them up.

Now, before the story of English is entirely hijacked by imaginary pirates, I should mention that this pirate captain had a reason to give Hengest a job, even if his original motive in snooping around Quidi Vidi was to find out whether the castaway had any treasure on him.

"Who are you?" the pirate captain might have called out.

"I'm a celebrity. Get me out of here," said Hengest. (Or something to that effect.)

"How much treasure do you have?"

"Treasure? Inglish hunk!* Do I *look* like I've got any treasure, thou damnèd bitch-hag?†"

"Oh, okay, sorry," said the pirate captain, probably. "My mistake. Bye."

The boat turned to go.

"Come back here, cavelly, havelly, javelly Sodomyte," hollered the hero, approximately. This was one of Dunbar and Kennedy's most vicious insults, a supremely tough alloy

* A "hunk" was a sexually promiscuous woman, not usually a man. "Inglish" is the homophobic term mentioned earlier. Hengest might equally have called the pirate captain a "sodomizing slut."

† Although "bitch" always literally meant a dog's wife, it began its long career in verbal abuse as a unisex insult, turning against women later, as "harlot" did, only after centuries of being lobbed mostly at men.

of poetry and abuse, the likes of which the pirate captain might never have heard, despite his rough trade.

"What did you call me?"

The pirates began rowing their boat away a little faster, no doubt.

"Semi-pistated old nun's twat! I'll deruncinate each follicle on thy scalp, oh, bawdy Jesuit-boxer. Jezzy bastard. Pope's turd of a Papyste most foul. Papistical, papish, popestant popeling! Yadswyver! Kite-fucker! Hostand-hipped carling's pet!*"

Under such a browbeating, once-brave pirates hauled on the oars like never before, I'd bet. At a hefty speed of eighteen knots (roughly equal to an Olympic men's-eight sprinting across Quidi Vidi lake in a modern raceboat), they would be out of earshot within fifteen seconds, and nearly three hundred metres offshore by the half-minute mark.

"Hold it," said the pirate captain, if he was smart.

Unlike the boss of a typical herring boat, a person in charge of unruly, disobedient, and often liquored-up pirates needed an on-board "roarer" in exactly the sense of the word suited to Hengest's abilities. The position was usually titled "first mate" or "quartermaster," but roaring and ruffling was the job. A candidate with the hero's rare depth of training, able to scare pirates into uncharacteristic hard work, must have seemed as good a prize to the pirate captain as a medium-sized box of gold.

And lo, the pirates took Hengest into their company, and the ancient ex-warrior put his strange qualification to work

* Please refer to your *Dunbar and Kennedy Primer for Ritual Scottish Insults*, modules 1A and 1C.

after all, yelling abuse at miscreants, whipping the lazy with his sharp tongue. The ruder he could be, the more lavish the pirate captain's praise became, not to mention the bonuses and perks (access to the captain's private reserve of beer and hooch, for instance), plus the underlying satisfaction that comes from doing good work *and* serving his country, helping to fill the royal war chest back at home.

"Finally," Hengest probably said to himself. "The perfect job."

"Argh!" squawked the parrot that he surely adopted, as part of the uniform.

The hero lived in pirate mode, I imagine, for as long as he could get away with it.

## 3. GOD'S GIFT, 1610 TO 1640 AD

But all good things come to a government cut. James of Scotland took his throne to London in the early 1600s and declared a new moral era for all British people. Specifically, he refused to be a pirate king. Put away those peg legs and eye patches, said James. Stuff the parrots. We'll use our boats for something else. And by the way, no swearing either.

"What?" said Hengest, probably, when the news finally reached his boat.

"This is straight from the top," announced whichever pirate captain was now in charge, eighty years later.

King James's royal decree meant that anyone caught using foul language on British soil or ships would need to pay a fine, calibrated to a scale of profanity fixed by the king.

The levies went to the government. It was a sin tax, really.

"A shilling just for saying 'villain,'" Hengest would moan, upon learning the new rules. "*Ten pounds* for yelling 'Jesus Christ!' in a public venue?"

"I'll pretend I didn't hear that," the pirate captain might have said because, despite being a pirate, he was also His Majesty's legal agent aboard ship. "But Hengest, we're going to have to let you go."

"This is obscene."

The hero probably sulked on a nearby pile of stolen beavers while the pirates discussed how to manage their switchover to an honest trade. A logical port of call was New England, where human trafficking and rum production were beginning to take off. The crew probably offloaded Hengest at the port city of Boston, where, without a severance package, because pirates hadn't unionized, he'd find himself back in a state of wretchedness again. Stumbling hungrily down the wooden sidewalks of Boston, he must have looked like any other unwelcome misfit, cursing loudly, demanding food, claiming to be somebody important.

"I edited *Beowulf*!" he might have growled at the uncomprehending Puritans. "I *am* the Wanderer. I used to drink with Chaucer!"

It meant nothing in the New World.

Luckily, there was a place nearby for such people. The community of Providence branded itself as a sanctuary for the displaced, the disliked, and the distressed of conscience. Its founder, an Englishman named Roger Williams, actively recruited "quite a collection of dissenters and otherwise-minded individuals," as his Wikipedia entry puts it. Roger was himself an exile, forced out of Boston society after he declared King James to be a "solemn liar" who had stolen land from the First Nations. Judges in Boston charged Roger with harbouring "diverse, new, and dangerous" opinions, and banished him. In 1636 AD, having learned a local Narragansett dialect, Roger negotiated a half-decent treaty with the nearby princes, took his patch of land, and spread word that wastrels of all types should join him on what became Rhode Island. If Roger lived up to his promises, he ought to have opened his gates to Hengest, who was a fellow conscientious objector to King James's policies.*

Having set himself up as a magnet for outcasts, Roger Williams knew plenty of crazy people. Nothing Hengest could say would shock him. It's not that Roger was open-minded. He just considered everybody's head to be full of garbage, except his own, and that's why he wanted a fresh society on Narragansett land, or *his* land, according to a treaty that, as a matter of minor irk, he'd lost and rewritten later from memory, but the point was that he owned Providence, thanks be to God, and human culture could start a glorious new day with no mistakes in it.

Roger felt a second inner prickle, a nagging backwards bite. His opening move as leader of the idyll had been to persuade Narragansett chiefs to support English settlers in

* James died in 1625, but I assume there was a time-lag between his anti-swearing and anti-piracy edicts and their implementation by reluctant civil servants, pirate captains, etc., especially in distant colonies, delaying Hengest's arrival in New England until around the time of Providence's foundation.

Boston while the latter committed genocide against the Pequot nation, overcoming the chiefs' initial impulse to team up with the Pequot and turf the Bostonians instead.* Thanks to Roger's diplomacy, English Puritans were permitted to set fire to hundreds of men, women, and children, cutting down the ones who tried to run away, and later corralling any survivors so they could be packed in ships and sold to overseas plantation bosses. This was a strange way to thank God for his providence, and Roger knew it – biographers say he felt awful about what happened – but as long as he avoided thinking too hard any time he stepped on a knucklebone in the woods, or when he bought provisions from a merchant ship headed for the Caribbean with its cargo of children, then he could focus his mind on becoming a noble defender of liberty and a constant friend to the Native American.

He loved poetry. He wrote this:

The courteous Pagan shall condemne
Uncourteous Englishmen,
Who live like Foxes, Beares and Wolves,
Or Lyon in his Den.
Let none sing blessings to their soules,
For that they courteous are:
The wild Barbarians with no more
Then nature, goe so farre

* Early English accounts of the genocide blame the Pequot people for starting it. Supposedly they mixed up England with Holland and retaliated against *English* colonists after *Dutch* pirates murdered a Pequot prince. It seemed that everybody was having a hard time telling one tribe from another.

If natures Sons both wilde and tame,
Humane and courteous be:
How ill becomes it Sonnes of God
To want Humanity?

Even if Roger didn't trust Hengest's claim to be a star of ancient epic poems and a personal friend of Geoffrey Chaucer, the Angle's weird ravings probably gave Providence's founder an excuse to show off his own verse.

"Argh, yadswyving baird rehator!" Hengest might have said, after reading the above doggerel.

"Excuse me?"

"Wait thou nocht whereof to make nor indyte?" asked Hengest, approximately. "Blow down me top-sail and shiver me timbers!" The problem with spending a century on a pirate boat is that one can lose track of English's mainstream. Hengest's dialect would be a mixture of early sixteenth-century Scots with a hundred years' worth of grumpy pirate.

Roger, no doubt, looked perplexed.

The hero must have cast his gaze around Roger's cabin and spotted the books. Roger had studied languages and rhetoric at England's Cambridge University, and grew up in the liberal literary set, so he almost certainly told British merchants to fetch him the latest titles from London whenever they had spare room in their boats. In 1640, those bestsellers included Ben Jonson's *The English Grammar* and William Shakespeare's *The Compleat Works of William Shakespeare*, so it's likely that both titles lay on Roger's bedside table at this moment.

"Give me a minute or two," Hengest probably told Roger.

The ancient Angle's adventures have propelled the word "Hengesty" toward two potential meanings connected to language acquisition:

(q) (i) tin-eared with regard to foreign languages (e.g., Mi'kmaq)
(ii) fibre-optic-eared with regard to English, esp. in terms of adapting to current standards as time goes by

Extrapolating from sense (q)(ii), I guess Hengest quickly updated himself upon exposure to Jonson and Shakespeare (although he probably fell asleep during *Cymbeline*, slowing him down by several hours). By the time the hero finished *Two Gentlemen of Verona*, he would have become state-of-the-art again.

Shakespeare's plays offer many suitable put-downs to fire at a seventeenth-century liberal like Roger Williams. Hengest, however, lacked any motivation to say, "Thy sin's not accidental but a trade," or some such, pointing out how the Puritan crackpot's project colluded in a grand heist aimed at enriching Europe. Roger's preening poem likely disappeared from Hengest's thoughts as he began to read the Jacobethan* luminaries. From his perch in the New World, the hero might have felt struck by the anxiety of Jonson, a star English writer who gaped out at the widening global expanse like a kid new to high school, suddenly conscious of how much bigness existed, how small his home-world felt. In *The English*

* "Jacobethan" refers to the time of King James and Queen Elizabeth, combined.

*Grammar*, Jonson placed Latin examples opposite every comment on how English worked, in hopes that neither his book nor his language would come across as too niche, provincial, and temporary.

"This would seem to represent the mental attitude of the scholars of the age, Jonson and [Francis] Bacon," wrote a professor introducing the *Grammar* in 1909. "Bacon rendered his essays in Latin that they might be enduring to posterity; Jonson supported every statement on the formation of the English language by Latin authority."

Smart seventeenth-century writers were hedging, scared to trust their artistic immortality to the fate of English alone. This should have bothered Hengest. Bacon and Jonson's ambitions for their names after death mattered only in a mystical ego-worshipping way. Hengest had better reasons to worry. His track record suggested he would meet posterity in person someday, and he didn't want it to be as the only English-speaker left standing. To be solitary in one's language community is a special kind of wretchedness, even for a rude misanthrope, and having just escaped once again from cultural isolation, the hero shivered, I would imagine, at the thought of being sentenced to it permanently in the future. England had long been Europe's afterthought. Now that the country was spreading overseas and playing the game of empire, and now that its best writers showed some international clout, the little island looked more puny than ever. It's the paradox of growing. Fragile earthlings felt a similar pang upon seeing the first photo of their planet from space.

Hengest's existential fears would have dwarfed any minor annoyance he felt at Shakespeare's verbal tics, although these might distract him briefly. The playwright often stuck an "un" at the front of words, for instance, rather than choosing a proper opposite.

"'Unhand' me?" the hero probably scoffed while reading *Hamlet*. "Why not 'free' me? And 'unhappied' him?" (He was now reading *Richard II*.) "What's wrong with 'saddened' him? And 'unmask'? Ridiculous!" Then Hengest perhaps recalled that this "un" habit revived an old Anglish word-trick that had fallen out of fashion during the early Middle Ages, so while Shakespeare was gratuitously minting new terms, he was also being ultra-conservative, or ironically old school.

As for Jonson's *Grammar*, I expect Hengest just chuckled at the man's rage over spelling conventions, and admired the success of his own meddling in the days of Caxton.

"The *g* in 'cough' sounds nothing, only the writer was at leisure to add a superfluous letter, as there are too many in our pseudography," said Jonson, as if he planned to fix this problem.

"Anger at wasted letters," Hengest might have retorted, "sounds nothing, only the writer was at leisure to add a superfluous complaint."

Unfortunately, before a full-fledged inner dialogue could erupt between the founder of English and Ben Jonson and Shakespeare, someone probably interrupted. A young settlement like Providence is a busy place, always on the brink of panic. For example, Roger Williams may well have rushed in, blabbering something about how it was okay for Hengest not to like his poems, but please spare some praise for this other piece of work, which Roger had put a great deal of thought and care into.

If Roger did say this, he then presumably dumped a manuscript on Hengest's lap.

*A Key Into the Language of America*, the front page declared in Roger's handwriting, and underneath: *By Roger Williams.*

"We all have to learn their language sooner or later, if we plan on sticking around here," Roger probably said to Hengest.

Neither of them could have known that this book would become the publishing sensation of the 1640s, making Roger Williams a household name in London for decades afterward. It caught two co-operating waves, one of curiosity about American indigenous people, the other of lust for dictionaries. Robert Cawdrey's *A Table Alphabeticall* had blazed a trail in 1604, the first book aimed at defining English words for English speakers, employing plain words to describe how to use more tricky words. It was followed by John Bullockar's *English Expositor*, Henry Cockeram's *English Dictionary*, and many other titles by men with unlucky names, culminating in a book of thieves' slang called *The Canting Academy*, by Dick Head.* Every urban, well-heeled English person in the seventeenth century hungrily picked up these dictionaries at the store, bought them, flipped through their pages once or twice that evening, and then slotted them into a visible spot on the mantelpiece or bookshelf, where they sat untouched,

* For obvious reasons, he tried to get his friends and colleagues to call him Richard.

motionless, silently performing their true role as architecture.

Roger's *Key Into the Language* guided readers toward speaking a Narragansett dialect. He promised they could easily progress to other Algonquian languages having mastered this one, allowing an English person to live and work anywhere in North America. (He was forgivably ignorant of Iroquoian, Siouan, and all the language families further west and north.) Roger championed a scenario-based pedagogy. Imagine, he proposed, that you have offended someone.

"Cawaúnckamish – *I pray your favour*," supplied his book, adding a usage note: "Upon some offence conceived by the *Sachim* or Prince against any, I have seen the party reverently doe obeysance, by stroking the Prince upon both his sholders, and using this word."

Roger offered back-up spellings and forms, as all good dictionaries do. For instance, "cawaúnckamish" might elsewhere be "cuckquénamish."

The guidebook contained word lists for use in trade, ordering and complaining about one's food, praising children, asking for directions, and arranging accommodation.

"Kukkowétous – *I will lodge with you*," said the book. And also, "Squuttame – *Give me your pipe.* Wúnnancáttup – *I am very hungry.* Teáguunnumméitch – *What shall I eat?*"

Hengest was probably horrified.

"Jesus Christ!" he might have shouted. "Learn their language? Are you crazed?"

"All citizens of this sanctuary are expected to study American," replied Roger. "And by the way, stop taking the Lord's name in vain. Swearing is outlawed in Providence."

A colony of madmen who nurtured foreign languages and chose to obey King James's vicious ban on rude words was no utopia for the likes of Hengest. I doubt he wanted to spend another minute there.

"This place is worse than Quidi Vidi," he might even have said as he marched down to the dock, calling out for a boat, a boat, his kingdom for a boat.

## 4. SEMI-COLONY, 1641 AD

If Hengest left Providence by sea, he could have gone in many directions. A British ship might have ferried him to other ports on the North American coast, or south to the Caribbean islands, east to Britain, or southeast to Africa. The Atlantic journey that came to define the epoch followed a clockwise "triangle route," a swirl of goods and people and wealth and misery around the ocean. Humanity had never seen its like before. Money and treats silted north. Captured Africans found themselves in the west. Europe sent weapons and remittance men down south. Triangles are famously strong members of the shape family, and this one props up roughly half of the modern world economy, holding in place much that is terrible and wrong. Lovers of art feel bound to mention that many beautiful items dangle from it too – genres and pieces of music, poetry, and painting. Without the Atlantic slave trade, for instance, no one could have drawn this charming sketch:

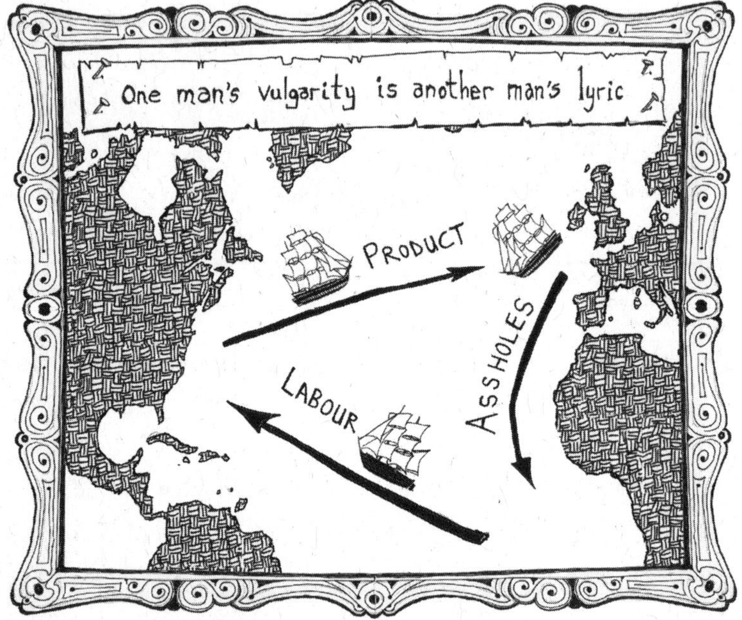


*Figure 4.1* – "The Triangle Trade"
*Courtesy of the Royal Anglish Merchant Adventurers Club and Lounge*
*(Artist virtually unknown)*

Europe acquired its taste for West African labourers by mistrial-and-error, gradually. In 1641 AD, English imperialists hadn't yet caught up with the Portuguese and especially the Dutch, who at that moment were setting pace in fishing for humans, as they had previously done with herring. The Dutch boats dominated the Middle Passage between the Bight of Benin and the New World, while most English merchants traced a less dangerous triangle, an anti-clockwise isosceles route around the northern half of the ocean. Ships left the British ports with their hulls full of cutlery, cloth, and ethnically British slaves (who preferred to be called "convicts," "bankrupts," or "indentured labourers," please), then stopped in New England to sell cargo, pick up lumber, and buy a few more slaves (indigenous Americans, usually). They lugged it all down to the Caribbean to swap for sugar, cotton, and smokes. Then back home.

Caught up in their momentum, Hengest's journey could have curved south from Rhode Island to where a colonial sugar industry was exploding out of Holetown, Barbados, at which point the hero must have asked himself a question – to disembark, or not to disembark? If he stayed on board and rode around the triangle, he could return to London, a known territory. He might locate Horsehair and perhaps mooch off her earnings for as long as it took to plan his next heroic move. However, on the cruise to Barbados, he presumably dined with the captain and crew each night, and heard their gossip about a brewing civil war in England, set to erupt any moment now. (For all the mariners knew, it had already begun in their absence.) This surely gave Hengest pause. Meanwhile, as his taxi sloped past the land of Haiti-to-be and along the arch of the archipelago, Hengest would have glimpsed for the first time what northern Europeans have always branded a paradise, an endless promise of sandy beaches ripe for a good conquer. He had just read *The Tempest* too. If an old idiot like Prospero could get rich in this part of the world, Hengest probably figured, I'll have no trouble.

So I expect the hero chose to leave the boat. He struggled to his feet and straightened his knees, I guess, quoting his favourite Jacobethan pep talks. "Nothing ventured," he might have said, shuffling toward the ship's off-ramp. "To mine own self be true. The world is my oyster; I shall not want."

"That'll be fourteen pounds and six shillings," the boat captain said, approximately.

"What?"

This has happened to me. One thinks one is in civilized company, an oasis where the good-natured hotel manager has stocked one's mini-fridge, and the buffet and bar remain open all day long, free of grubby transactionalism, which so often profanes the sacred bond between host and guest. And then, a rude surprise. One has been running up a tab.

"*I* don't have any money," Hengest would have explained.

"You can't just cruise around on boats for free, mister."

The hero probably thanked the merchant adventurer for this advice, and vowed his solemn warrior's oath to recall it next time he boarded a vessel. He'd then have asked why his hands were being tied behind his back.

"Argh!" said Hengest, in all likelihood. "Unhand me. And give me back my hands."

Down on the beach, where the sand-line met the palm trees, a gang of whip-wielding brokers would be guarding the holding-pens full of new arrivals. Hengest joined their manacled cargo, perhaps in the company of Narragansett people who'd been imprisoned by the Boston settlers – New Englanders betrayed their former allies as soon as the Pequot population fell low enough. Chances are that the Narragansett captives stood beside Europeans whose social or fiscal debts had been bought up by merchants, converted into promises of labour, and bundled together for sale to farmers. This "indebted" type of slave was the category into which Hengest now fit.

"I see," said the hero, no doubt suddenly anxious. "My mistake. Take me back to Providence, then. We'll pretend this bit of history never happened."

"Sorry, mate. That's not how it works."

The merchant captain could barely have recouped half the Angle's fare (including hospitality) by selling him. Even at the low-ball price of five pounds, old men were hard items to shift. Colonial sugar farmers needed strong specimens for the fields and attractive ones to keep around the house. There wasn't much call for sour-tongued wizards with a history of megalomania. According to bills of sale and auction-house rules recorded throughout the eastern Americas, slave-sellers solved a problem like Hengest by lumping people together in "families," supposedly because a trader couldn't bring himself to split apart a husband and wife, or cruelly separate a nephew from a great-uncle. No sensible observers believed that story. As Horace Greeley of the *New York Tribune* put it in 1859, "There is perhaps as much policy as humanity in this arrangement, for thereby many aged and unserviceable people are disposed of, who otherwise would not find a ready sale." Like a cable company padding its basic package, the Holetown brokers probably used this trick to impose Hengest on a reluctant British-Barbadian farmer, who chucked the hero into a donkey wagon along with other, more desirable purchases.

"He doesn't look like their grandpa," the farmer might well have complained, when handing over his money.

The rest of Hengest's alleged family didn't necessarily know each other or even come from the same part of the world. Captives often got mixed up, separated, bound together, and reshuffled at several nodes along the wretched way from home to a Caribbean slave market. There was policy in this too, because slave traders became nervous if their properties understood and spoke to each other. Hengest's donkey cart may therefore have carried people who grew up learning Spanish, Igbo, Portuguese, Wolof, Yoruba, English, or any of the Algonquian languages of the eastern seaboard. Some might speak Gaelic. Dutch, French, Bantu, Edo, Boko, Bokobaru, Ashanti, Wendat, Welsh, and Pirate were all possible too.

Modern scholars have very little idea what people said to each other, or how they said it, in the fields and big houses of early Caribbean sugar plantations. No first-person accounts from slaves in the 1640s exist to tell the tale. To a tiny degree, one can extrapolate from the words of slave masters such as Mr. Ligon, an English arrival who tried to run a sugar farm in 1647 and wrote about it later. Ligon remembered meeting one African slave who spoke fluent English, for instance. The slave politely asked his boss how a ship's compass worked, and what was involved in practising Christianity. Then Ligon wandered onto a neighbour's farm where a group of people, also African, were playing a game. The Englishman asked to join in, but "could never learn because they wanted language to teach me."* Perhaps these slaves spoke an African language,

* From Dick Ligon's *A True and Exact History of the Island of Barbadoes*, published in 1657.

or a new island mix of vocab they'd picked up since losing their freedom. That depends on how long they'd been enslaved and whether the game players shared the same homeland. It's also possible they spoke several languages from West Africa plus the newly minted "pidgin" codes of half a dozen forced-labour camps on the island, *plus* a smooth Shakespearian English, and they simply wanted Mr. Ligon to piss off.

Malcolm X famously contrasted the cultures of house slavery and field slavery, the former producing people who would rush to help put out a fire in the boss's house, while members of the latter prayed for a wind to burn the place down more furiously. The two worlds created separate types of talk as well. In the sugar fields, the permanently owned slaves and temporarily indentured labourers might be left to their own devices when the bosses didn't need to directly abuse them. To communicate among themselves, they invented whatever codes and tricks served a short-term goal, and also borrowed from habits formed by colleagues who'd lived on the farm longer. The results would vary depending on who took part. On one farm, if enough recent arrivals spoke the Ashanti language of Ghana and Ivory Coast, they would naturally form a hub among the enslaved workers, and if a Narragansett minority wanted in, these people needed to learn basic Ashanti. On another farm where no single group dominated, labourers might assemble a general toolkit of phrases – greetings, instructions, warnings – and some other useful bits of language drawn from the stock of, say, Spanish, English, Igbo, and Yoruba, biased toward the more talkative or powerful among them.

Unlike the slave traders, English sugar bosses often wanted their labourers to be capable of conversing, partly because this could raise morale and prompt people to work harder and produce more sugar, but also because many plantation jobs needed special skills, such as knowing how to operate the boilers or milling tools or what-have-you. Some slaves managed small crews or trained their own replacements. Chaos and miscommunication, in these cases, did not help. Picking up some basic English was one way to attract favouritism or a promotion from the plantation manager, who found bilingual foremen handy. Thus a pulling force drew some slaves toward the English vocabulary at the same time as the ruling class pushed it upon them.

In Hengest's case, a farmer would most likely have put him to work in and around the large farmhouse because such a decrepit creature couldn't cut much cane. Owners expected their house slaves to obey direct and varied instructions, mostly given in English. This automatically put Hengest, native English-speaker, into a foreman-like role. While new conjugations and grammars got cooked up among the planted rows and labourers' huts, Hengest would sell his language directly to the other prisoners of the house by helping them understand what the boss-man and boss-family members wanted. A haphazard style of English-teaching could have been Hengest's best service to the sugar farm, although I'm sure he mostly spent his hours on hands and knees, scrubbing tubs, emptying chamber pots and refilling them with water (for which he needed to stand up again), cleaning out the chicken shed (bent over), rescuing pans in which the farmer's children had attempted to make toffee (standing up but hunched), endlessly sweeping sand out of the front hall while the wind blew it back in, rfshft.

While he laboured, the diseases of malaria and yellow fever got busy too, killing thousands of immigrants to Barbados, including a chunk of the English land-owning class. Smallholders, Ligon among them, gave up and fire-sold their slaves down the road to larger farms, which consequently grew bigger and more gulag-like than ever. The remaining sugar bosses in the Caribbean, along with their peers on the American mainland, began paying more for African slaves, who were less likely to get sick because their blood often contained the right antibodies. (The major viruses and plagues that scoured the New World in the 1600s have been blamed on imported African mosquitoes.) By mid-century, almost all the people sold into forced labour on Barbados came from sub-Saharan Africa, so the longer Hengest remained in captivity, the more he'd hear his fellows speaking Luganda, Igbo, Wolof, or Ashanti, and the less he'd hear of Manx, Scouse English, Gaelic, Dutch, and so on. He'd also hear the rise of a new language, a mishmash, the merger of the most popular ideas for how to confer, all of which bore the impression of the workers' common exposure to one tongue of power. For Hengest to survive long enough to experience this, despite his daily congress with germ-filled slop buckets and dirty laundry, sounds like a miracle. We must remember he was blessed – or cursed – with an immune system hardened by multiple centuries.

Traditionally, the last five-hundred years form the least-cool part of the story of English. It's been especially tough for storytellers who wanted to make a hero out of the language itself, portraying it as a plucky, joyous child, hungrily absorbing a world of delights.

"The indefinable genius of the English language," wrote one fan, "has always been to adapt itself, like mercury, to every new contour."*

"Of all its many triumphs and cunningly rich compromises," said another, "there is little, I think, that so singularly characterizes English's resources as its encounter with the African languages through the slave trade."†

No, the recent centuries mean that the English language personified is too rude to be heroic. Time has cured the first millennium, not the second. I can cheer for a beast that once piggybacked on the massacring of the Celts etc., but there's a limit, or a threshold, where the organism passes into the dark side and any cheering must stop. To be sympathetic to English, one may single out the language's praiseworthy traits – the limericks, the pretty speeches, the songwork of Odetta – but set against its complicity in the North American holocausts or the extractions from Africa, these apologies ring as empty as pointing to Joseph Stalin's inspirational effect on his grandson, or Idi Amin's mastery of the consoling hug. Nevertheless, having made it this far, loyal biographers of the Angle-born tongue cop a grin, microscopically twitch their facial muscles, and strive to pick off their polite, harmless interest from the mighty unkindness.

* *Globish*, by Robert McCrum.

† *The Adventure of English*, by Melvyn Bragg.

The two substances part about as easily as melted candlewax and corduroy.

Many word-lovers have beachcombed early-modern English for shining moments of resistance, their detection tools powered by the odd marriage of wishful thinking and precision. I see it as a worthwhile hobby even when it draws mockery and skepticism. For instance, in a book called *It's Bigger Than Hip Hop*, the poet and scholar M.K. Asante Jr. told of how Wolof-speakers planted their word "xonq," meaning "red," into the English vocab. Since the letter *x* in Wolof is a guttural sound, often spoken as "h" by outsiders, the word became known as "honky," our rude term for the pinkish-skinned. This is a tiny landed punch, a shot of victory scored by seventeenth- to nineteenth-century labourers from Senegal and Gambia, to be heard and quoted forever when modern people damn whitey.

Jesse Sheidlower, the editor of the *Oxford English Dictionary*'s American content, has called this account plain wrong, and wishes people would check the big English book instead of making stuff up. As the dictionary tells us, in truth, "honky" came from the land of "etymology unknown." If we must asterisk something, the word could be a clipped version of "Hungarian," but that's just *perhaps*, and since almost anything may be wrapped in perhapses, we should proceed timidly, mutely, obediently. What the human race knows for certain on the issue is this: nothing. Matched against the awesome power of zero, the survival of a competing but puny "xonq" origin exposes to Sheidlower how "weirdly lax" people are on matters of language.

"This linguistic sloppiness does no one any favours," he wrote, responding to yet another writer's xonqy rumour-mongering.*

Lexicographers show their hidden vigour by leaping to defend new uses of words, especially ones that are premised on error, because such things help build a case for funding dictionary departments. The same people never approve of anyone who coins stories *about* words, regardless of whether the inventions add a useful layer of meaning. For instance, M.K. Asante put his "xonq" explanation into the mouth of a composite character named Hip Hop, a figure of no fixed gender who generously gave the poet an interview over the phone. In their conversation, Hip Hop tossed around a bunch of word histories not found in the *Oxford English Dictionary*, and on some topics, such as his/her own name, one could hardly call Hip Hop the less-important voice.

"My first name means 'to see or to be enlightened,'" Hip Hop told Asante. "In Wolof, there's a verb 'hipi,' which means 'to open one's eyes and see.' 'Hop' is an Old English word that means 'to spring into action.' So what I'm about is enlightenment, then action."

The world's leading authority on English disagrees. "Hip" in the *Oxford English Dictionary* derives from the vast and mystical "origin unknown." "Hop," during the heyday of Winchester House, meant simply to leap or jump about. The dictionary's historical principles don't allow for a modern word "hip hop" that literally implies "open your eyes and take action" with help from Wolof and Old English. But that word,

* "Crying Wolof," by Jesse Sheidlower, writing for *Slate.*

and derivation, exists over in the asterisk reality, where Hip Hop lives and breathes.

The two parallel universes, like taboo and totem – or asterisk and obelisk – aren't as contradictory as they appear. "Hipi" in Wolof does mean "open an eye," though current Wolof lexicographers spell it "xippi." "Hop" does have a special sense that we inherited from *old* English, i.e., the slang of the 1920s, when "hop to it" was chosen as the title of an Oliver Hardy movie. The phrase, still vibrant today, denotes "spring into action," just as Hip Hop said. For people who know this stuff, the English "hip hop" will carry a literal sense of enlightenment and action, and anyone who silences that thought is shooting their own toes off.

The widespread telling of a story about "xonq" recommends "honky" for certain jobs in conversation and poetry, just as the alloy of Wolof with English in "hip hop" could push that word to show up at a certain place and time. The history of forced labour for Wolof-speakers in Barbados, or Saint-Domingue, or Cuba, adds potential weight to both modern terms, affecting their orbits, and while the role of long-ago enslaved workers in either word's career arc is small and hard to detect, it isn't zero, or insignificant.

The English language is as personal as it is public. In my private universe of whims, I like Hip Hop's story about his/her name partly because "open your eyes, then spring into action" upends the favourite slogan of Napoleon Bonaparte, who tried to quash the Haitian Revolution after Toussaint L'Ouverture led the workers to rebellion and freedom. "*On s'engage puis on voit*," said Napoleon in those days, over and over, until everyone was sick of hearing it. "We act, then we see."* It was his trusty rule of thumb, but the opposing and more rational philosophy of hip hop, of "we see, then we act," won the battle that time.

The name "Hengest" benefits from a rough translation into Wolof and back again too. A Wolof-speaker today may hear it as two words: "xeen," which sounds like "hayng," followed by "gis." The final letter *t* would be ignored because Wolof words never end with an "st" sound. (This mirrors the way English-speakers skip the throat-noise in the Wolof *x*.) Since "xeen" is to smell and "gis" is to see, Hengest's name literally means, "smell, then see," perhaps espousing the view that accurate perception begins with a sniff test. This translation doesn't destroy the word's older ties to stallion-like behaviour (German/Angle) or oldness-and-hunger (Welsh/Brythonic), and if the hero of English's name somehow evokes all versions at once, so much the better.

"Smell-see," one of Hengest's housebound colleagues might have smirked to herself, long ago. "I guess you smell him before you see him."

I expect Hengest's ability to help other slaves understand English commands was hampered on many levels. First, he lacked any skill with foreign languages, making him a weak partner in the multilingual sense-making game. His bad mood probably didn't help either. Even more debilitating, all the house-slaves may have worn the "iron muzzle," an oval

* Some writers, including C.L.R. James, record it as "*On s'engage, puis s'envoit*," i.e., "One gets engaged, then one gets laid." It's hard to say whether Napoleon intended the double-entendre.

plate tightly bound and locked onto the mouths of servants to keep them quiet and prevent them from eating food from the kitchen. Olaudah Equiano, a former slave, described the tool in his autobiography (written in the 1700s). Writing would also have been tricky because a farmer certainly didn't lend precious paper and pens to his slaves, and blackboards hadn't been invented yet. Hengest's best mode of communication may have been emphatic miming, along with drawing rude pictures using a sharp pebble and a slate.

There were consequences.

Out in the fields, pronouns got mixed. Just as Anglish picked up "they" and "them" from Viking, English locally adopted Igbo's "unu" to replace the derided and confusing "you" (plural). Today, Barbadians who learn this word tend to say it as "wunna." A fashion caught on, and stuck, of skipping English's verb "be" in phrases like "Hengest is smelly," making it, "Hengest smelly." People either did this because they liked the sound of it, or to save effort, or because the word "is" never belonged there in the first place – perhaps the English terms were riding another language's grammar, such as Uganda's Luganda, where putting a verb between "Hengest" and "smelly" would sound weird. Hardly any African words from the 1600s stuck around to be spoken in English today, but these core pieces of grammar, now spoken mostly by Barbados's working class, may echo the speech of enslaved people on the island long ago.

For Hengest, the finger callouses, the backache, and the scars of physical abuse confirmed that he had discovered a new low.

"To think," he probably thought, "how a thousand years ago, I felt as if life couldn't get any worse."

His escape route from the Caribbean is even tougher to sketch than his arrival. Sugar farmers in the mid-1600s did not leave behind lists of their slaves' or servants' names, so there's no hope of finding a record of him, and in any case, Hengest tends to deke the nets of written evidence like a pro hockey star playing shinny with relatives. In the 1660s, a tide of British emigration from Barbados to Jamaica might have carried the enslaved hero along with it, but only into the same unhappy predicament.

The standard cures for enforced house-work were to buy one's freedom or serve out one's time (in cases of indenture). Although an ethnic Angle couldn't technically be a slave within the British Empire, in practice, without a contract or access to a lawyer, Hengest's so-called temporary sentence had no endpoint. He couldn't write to Horsehair for money because, even if he knew a way to send mail, he didn't know her address. His sole hope for cash lay in his marketable skills or crafts, namely (1) literacy, (2) virtuosic rudeness, and (3) some familiarity with canonical poems. Strangely, number three could have been his saviour.

In 1717, a printer set up shop to serve Jamaica's upper classes, publishing the *Weekly Jamaica Courant* out of Kingston and spawning a scene for aspiring colonials who wanted to feel civilized, urbane, more English than the English. This begat bookstores, which competed against each other. To edge ahead, one of them needed a professional book buyer, someone with taste (or a claim to taste) who could pick sure sellers for his Jamaican-English client base – the latest Defoe, yes, the latest *Dictionary of Difficult Words*, yes, but not that Eliza Haywood chick-lit, *An Unequal Relationship*.* The hero could have spent his few leisure hours doing low-wage work at the bookstore, or if travel and time constraints prevented this, maybe he inspected the publishers' catalogues from his workplace, snatching moments between pinning clothes on a line and folding bedsheets, and then sent his picks into town with the newspaper delivery kid or some other messenger. If he chose well (as I'm sure he would have done, given his long history in Eng Lit's company), he might have saved up the price of his manumission within a couple of years, especially if the bookstore owner took pity on him and slipped a bonus or two his way. Luckily for Hengest, he wasn't very valuable.

## 5. MORE PIRATES, 1720 AD

In Kingston, homeless but free, I suppose the hero of English beelined to the bookstore, the only place where somebody knew him. He probably asked to work there and began saving money, as one could do with a bookstore clerk's salary in those days.

It makes an upside-down sense that his path becomes harder to discern, the closer he travelled to current affairs and the information-overload era. If Hengest spent time in

* Haywood wrote several takedowns of patriarchy, including *The Fortunate Foundlings* and *Anti-Pamela*, a 1741 parody of Samuel Richardson's *Pamela*.

the public eye or even a major literary scene after the mid-seventeenth century, sooner or later he would have bumped into an Aphra Behn or a Daniel Defoe (parents of the English non-fictional novel). We'd now have his *True History* or *Life and Strange Surprizing Adventures*. J.R.R. Tolkien wouldn't have been left to cut brush through the forests of asterisks, I wouldn't need to extend his trail, and the story of our language never would have run into so much trouble. (Scholars will fight over anything, though. I suppose they'd call foul on some aspect of Behn and Defoe's journalism.)

The rampant weeds of European capitalism had shot up on either side of Hengest while he laboured, lifting nobodies into the class of emperors, through the mechanism of buying cheap on one side of an ocean and selling high on the other. Hengest must have yearned for a piece of it. A Kingston bookstore made a weak springboard for a vault into the super-rich, but it's all the hero had. If he could persuade the bookstore owner to send him on a buying trip to London, in order to strike bargains with publishers, ferret out offbeat titles that competing booksellers couldn't stock, and copy the latest trends in window displays, then he could invest the wages he'd earned in a few bottles of rum to bring for sale in England, where Jamaican booze was catching on. By burying the transport costs in the store-owner's books, so to speak, and hiding the rum bottles on his bony frame, the old Angle could hobble past the London customs officers and pocket the margin as profit. Rinse and repeat.

Let's just say he talked his boss into it.

Such a scheme would have led the hero of English up another gangplank onto another boat, leaving Kingston via the world's most dangerous waters, pirate-wise. He was also in history's most misogynistic company, swearing-wise. The historian Geoffrey Hughes has pointed out that between 1600 and 1850, English suffered a "glaring hiatus in the creation of favourable terms for women," while men wrote binders full of nasty assaulting nicknames. Their ebullient dictionaries of slang bellowed the words "moll," "punk," "baggage," "hussy," "fuck (noun)," "goose," and the like. One explanation for the uptick in anti-women slurs at this time is the state of the English penis, thanks to a sexual revolution inspired by the rise of rational thought and the decline of church control over bonking. Condoms existed, but were made of pure catgut and therefore expensive. If a man bought one, he tended to keep rinsing and re-using it until it broke. Thus, widespread itches, regrets, recrimination.

"Should never've swivved* the bloody slattern," an able seaman probably said to his friend as Hengest hobbled past on the deck of the merchant boat.

"Oo, arrrr," said the friend, perhaps. He wasn't a pirate. He came from the highly "rhotic" southwestern patch of England, like most sailors travelling to the Caribbean. They enjoy their letter *r* there, for pleasure and – as in this case – for pain.

"The goose, the goose!" tutted the able seaman, arguably. "Goose" sounds childish now, but in 1720 it was harsher than

* *swivved*: screwed/fucked, as in "yadswyver."

"bitch." It meant a prostitute who made your groin swell up in a bad way.

"Fireships all over the place these days," a third voice could have added. Maybe he was about thirteen centuries old.

The two younger sailors, who hadn't noticed the ancient hero until then, probably gasped.

"You too, old man?"

"Blimey."

A "fireship" was a prostitute with a venereal disease. I haven't counted, but it looks as if roughly one out of every three English words coined during the early 1700s meant this same thing.

Before the men's conversation became more detailed, however, the odds are that the merchant boat would have been attacked by pirates. In all the movies set near the Caribbean in the early eighteenth century, I don't believe a single merchant ship has sailed through without a pirate fight, and I fail to see why the story of English should be any different. History boasts two particularly good pirates, named Anne Bonny and Mary Read, a pair of cross-dressing warriors on the run from British naval authorities. Read began wearing boys' clothes as a kid in England, to fool relatives into giving her single mom more money. (Her extended family wouldn't waste resources on a girl-child.) Bonny pretended to be male to score a job on a pirate boat in Jamaica. She cursed her fellows for their cowardice and out-dared every one, took her pick of lovers, and tossed the used ones overboard like apple cores.

It's hard not to idealize Anne Bonny and Mary Read, as many others before me have found.

They broke shit. They somersaulted onto slave ships, killed the captain, pocketed the cash, set everyone free. They said, Hey, join us if you want to. We're pirates. (Argh!) The intrepid journalist Daniel Defoe reported their story:

> They took a great Number of Ships belonging to *Jamaica*, and other parts of the *West-Indies*, bound to and from England; and whenever they met any good Artist, or other Person that might be of any great Use to their Company, if he was not willing to enter, it was their Custom to keep him by Force.
>
> —*A General History of the Pyrates* (1724), by Daniel Defoe*

Sadly, Defoe didn't explain precisely what Bonny and Read meant by "good" art. Did they prefer Rococo or the emerging Enlightenment movements that extolled virtue and moral sense over frippery and decoration? If your boat was attacked by pirates in 1720 AD, this suddenly became a life-and-death question. Some poor artist must have quivered under Read's cutlass, desperate to show his usefulness, pencilling a lavish sketch of the Last Supper onto the ship's deck.

"Tsk, baroque," Read said, maybe, as she swiped off the man's ears and then his head.

Meanwhile, back on the main plotline, Hengest and the two seamen were scratching themselves from head to groin

* Some of Defoe's biographers dispute that he really authored this book. By the mid-1720s, he'd become such a bankable name that booksellers began sticking "Defoe" on any novel or non-fiction title to help sales, genericizing him like kleenex or escalator or Webster's dictionary or Roget's thesaurus.

and, in all likelihood, serving up more choice cuts of sexist slang when they heard a crash behind them.

"Arrgh," shouted Mary Read, somersaulting aboard.

"Arrgh," growled Anne Bonny, doing the same thing.

I suppose any gang of pirates could have shown up, but these were the most appropriate. My sense of conventional pirate behaviour tells me the women began their work by chopping up anybody who looked rich or got in the way or put up a fight or tried to run somewhere. It must have seemed an indiscriminate massacre. In his salad days, Hengest had sword-skills enough to defend himself and maybe triumph, but after so long wandering the world, he probably just sulked. Finally, he stood to be released from his immortal coil, or so it seemed, as Bonny and Read turned their blood-thirsty gazes on him.

"Go ahead, you brims, you bawds, you jilty conveniences. Crawl-down, cunt-bitten slammerkin shrews! Husbands for Whores and Bawdes, away you wind-suckers, ass-buggeres, poxed trollops, wanton draggle-tailed wenches. Foul limmers! Dirty loons! Strumpet sodomizers! Why the fuck are you still standing there?"

I imagine the admirable pirates grew curious. For them, effective cursing was a professional development topic.

"Why 'the fuck'?" Mary Read might have repeated, for instance. "That's interesting. I've heard of 'why the devil' dot-dot-dot, of course . . ."

"But yes, this is something new," Anne Bonny agreed (as long as I'm not idealizing her too much). "Some folks say, 'Why *the puck*,' or, 'Who *the puck* are you?' Perhaps that's a minced form of this old man's oath, spoken to protect the kids."

"No, no, no," Mary Read could offer, as she'd grown up in England, with more access to the relevant literature. "A 'puck' is a devil or sprite, like the guy in *Midsummer Night's Dream*, so when Shakespeare wrote, 'What a divell hast thou to do with the time of the daie,' he could equally have said, 'What a *puck* hast thou,' etc."

"Oh," Anne Bonny maybe replied. "'What the devil,' hence, 'What the puck,' hence, 'What the fuck.' That's really cool. Do you *know* each one pushed the other, or are you just making it up?"

"Thinking out loud, as usual. You know me," Mary Read perhaps admitted, "but it *would* be awesome because of what happened long ago in the Germanic languages, when *p*-words became *f*-words, like 'pater' turning into 'father,' or 'pisces' into 'fishes.'"

"Arrrgh!" Anne Bonny might have exclaimed, enthusiastically. "A rum-gullion good coincidence, blow me. The legendary *p*-fuck, as told of in the shanties of old!"

Talking of fucks, the two idolized and idealized pirates also liked to have sex with the men they found on boats (or so Daniel Defoe believed). For instance, this one time, Mary Read found a "young Fellow of a most engaging Behaviour," as Defoe put it, and since Read was dressed "as a Man, she suffered the Discovery to be made, by carelessly shewing her Breasts, which were very white. That young Fellow, who was made of Flesh and Blood, had his Curiosity and Desire so rais'd by this Sight, that he –"

"Excuse me." Mary Read probably interrupted the story of English at this point. "We're having an important scholarly discussion here. Now, come with us, strange old man. We have uses for your art. Tell us more new ways we can curse, slander, and offend."

## 6. DITTO, 1720 AD

Here is the thing to know about eighteenth-century British men – nerds. Out they came, arms linked, marching to the beat of Samuel Johnson's *A Dictionary of the English Language*, Robert Lowth's over-long *A Short Introduction to English Grammar*, and Jonathan Swift's pithy *A Complete Collection of genteel and ingenious Conversation, according to the most polite mode and method now used at Court, and in the best Companies of England.* They blared their brainy prowess in tones of England's first native typeface (composed by William Caslon in 1722), debating the correct usage of the "long *s*" character, which looked almost identical to an *f*, as in "fong of fpring," "the confcience of a faint," "a Thoufand fhining Queftions," rffhft. With hindsight, we can see the answer in every case: "Stop writing *s* as if it's an *f*. Don't do it ever!" But three hundred years ago, it remained a question for serious dispute between conservatives and progressives at society's bookish end. All this delightful discussion is well and good until the nerds cashed their dividends from the Royal African Company, whose violent activities paid for their spare time.

While the London brainiacs disputed the fixing of English

grammar, Hengest must have bewailed the ill forces that tossed him around the ocean against his wishes. His plans, in tatters. His story, hijacked by these bloody pirates. How absurd it would seem to him, if he could see the whole picture, that a dinner-club of squares aimed to bring order to the language he invented, a figurative, semi-spiritual creature, yanking the ex-warrior around like he was its chained pet rather than its hero. Control the thing? Once upon a time, maybe, but too late now. That butterfly representing the composition of English vocab wasn't looking so pretty any more.

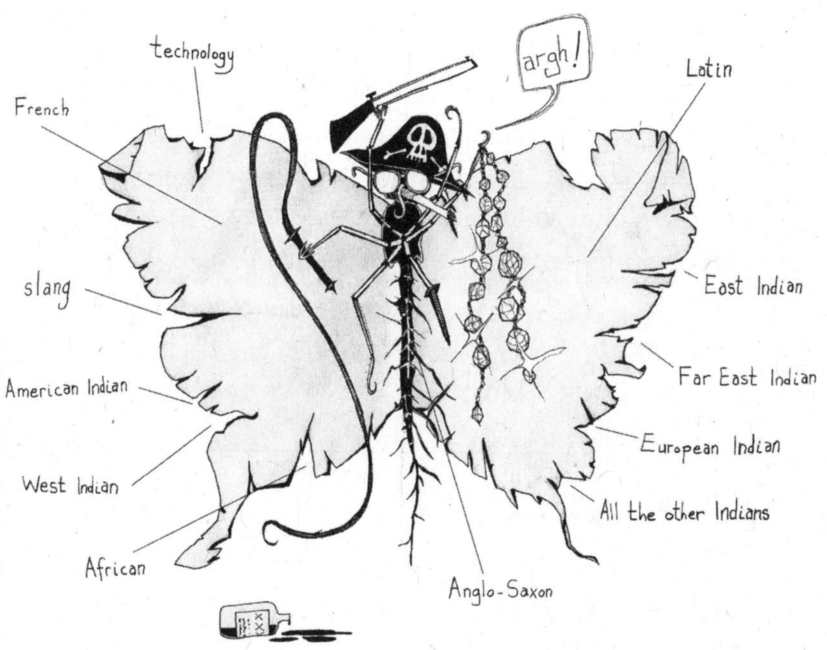


*Figure 4.2* – The English language, modern period

Mental pictures are most often drawn on the fly and propelled by habit. My image of Mary Read conflicts, for instance, with the vision of the eighteenth-century governor of Jamaica, for whom the word "pirate" didn't evoke somersaulting folk heroes. He'd heard too many stories of innocents murdered, stuff stolen, wrenches thrown into the economic engine upon which social cohesion apparently depended. Being a man of action, not words, the governor sent his best employee, Captain Barnet, to risk his own life and the lives of his sailors by attacking Read and Bonny's boat.

In the end, it was rum that undid the outlaw duo.

To get an idea of how rum fit into a pirate's mental landscape, one can look at how their tribe used the word, as recorded in Francis Grose's *Dictionary of the Vulgar Tongue* from 1785, or Richard "Dick" Head's *Alphabetical Canting Dictionary* from 1673. It's not so much that pirates and their outlaw friends had fifty words for the stuff, but rather that they made this one word mean everything else:

| | |
|---|---|
| **rum** | good |
| **rumbeak** | a judge |
| **rumbo** | a prison |
| **rumbob** | an apprentice |
| **rum boozing welts** | some grapes |
| **rumboyle** | a watchman |
| **rumbumtious** | obstreperous |
| **rum chant** | a song |
| **rumclout** | a handkerchief |
| **rumcully** | a rich idiot |

| | |
|---|---|
| **rum diver** | a pickpocket |
| **rumdubber** | somebody who picks locks |
| **rum gagger** | a storyteller |
| **rumhopper** | a drawer (in a chest of drawers) |
| **rum-pad** | a road |
| **rumtitum** | in good condition |
| **rum quids** | booty, stolen goods |
| **rumville** | a capital city |
| **rum wiper** | silk |

Rife mentions of booze are a sign of alcohol dependency. The pirates clearly had a problem. If you attacked them after 4 p.m., there was a good chance they could barely see you, let alone fight you. Captain Barnet knew it, and took advantage. He snuck up on Read and Bonny's ship late one evening in October of 1720 AD, boarded, and easily disarmed everyone. According to *A General History of the Pyrates*, only the two women struggled at all, and without solidarity among co-workers, resistance was futile. Barnet hauled the gang back to Kingston to see the rumbeak.

Calico Jack, pirate captain and ex-boyfriend to Bonny, was publicly disembowelled for his crimes. Bonny herself lucked out. Her rich dad in Carolina bought her an unofficial pardon. Mary Read escaped execution by pleading that her belly housed an innocent fetus, then – according to fans – she faked her own death and returned to pirating, more carefully this time. If so, her trick was so rum and her work so clandestine that she never again caught the attention of authorities, be they judicial, scholarly, or creative writerly. For all we know, she slummed around with Hengest.

*A General History of the Pyrates* doesn't mention what happened to the artists and other useful captives adopted by Read and Bonny. I trust the soldiers knew enough not to disembowel them too. Most likely, Hengest got dumped back where his voyage started, Kingston, still angling for a ride to England to pick a reading list for the New World. With Calico Jack's carcass rotting on a stick, warning other pirates to lay low, perhaps order was restored long enough to let a few merchant boats make it safely out of Caribbean waters. However, Hengest's money had gone the way of the rum, and I doubt a Kingston bookstore could afford to stake him for a second dangerous junket. Like many a budding entrepreneur, Hengest needed a Plan B.

"My name is Daniel Defoe," he might have said to the most gullible-looking ship captain on the Kingston docks. "I'm writing a book about swashbuckling seafarers, and you strike me as exactly the sort I need for a model character. No promises, but can I ride in your boat, and watch what you do?"

Any merchant adventurer would be thrilled.

"Mr. Defoe, what an honour," the captain must have said. "Step this way."

That took care of his transatlantic fare. However, the hero needed cash to start his trading empire. He might have offered some vanity scribing services to the sailors, writing down their fishermen's tales on pinched paper from the captain's log, selling it back to them with a genuine "Daniel Defoe" signature on the bottom, for a few pennies each.

With that, plus a few nabbed bottles of the captain's rum taken after the man fell asleep while recounting his adventures, Hengest could afford to nip out to a bookstore when the ship arrived in Britain's western ports, where most trade ships from Jamaica arrived. Then he needed to find another ship captain heading west, try the ruse again, arrive back in Kingston, and sell his books at a markup.

"Boy," Hengest said to himself, I expect, as he hauled his load up Kingston's Hanover Street toward the bookstore after another return journey. "This is a real get-rich-slow scheme I've found here."

Over time, other drawbacks would present themselves.

"Mr. Defoe? I love your books," a passenger might have said one day, perhaps a Liverpudlian woman who'd bought passage on a merchant ship bound for Jamaica in order to join her partner in abusing labourers. "But I have a quibble."

"Really?" Hengest probably replied, thinking, play it cool.

"Yes. In your first book, *An Essay on Projects*, published in 1697, you evinced an ideal that within the English language, it should be, quote, 'as criminal to coin words as money.' End quote. But English itself is a bricolage of coined words, imported words, and extrapolated meanings, is it not?"

Hengest most likely nodded. "Yes, in a way, it is," he might have said. "That sounds like an oversight. Or a joke."

"Next," said the Liverpudlian, I imagine, "you aver that 'reason must be the judge of sense in language, and custom can never prevail over it.' If this were true, would we not have to overrule almost every development since Hengest landed on the beach of Ebbsfleet? And does this not contradict your other desire, to freeze English exactly in the form you feel yourself to have mastered?"

"You might think that," Hengest said, alert to the risk of exposure. "I couldn't possibly comment."

"And another thing –"

"Now, look –"

"Just one more."

"Oh . . . all right."

"You proclaim English to be 'the noblest and most comprehensive of all the vulgar languages in the world.' Yet, as you told Jonathan Swift in *The Examiner* magazine, you are barely bilingual, speaking only functional French, plus some rudimentary Italian and Spanish. How does this paltry sample justify your conclusion?"

I expect Hengest tried to walk away from his questioner.

"Must have been in a hurry that day," he may have told her.

The fan probably pursued him.

"That brings me to *Robinson Crusoe.* I have questions about your portrayal of Man Friday."

"God damn me, enough questions! Go away."

"Swearing, Mr. Defoe? You've called swearing 'a lewdness of the tongue, that scum and excrement of the mouth, of all vices the most foolish and senseless.' End quote."

"Did I?"

"Yes. A 'mere frenzy of the tongue,' you wrote. 'A vomit of the brain.'"

"Well then, by God, I didn't mean it, damn you."

"Mr. Defoe? Aren't you responsible for your own words?"

"For Christ's sake," Hengest probably said, eyeing the

rigging as a means of escape. "We all gotta make a living, okay kid? Leave me alone."

Then, in or around 1732 AD, the hero would have bumped into his scheme's most serious flaw, when instead of welcoming him aboard, a merchant adventurer gave Hengest the hairy eyeball.

"Daniel Defoe, you say?"

"Yes," said Hengest, roughly.

"*Daniel* Defoe?"

"Right."

"I heard you died in the year 1731."

Rather than confess to fraud, Hengest likely opted to lie-and-deny, winking at the merchant and commenting that rumours of his death had been greatly exaggerated.

"Oh, good," the merchant would have replied, if Hengest was unlucky. "I thought I'd never get my money back."

Defoe spent most of his adult life running from creditors. Literary historians have counted 198 pen names the author is thought to have used in order to collect income on the sly – dull examples like Andrew Morton or Tom Taylor, plus more exotic ones, such as Eye Witness or "Heliostrapolis, secretary to the Emperor of the Moon." Defoe died (or faked his own death) in a cheap rooming house near London, more than ten thousand pounds in debt.

"I suppose this box contains my ten thousand pounds?" the merchant probably asked Hengest, pointing at the hero's trunk full of books destined for sale in Kingston.

"No," replied Hengest, obviously. "That's just English literature."

"Then you're paying me . . . how?"

One person's debt is tied to another's asset. However, a debt isn't bound to any chemical content. If the parties agree, ten thousand pounds in cash may be transmuted into, say, one pound of the debtor's flesh, or more conventionally, a term of labour.

"Not *that* again," Hengest surely said. "I will not wash dirty laundry. Your underpants are off the table."

However, the hero held another asset, literacy, which a seagoing merchant valued. Many trading ships hired full-time "captain's clerks," to render the ship's business onto paper. In 1748, Tobias Smith portrayed such a sea-scribe in *The Adventures of Roderick Random*, in which a fictional clerk records inventories, takes dictation for the captain's log, and pretends to be a source of authority on law whenever the captain needs backup. Non-fictional sources add that whenever a sailor died, the captain's clerk made a list of the dead man's belongings and filled out a report denying that the shipping company could be blamed for whatever accident had occurred. It was a terrible job, and nobody wanted to do it.

"For as a captain's clerk is no poft of honour, and of very fmall profit," wrote the *London Gentleman's Monthly Intelligencer* in 1758, "no captain can get a gentleman of character and education to ferve him as his clerk, much lefs one who could give him good fecurity for his diligence and fidelity."

(They really needed to fix the *f* problem.)

If the merchant's likely trouble in finding a clerk collided with Hengest's accidental absorption of Defoe's debt, then the hero landed up in hock, earning his way out by use of the pen, at roughly three pounds per month. At best, this let him keep pace with the interest on Defoe's loan. To look on the bright side, many writers find themselves in worse situations today, and Hengest's role as the scriptal arm of an eighteenth-century trading ship posted him to English's cutting edge during the period of his language's great engorgement. While the capitalists partied in the capitals, the English language broke open the world's pinata, seizing "chintz," "jungle," "yogi," "guru," "harem," "odalisque," "orgasm," and a thousand other fireworks to light up the tongue. (Even lexicographers got their rocks off in the 1700s.) Not that Hengest had fun, though. English's million-fold gain was paid for with others' losses. To the hero, Europe's age of international trade brought drudgery, a data entry job recording items bought and sold, sold and bought, year after year, port after port, chained to the ride around the Atlantic triangle and its cousin shapes – the East Indian kite, the Mediterranean rhombus – a repetitive spiral in the spirit of the most popular new word during this explosive time: "ditto." English merchants borrowed it from Italians.

"Cofsacs, fine, yard and half broad, one thousand," Hengest would write, for instance, watching a crate of miscellaneous Indian fabric get loaded into his ship's hold.* Then, when more cofsacs came aboard, he'd write, "Ditto, of an inferiour Sort, five hundred."

* Most trade names entering English usage in the 1700s fell right back out again. My dictionary stops bothering to figure out what all the items looked like. It doesn't mention "cofsacs," which appeared (as quoted above) on an East India Company document from 1730. The closest word in the dictionary is "coffoy," defined as "some kind of imported fabric."

Then, "Ditto, fine, yard and three-eighths, eight-hundred." (More cofsacs.)

Then, "Ditto, of an inferiour Sort. Four hundred." (Still more cofsacs.)

"This morning, I'd never even heard of cofsacs," Hengest probably said to himself.

Finally, when different fabric arrived, Hengest might have a chance to write "gingham." And then, more dittos.

"Ditto" showed up so often on lists of imported cloths that people mistook its meaning and began to order suits made from ditto. The mistake was repeated until it stopped being a mistake and tailors obligingly sold it as another miscellaneous Indian fabric.

"A snuff-coloured suit of ditto with bolus buttons!" a merchant advertised in *Connoisseur* magazine in 1756.

If Hengest picked up another pet parrot during his voyages, as he surely did (for company), this word must have entered the bird's vocabulary. I suppose the parrot sat on Hengest's shoulder, watching the stevedores cart their crates down the dock from Bristol's or Liverpool's portland warehouses. Whenever the cargo inspector called out the goods to the ship's clerk, the parrot heard what Hengest heard.

"Sqqrrraweek! Ditto!"

"Shut your beak, asshole."

"Ditto!"

Of course, the parrot didn't mean "as aforementioned," but something more like, "Feed me," or perhaps, "Take me home."

When the merchant ship had drunk its fill of wool, inferior fabrics, and rifles, it probably headed to the Bight of

Benin to trade them for slaves. Hengest's task and language remained the same.

"Negroe man," he'd write. "Ditto woman. Ditto girl (meagre). Ditto man. Ditto man (old, meagre). Ditto."

In 1781 AD, the British Chief Justice Mansfield read an inventory much like Hengest's and tallied the ditto-men, ditto-women, and ditto-girls, meagre, who'd been thrown overboard by a boat captain heading to Jamaica on a ship called *Zong*. The captain tossed the slaves into the ocean because he'd got lost and hadn't stocked *Zong* with enough food. Rather than treating the case as a criminal trial, the judge viewed the line items as property data because he worked from within a context, having been hired to decide whether the ship's owners deserved an insurance payment to cover their loss. If Justice Mansfield had refused and said, "To use the language of property ownership in this case is wrong. We are talking about a mass murder," then he would be remembered today as a hero. But custom holds more power than reason for most of us, most of the time, and the judge let himself get swept up in the current of nonsense. He ruled in favour of the insurance company because, in his reading of the law, the ~~murderers'~~ slave owners' negligence voided their policy.

One good reason to pay attention to poets is that they are hired to notice parts of words that lawyers tend to miss.

"The language in which those events took place promulgated the non-being of African peoples," wrote the poet NourbeSe Philip, for example, reacting to the *Zong* case. "I deeply distrust this tool I work with – language," she continued. "I distrust its order which hides disorder, its logic hiding the illogic, and its rationality, which is simultaneously irrational."*

Humans have devised some rum tricks for ridding themselves of a sense of meaninglessness. A good one is to picture a non-conformist, an undetermined being, who does better than reiterating what he or she has been told. Religions offer prophets or trickster figures. Action movies have heroes and heroines. Languages offer poets. Hengest never showed much interest in religion, and he was neither a lawyer nor a poet by training, but he did like to think of himself as a hero, despite the evidence against it – his job, his rut, his banal participation in a system he couldn't be expected to understand. Spying a hero in the mirror was still possible, somehow. He just needed someone who could show him what the word meant.

## 7. OLD FRIENDS, 1802 AD

When the city of London opened its West India Docks in 1802 AD, many boats arriving from the Caribbean veered there, favouring it over Britain's west-coast ports. If Hengest's ship joined this trend, the hero would be filling out permit papers and customs forms just two short bends in the river away from his old favourite pub, the Tabard Inn. Also, his daughter-sister and erstwhile partner, whom he hadn't seen for three centuries, might still be alive and

* From *Zong!*, by M. NourbeSe Philip.

working in the neighbourhood. There could hardly be a better time and place to make his escape.

Either of two appeals might have earned Hengest a temporary release from the current merchant ship captain (presumably a grandson of Defoe's loan shark):

(1) The compassion plea –

"I haven't seen my daughter in three-hundred and twenty years. Or my sister. She's probably around the corner, and I'd love to find out if she's alive"; or

(2) The honesty plea –

"I'm not Daniel Defoe."

"We had started to wonder," the ship captain probably replied. On the one hand, the hero's confession invited accusations of fraud. On the other, the merchant captain lacked any motive for pressing charges. "Don't forget your box of books," he reminded Hengest, I expect, as the hero hurried to leave.

The trunk containing first editions from 1732 gave the old Angle an asset to exchange in London's second-hand bookstores, so Hengest could finally get back to building up his global trading empire. Here in the capital city of English Literature, he could track down obscure or short-run editions, or delve into whole stores specializing in a single niche. Porn-with-big-words, for example, was enjoying a boom, after soft-core crowd-pleasers had carved out a market – works like *The Authentic Memoirs of the Countesse de Barre*, or *The Confessions of a Young Lady*, or *The Adventures of a School-Boy*, and the now canonical *Fanny Hill*. The inner reaches of a dirty bookstore in the Covent Garden market district must have held plenty of novelties not yet seen by the gentry of Jamaica. Checking over both shoulders first, the ancient warrior probably slipped a slim volume out of its dust jacket and gently opened it somewhere near the middle, careful not to crack the spine.

> . . . the breast and belly of the woman are not unenjoyed by the roving and pressure of the man's hands; and moreover there are certainly two additional gratifications not known in the former instance, namely, the feeling of her plump, warm buttocks planted in his lap, and the pleasure of handling the delightful mount of Venus, at the same time that he is fixed in, and enjoying it behind . . .
>
> —*The Battles of Venus*, Voltaire, 1760*

"Ahem," said the store owner, I expect, pointing to a sign that said, "No sampling, please."

Friends of mine who remember life before the Internet suggest that the bookseller would have wrapped up Hengest's purchases in a brown paper bag. Also, I'm told that if ever the hero was likely to run into someone he knew, it would happen a few seconds after he emerged from this bookstore.

Twenty paces later, then, I suppose he trod in a puddle of horse muck, and then heard a woman's voice calling his name.

"Hengest?"

He wouldn't immediately see who had called him. The city had entered its most successful stage as the hub of Britain's Second Empire. Its population had just pierced the

* Pornography from the time often bore spurious author names on the cover. As one scholar has pointed out in describing this work, "It is superfluous to add that it is not translated from Voltaire."

one-million mark. Covent Garden's market streets almost certainly pulsed on every side, with crowds of shoppers, schleppers, tourists, and fashionistas costumed in the tastes of this gilded age. For women, this meant corsets, bird cages, and horrendous feather hats.

"Dad!"

He spotted her eventually, of course. The familiar hair.

"Horsehair."

"I thought it was you!" Horsehair probably said.

I expect Hengest fidgeted with his brown bag.

"I haven't seen you in – is it centuries?" said Horsehair, perhaps.

"Yes, it *is* centuries."

Maybe they moved to dodge a taxi-carriage as it rattled over the cobbles.

"God, the time whips by, doesn't it?"

"So far."

They might have uttered any old thing. I suppose they conducted what Jonathan Swift called "polite conversation." Often the first few moments after a long parting can be strangely stiff.

"You're just here shopping?" Horsehair probably pointed to his bag.

"Er . . . yes. You look rich. What a lot of jewellery."

People at the top of the legal profession can grow wealthy in the course of a normal working lifespan, so Horsehair must have been able to pile up a huge stash since the 1380s, especially if she invested well. She jangled her sapphires, I guess, or whatever the stones were.

"That's the law trade. Who says crime doesn't pay?" she may have said. "Oh, look out – donkey."

"Huh?"

In cramped downtown areas at this time, any extended conversation would be interrupted by passing vehicles, livestock, and donkeys, etc.

"These streets need a redesign," Horsehair probably said. "It's so hard to have a proper chat with the traffic whizzing."

"What did you call it?"

"*Traffic?* I know, anachronism. Slap on the wrist. I'm terrible. But we're only fifty years away from its oldest surviving written record."

"No. I meant the ass."

Horsehair blinked, I expect, then remembered. "Oh yes, ass and donkey. Right. You *have* been away, haven't you?"

The long-lived Angle pair couldn't have known the danger they were skirting. It may look like any other soupçon of word-science, but the bubbling triangle of "ass"/"arse"/ "donkey" has swallowed more minds than we know about. Most students of the English language never go near it, but I will sail as close as I dare just to prove I'm not chicken.

The word "donkey" presented itself on both sides of the Atlantic moments prior to the year 1800. It was spotted in England first, and the storyline there is easy. Since the days of stiff-boned bodices, any Londoner who mattered would drop the letter *r* from many words. It was a sliding scale. The more you mattered, the fewer *r*'s you said. This cunning way to stratify society along clear and sustainable lines was flawed because the underclass could hack the system simply by keeping their jaws down while saying things like, "Airy-fairy." As more plebs exploited this loophole to scale the social ladder, rich kids rushed to place further obstacles in the way. One splendid wheeze was to say the letter *a* as if it were the letter *o*.

"Oh, rather," said a young heiress, strapping herself up for the hunt. The word sounded like "woth-uh" or "waw-thuh."

"A real 'aw-haw' moment, I'd say!" her friend quipped. "Plebs won't cotton on to us this time."

Unfortunately, she was wrong. The social climbers learned the *o* trick too, inflicting tragic collateral damage on "ass," the animal's name, because it now shared the noise of "arse" for many speakers at prestigious or aspirational events. Worse, both terms squished against the word "oss," the working-class Cockney London term for "horse." I imagine this caused a number of minor commercial mishaps and major eye-opening experiences when the agricultural fairs visited the city and people from different groups attempted to buy and sell livestock. Whoever suggested a new word, "donkey," probably did so after a devastating cock-up of one type or another. My big dictionary today refers to "donkey" as "a recent word of slang origin," which either reveals how long it's been since an editor peeked at the entry, or confirms that lexicographers really do need to get out more. The point is, "donkey" popped out of some orifice where the sun doesn't shine, like most everything else I've wanted to know about. No serious confusion exists, however, about why southern English people chose to stick a new label on their asses. It was clearly a wise move.

Most people living west of Barbados didn't mimic England's upper-class plummy accents, but they began calling their bums "asses" and found a need for "donkey" too, alongside "jack-ass." The Democratic Donkey became an icon of that political party, not a Democratic Ass.

One might very well think: "Huh."

At this point, nervous word-nerds sense they are approaching the point of no return and head back to safety. Oh, sure, they say with a tremble, some gallant Londoner dropped into New York or Boston, flung a "donkey" or two around, and Americans copied it. Big whoop. Happens all the time. Clears up that nasty mix-up of "ass" the animal and "ass" the buttocks. Easy-peasy, go the skitterers, enough of this ass-talk, please.

Their caution is prudent. I've studied the expedition maps and notebooks left behind by philologists who tried to venture further, who felt obliged to find out why the *r* disappeared from the American "arse," why that word merged with "ass" instead of rhyming with "farce" or "cars." Before vanishing, these unwary wretches sketched out links between various cell-like groups, whom they believed to be colluding in the arse-to-ass movement, though the means of communication were opaque. The cells contained speakers who'd grown up in Britain (various parts); speakers who just wanted to *sound like* they grew up in Britain; speakers with African heritage, whose families had never said "r" because it clashed with their (or their grandparents') *r*-less mother tongues; and speakers like Anne Bonny's grandchildren, secretly pirates, but following the first and most important rule of pirate disguise: "Don't say, 'A*rrrr!*'"

The main agitators lived down south, speaking of their "horses" as "hosses." For them, to "curse" was to "cuss." To "burst," to "bust." Today, none of these yokel words has yet knocked its fancy equivalent from top spot in American society. But "ass" blasted "arse" out of the North American water, sucking the British "donkey" across the Atlantic to jostle with "jack" and "jenny" and "mule" in naming the lesser horsey beasts. How did this happen? Well, now I hear the trouble in the water and see the circling currents. Maybe those southerners swore more often. Maybe all the *r*-reluctant cells in America teamed up at the right moment, by coincidence, as when a freak election puts an underdog in power. Maybe being rude and crude gave "ass/arse" greater flex than "cuss/curse." But the paper trail is murky and the answer, if there is one, lies in missing conversations. To chase them now would be to take an enquiring mind and bury it in asterisks for the rest of its natural or unnatural life.

What saved Hengest and Horsehair from this black hole was the hero's total lack of intellectual curiosity, I'd wager.

"*Donkey*," he probably repeated. "Good word. Do they still have pubs in London? I want a drink."

"Ditto," said Hengest's parrot, if he still had it.

## 8. WALK SOFTLY AND CARRY A BIG DICTIONARY, 1802 TO 1945 AD

When I was young, I was taught a thing or two about the colonies. Let me tell you both of them.

Number one: the sun set twice on the British Empire – first when it lost the cowboys, then when it lost the Indians. This was a joke, referring to America's independence of 1776 and India's independence of 1947.

Number two: "We seem to have conquered half the world, as it were, in a fit of absence of mind." Teachers told this as a joke in the other sense – an object of ridicule – because they'd seen the movies and knew the old empire was red in sabre and claw, rather than politely humorous like Sir John Seeley himself, who'd written those words in 1883. Even as a kid, I pitied Seeley, the straw man of xonqy guilt. He'd never strongly desired the role of eminent professor and public intellectual whose opinions on colonialism mattered. It just sort of happened to him. Accidents do. In another flight of whim, the historian built the world's largest-known private collection of port wines, which he stored in a special apartment at the University of London, and drank with doses of laudanum that sentenced his brain to violent mood swings and an early death. His name only showed up in our history class as a foil and the set-up for an easy but instructive pun: "When writing about the British Empire, don't be Seeley."

Funny, what one remembers from high school. My teachers grew up believing in the glory of empire but had fine-tuned their views after watching Ben Kingsley's Oscar-winning enactment of Gandhi in blackface, and by the time my classmates and I showed up for school, the old folks seemed anxious. The charm of certain absent-minded humanists was now in doubt. Even spelling was dangerous. Linton Kwesi Johnson wrote "Inglan Is a Bitch" in 1980, using a phonetic style that wrought havoc on English schools and created "a generation of rioters and illiterates," or was alleged to have done so, in the *Spectator* newspaper. Pink-ish liberals began to forgo their most comfortable and reassuring traditions, such as having lunch at a London pub called The Elephant & Castle, which was named after the Royal African Company's logo.

Snap trivia: What's the most popular tattoo in the history of the English language?

Answer: RAC, the royal company's initials, though technically it was less a tattoo than a brand in the literal sense, a stamp applied with hot iron to West African chattel, much as a farmer spray-paints a tag on his or her sheep. I doubt anybody was nerdy or flippant enough to notice how in Old English the tag would be pronounced "ratch" and sound just like the word for a wretch/hero far from home.

The pub's branded sign shows an elephant carrying Anglo-Norman architecture on its back. Many years ago, unnamed sources familiar with the brewing industry spread rumours that the pub got its name by mangling the Spanish words *L'infanta de Castile*, meaning a child from Castile. This is still the version told by London tourist literature (the pub is old and famous), despite the exact match between the pub's sign and the RAC's elephant-and-castle icon, stamped into English guinea coins during the 1600s. In the fake tale, the phrase "Elephant & Castle" is cast as folk etymology, a phrase born of harmless misunderstanding, like the term "kitty-corner," which is a tattered version of the French "quatre-coins" and was originally free of cats or kittens. Likewise, the Elephant & Castle sign had no link to profits from slave labour, or so folks were told with a puff of philological smoke that masked the stench fairly well, such that a North American company in 1977 felt okay about borrowing the name for its line of British-themed pubs, and hasn't suffered from the connotations yet. To be fair to this company, I visited their Elephant & Castle pub in Toronto and found it not half-bad, but it is also funny, the things people *don't* remember from high school, or were never taught.

Liberal guilt predates my schoolteachers, by a long shot. In the late 1700s AD, many Londoners also felt icky that a poor elephant was carrying a European military fortress, blatantly symbolizing the southern-drawn labour, the northern-based headquarters. Those with loving hearts began to think up ways to make amends. For many, the *Zong* ship and its murdered captives became the straw too far, and I suspect Horsehair numbered among those who felt torn in two by the court case. Perhaps it woke the sleeping half of her lawyer-poet self. Surely she saw a conflict between enjoying life among the powerful while regretting the etymology of it all. And yet, who is good enough to give up their own privileges without being forced to? Some people did, or tried to, often propelled by doubtful theories of cosmology, but a more common behaviour in northern capital cities was to gesture with small, tolerable, even enjoyable sacrifices. A woman like Horsehair, blessed with wealth and a generous spirit, certainly would have supported the abolition cause, and very likely felt moved to act, raise cash, and hand over (some of) her own, striving – within reason – for meaningful change in the world. If so, although her route to 1802 AD varied spatially from Hengest's, the two shared a common spirit: the fear of meaninglessness.

"I *want* to be greedy," the hero was probably moaning, less than a beer into their meeting. "But it never works for me. A job here, a job there. Life doesn't get better. It just goes on."

"Chin up, Dad," Horsehair might tell him. "I've got an idea. You'd be great at this."

If Horsehair had worked at the heights of the legal-governmental trade, she certainly knew about the Sierra Leone project. To assuage her moral discomfort, she probably became involved as a financial backer. The fact that her name doesn't show in the written history of Sierra Leone proves only that she gave her cash and/or talents anonymously, which was a widespread impulse among donors, according to the project's director and spokesperson, Granville Sharp. Along with Horsehair and Olaudah Equiano and others, Granville had been driven nuts by the *Zong* judgment, with its talk of property rather than murder, and he vowed to work for a better world. He told the media in the 1780s that people funded his work in Sierra Leone "not with a view of any present profit to themselves, but merely, through benevolence and public spirit, to promote a charitable measure, which may hereafter prove of great national importance to the Manufactories, and other Trading Interests of this Kingdom."* After all, charity hardly counts if you paste your name all over what you pay for.

The project was this: English money put freed slaves from Nova Scotia onto purchased land in West Africa. These

* From Granville Sharp's brochure and press release, entitled *Free English Territory in Africa*.

Nova Scotians had escaped the U.S. after fighting for the British army during the American War of Independence.

"I don't see what ancient battles have got to do with me," Hengest probably interrupted, trying to steer Horsehair away from a long-winded social-hoping tirade.

"Giving people land isn't enough," Horsehair would have replied, or something. "Not after all we've done to disrupt their lives. They need education. A ticket to the good life, like we have."

"Like *you* have."

"Dad, they need to learn English."

"Don't Nova Scotians already speak English?"

"*Proper* English. And not just in Sierra Leone. I mean the world."

The precise dialogue between these two historical figures is a matter for speculation, naturally, but Horsehair's dream is based on a truth – teaching the globe to speak English seemed like a great idea. And while it took time plus a few false starts* before they got organized, the myriad societies of anonymous donors (SAD) had enough oomph and social connections to make great ideas happen.† Not that this

* The first Sierra Leonean settlement exported brown-skinned poor people from London, and it was named Granville Town after its main sponsor. Unfortunately, Granville Sharp failed to ensure the land was actually purchased from the local Temne nation. The town was soon attacked and destroyed, with most of its surviving citizens sold as slaves.

† No group formally called itself SAD as far as I know. The label arches over the many benevolent people whose names were not taught in my history lessons but whose small monthly donations made an extraordinary difference in the lives and cultures of other people further south.

would interest Hengest, whose fervent hope for the nineteenth century lay closer to home, specifically concerning a long-term improvement, re: the dinner situation.

"When in all this do I get –"

"Your dinner. I know, Dad. I'm getting to it. Charity isn't only putting cheques in the mail. There are governments, permits, policy changes, people to grease, insiders to get onside. It's endless work."

"I still don't taste –"

"The lobbying takes place over a meal. Almost always."

She'd done him favours before, despite his wayward parenting. If Horsehair held any sway at all among London's charitirati, she would surely steer a plum job toward her father-brother. A large philanthropic fund needed envoys to visit the target regions and meet with local power-brokers, especially the colonial officials and bureaucrats, to win their help and siphon their budgets. Talk of contracts and applications and matching funds sounds boring until you see what's for supper. While travelling in the world's less-fortunate zones, where SAD planned to funnel its money, Hengest probably enjoyed some of the fanciest cuisine he'd ever tasted.

For instance, with SAD's help, a Christian group working in the Sierra Leone colony built a school of higher education named Fourah Bay College, the first western-style university in sub-Saharan Africa, today billed by UNESCO as "perhaps the single most influential institution in Africa in accounting for the penetration and acceleration of the spread of Western education on the continent." Thousands of smart, ambitious kids made the pilgrimage to Fourah from across the landmass. Some alumni nicknamed the place, "the Athens of Africa." On the negative side, the native residents of Sierra Leone's Province of Freedom saw the Nova Scotians as an occupying force, even as the latter struggled for rights under the colony's English governors. Pouring stolen money into Africa's first English-language university hardly spelled freedom for Temne-speaking people in the territory roundabout, living under the "protection" of Britain's military, as the colonial government put it. But their problems wouldn't have impinged on Hengest's mood as he toured the new classrooms at Fourah Bay, en route to the governor's buffet.

Tales from Fourah Bay pumped up SAD's record, helping to market the habit of philanthropy to new givers. When Samuel Ajayi Crowther escaped from slave-traders at age twelve, then attended the college in Freetown, becoming a lexicographer, linguist, author, and the Anglican church's first African bishop, his career proved his own genius but also helped the cultural invasion. Crowther worked for decades to make dictionaries and books for the languages of Nupe, Yoruba, Igbo, and Temne. As he toiled all those years, the growing staff at his former college (and the other buildings it inspired) kept on penetrating and accelerating on a year-round cycle, non-stop, spinning their brand like a silver lure.

Really, the sums involved were minuscule. In batches of a few thousand pounds, a few tens of thousands, some prodigal wealth seeped back into the colonies from whence it came, falling from the pockets of donors. Usually, it was delivered via the evangelical pipes, and just like today, it was the gift that kept on taking. English knocked on doors and walked into homes, offering itself as a guest. To dramatize its behaviour, Kenyan writer Ngũgĩ wa Thiong'o tells the story of a lion who is invited to lay its head inside a man's hut, for shade on a hot day, but then the lion crawls in further, until it is sitting entirely in the hut, filling it, and the man must stand outside. For many years, Ngũgĩ believed that to write his books in the Kenyan language of Gikuyu would be career suicide, and until he became world-famous, he was probably right.

I recently heard a British scholar, named Andy Kirkpatrick, remark that any effort by England to press its language on the southern hemisphere looks titchy compared with the sustained work of southerners to pull English toward them.

"Far from forcing its colonial subjects to learn English," he said, "British colonial policy was in large part to provide an English education only for an élite rather than offer it to the great majority of the population. To argue then, that the colonial government imposed their language at the expense of local languages is to ignore the facts."

I live in terror of ignoring facts. But the manner in which I'm not imposing my language on anybody right now is different from how I'm not imposing Temne. The colonial policy was to get rich, and when money moves, it creates momentum. By busily filling their trunks, British colonists motivated those nearby to speak and hear English words more often. People who might otherwise have needed to learn Temne as a Second Language instead tossed it into their maybe-someday pile, along with notes saying, "Must revise Ancient Greek verbs," and "Write to Grandma!" One of the few moments when Temne enjoyed an up-spike of popularity among people from outside Sierra Leone was during the country's civil war of the 1990s, when UN soldiers received a handbook containing useful phrases and proverbs, such as the ones below. (The "ɔ" vowel rhymes with "dot," the "ɛ" with "bet," the "ə" with "uh." The "ŋ" sounds like "ng.)"

| **Temne**<br>*(two million-ish speakers)* | **English**<br>*(two billion-ish speakers)* |
|---|---|
| Mare məbɔthi kakarɔns. | A good beginning makes a good ending. |
| I yema na ye mu, kɛrɛ I ba-ɛ ankala. | I would have liked to give you, but I don't have, money. |
| An rɔŋ mɔ təpe ro yɛnki. . | Charity begins at home. |

In Temne, the third phrase literally means, "The devil, when he begins, is at home." The Temne speaker who wrote the guidebook assured peacekeepers that the proverb amounts to the same thing as the English one about charity.

As I am not from western Africa, Temne looked very foreign to me, until I learned that the language's word for "buttocks" is "ansa," which bears no direct relation to the English "arse" but perfectly matches an Ancient Sumerian word pronounced "ansa" or "anse" or "ansu," which begat "asnu," begetting the Latin "asinus," which begat "assa," the Old Brythonic word for a donkey that survived into modern

English. Some things were just meant to go together, as an old yadswyver* might say.

I doubt Hengest cared about imposing English on foreigners. His island culture had looked dangerously small in 1600 AD, but events since then dispelled the threat of becoming the world's only English-speaker in the foreseeable future. Instead, throughout the 1800s, the hero penetrated and accelerated through half the world, as it were, in a fit of absence of mind. We don't know his every move, but *somebody* whispered in the Indian governor general's ear in Calcutta during the 1830s, leading to that man's decision in 1835 that all funds available for Indian schools must go to solely English-language classes. Perhaps the same somebody referred him to SAD's solid track record of philanthropic work in the field of English-language teaching on each continent.

"Liberians are all speaking English now. And you should see what we're doing with Cree."

"Cree?" said the Indian governor general. "Never heard of it."

"And if all goes well, you never will."

"Jolly good. So you think you can, er . . . "

Somebody thought he could, obviously.

"Excellent," the governor general concluded, I expect. "Do we need a show of hands? No? Damn fine business. Brandy."

To quote a Sierra Leonean proverb rendered in Krio, which is the mixed language arising from imported English-speakers as they tried to negotiate with Temne-speakers and others, "*Dat bitul we de rol kaka, i no no se fo kaka i trangga.*"

* Please refer to your *Dunbar and Kennedy* verbal-abuse primer.

The dung beetle doesn't know it's not easy to poo. Hengest and his fellow envoys were just having a good time, acquiring a taste for canapés, chomping their way around with no malice in their minds as they accidentally helped English slip into more of the world's earholes.

Of all the junkets, the ancient Angle should have enjoyed Australia the most. There, the colonial rulers faced a traditional enemy of Angle warriors – the Welsh. A sizeable chunk of New South Wales's population spoke the Celtic tongue, toiling without the holy light of English education until someone persuaded the Australian governor general in the mid-1800s to sponsor schools for all citizens, be they labourers or farmers or sheep-shaggers. This reversed an old policy of leaving education to a few private tutors. It also helped purge Australia of its ignorant Welsh-speaking hordes. Hengest would have met with the moving-and-shaking set at the Australian Club on Sydney's Macquarie Street, where all major national decisions were made in those days, and where he must have feasted on the barbecued meat for which Australian culture is rightly renowned. No doubt he tasted kangaroo-on-a-stick, and washed it down with "lashings" of beer, as they used to say.

"There's more bloody beer here than bloody flies on your colonial-bloody pommie-bastard-bloody backside," an Australian Club member told Hengest, probably. "So help your-bloody-self."

Australians didn't invent the word "bloody." They just diluted it and applied it in greater quantities. As they did with beer, come to think of it.

The word gained taboo in England during the 1700s for reasons now lost, though the French "sanglant" had long sounded wicked to Catholic kids in that country, reminding them of the sacred blood they were forced to drink in one of the church's funny rituals.

A travel writer visiting New South Wales in 1847 found the taboo honoured only in the breach. He met a bullock-driver who said "bloody" twenty-seven times during fifteen minutes of conversation, from which the writer extrapolated that the average Australian man uttered it 18.2 million times during his lifetime. This is bogus reasoning, obviously, because the visitor didn't know whether the bullock-driver sounded average, or unusually profane, or rather priggish by local standards.

Sydney enjoyed an informal style in the nineteenth century. Higher-ups heard and understood the slang of lower-downs. In need of small talk with a visitor like Hengest, the well-to-do folks at the Australian Club might naturally begin to teach him some "Flash," a common code amongst the local felonry.

"'Spoony' – can't handle his bloody drink, 'whiddler' – talks too bloody much, and a 'dummy' is a bloody idiot," said an Australian.

"Spoony dummy," repeated Hengest. "Whiddling spoon."

"And 'bender' at the end means you didn't bloody mean it."

"How bloody fascinating," Hengest maybe said. He swigged a beer. "I mean, how bloody fascinating, *bender*. Bloody spoony old whiddler."

"You know," a club member replied, popping another bottle. "For a dopey bastard, you're no dopey bastard."

Roughly speaking, over the course of a three-day boozer without sleep, Hengest and the elite membership of the Australian Club swapped insults much too vile for print and, amid these, sealed a deal to spray English-language teaching into every dry shack in Australia, except the ones belonging to Aborigines, who weren't offered public schools until 1900 AD. Toward the end of the fourth day, Hengest had entered the process of passing out in a leather armchair, breathing wetly into his hat, pissed and contented. The rude Australians were going strong and kicked him awake.

"Henggy, you great cunt," they might have said. "A toast! To feeling bloody good about doing some bloody good."

I'd wager the hero of English managed to raise his glass one more time.

"To doing good," he said, possibly. "At long last, I'm doing really good."

"You mean, *real* good, you bugger," someone corrected him, or ought to have done.

"Whatever. Adverbs. *Zzzzz.*"

It was the best of times.

## 9. BOSSED BY AN ELF, (ONGOING)

In my childhood textbook, *1066 and All That* (published in 1930), the scholar-poets W.C. Sellar and R.J. Yeatman joked that after the First World War, "America was clearly Top Nation, and history came to a." Reading aloud in the authors' own vocab, it sounded like, "History came to a full stop," meaning that the end of Britain's ascendancy had killed the topic's appeal for them. But smart-ass Sellar and Yeatman wove a double-point out of their single one. The sentence reads differently in America, where history came to a "period," a statement warning the new empire that its time too will pass, while also alluding to life's continual churn. The pun saved Sellar and Yeatman from a face-plant like Francis Fukuyama's much-too-soon declaration of the "end of history," written in 1992, a full two decades ahead of the day in 2012 that embarrassed the ancient Mayan prophets – and at least *they* took the precaution of dying before anyone could tease them about it.

Britain's wane cycle began a few years into the twentieth century. This didn't stop British people from trying to rule the waves by subtler methods, such as the *Oxford English Dictionary*. When the first A–Z version of that book was released in 1928, lexicographers viewed it as a tentative rush-job based on too few shreds of shaky evidence. For the composers, a dictionary is always the result of (interrupted) hard work, of people doing their best while handicapped by insufficient resources, blind spots, and the daily need to break for lunch. Nevertheless, the Oxford dictionary immediately "took its place as the ultimate authority on the English language," as its marketing department likes to say.* In this minor arena – describing our tongue – the island culture hoped to remain Top Nation.

Meanwhile, at the newly minted British Broadcasting Corporation (BBC), managers fretted over their "great

* "The History of the *OED*," anonymously authored, published online by Oxford University Press.

responsibility towards the problems of English," to quote its founding chief, Lord-something. (His full name is provided by Google, but what matters here is his attitude.) He said: "Our responsibilities are obvious, since in talking to so vast a multitude, mistakes are likely to be promulgated to a much greater extent than was ever possible before. [rfshft, rfshft] No one would deny the great advantage of a standard pronunciation of the language. [rfshft] We seek a common denominator of educated speech."

People had hunted this whale many times before. In the nineteenth century, the chatter about how to sound educated in English grew into a roaring publishing trade on both sides of the north Atlantic. The BBC possessed a better tool, though. When a fashion leader during the 1800s handed out style advice, voicing her hatred of the new "is being" construction, for example – as in, "Hengest is being smelled" – she could only hope other people might choose to agree with and/or obey her.* By contrast, the BBC's army of speakers knew how to whisper directly into the minds of the masses all day long, to people living in India, Canada, the Caribbean, Australia, and across the misleadingly named "Commonwealth," where London's tones wafted via the shortwave Empire Service to "men and women, so cut off by the snow, the desert, or the sea, that only voices out of the air can reach them," as King George tactlessly put it. Lord-something thought his BBC

* An American scholar and father of two, Richard White, compiler of the first *Riverside Shakespeare*, said that when people spoke "is being" plus a passive verb, he felt "like a fellow whose uttermost upper grinder is being torn out by the roots."

announcers might be able to train the world's ignoramuses simply by modelling house style.

"Psst. *Am*-a-terr, not am-a-*turr*," the BBC management told its on-air talent in a 1931 booklet called *Broadcast English*. "And it's *add*-ult, not a-*dult*. Pass it on."

The BBC style of the early to mid-twentieth century became, arguably, history's most respected and ridiculed approach to speaking this language. Anyone who wanted to work for the public service broadcaster learned how to mimic it. Other people generally didn't. Instead, they carried on making mistakes, strangling vowels, going rogue, and seeking new alternatives. This occurred because (1) by Lord-something's own admission, the BBC's programs are "neither very interesting nor very good,"* so only a dogged minority has ever listened to them, and (2) most of us are not accountants.

The accounting profession managed to devise a worldwide standard called the Generally Agreed-upon Accounting Principles (GAAP), a set of conventions that are followed in all cases except criminality. Accountants succeeded at this project because none of them are cool, nor have they ever wanted to appear cool. (We know this because they chose to become accountants.) If they had been arty, unruly, rebellious human beings, they could never have learned to behave with such advantageous conformity. All subcultures make their little codes and agreements, of course, but it takes the personality-free to do so on a grand scale, top-line to bottom-line, margins matching, nation A to nation Z.

*Lord-something said this was a temporary situation (in 1932), and to be fair, he may yet be proved right.

Back on planet earth, while Lord-something sought the perfect set of guidelines for his radio announcers, kids in Los Angeles were looking to different models.

"A black musician who had a white woman and a Cadillac," remembered Hampton Hawes, the great pianist, "was a bad motherfucker. Anybody who *looked* good was automatically a motherfucker."

Now, Lord-something's democratic instincts led him to consult widely on the best approach to speaking English. He called upon poets, linguists, and even Americans, such as the New Jerseyan essayist Logan Pearsall Smith. But if he ever talked to the ten-year-old Hampton Hawes, I expect Lord-something came away feeling perplexed. For one thing, the BBC's founder had likely never heard the word "motherfucker" used in a positive sense before, and fair enough, because Hawes's memoir of 1930s California gave our modern dictionaries their earliest hint of this development. Lord-something might have learned "motherfucker" during the Great War, when the ruder breed of soldier used to say it in reference to the Germans, but this didn't help a radio boss figure out what pronunciation to recommend for the BBC Empire Service Radio, in hopes of teaching Hawes and other young people in Los Angeles to get it right. He remained uneducated in this regard, as did the wise men on his committee of advisors, which must be why the multi-year series of *Broadcast English* guidebooks always treated the word as if it didn't exist.

The first edition of the *Oxford English Dictionary* forgot about "motherfucker" too, due to a mix of ignorance, propriety, and a bias toward printed public material. To the extent that their choice was deliberate, omitting "motherfucker" must have seemed logical to the dictionary's editors, just as it did to the BBC. Neither authority saw a need to govern it. They knew that Los Angeles teens wouldn't check a multi-volume book published by a distant university for advice on when to say the word, nor tune shortwave radios to a dusty public service broadcaster to find out how "motherfucker" should sound. *The Oxford English Dictionary* and the BBC had set ambitious goals for themselves already, well beyond the reach of their funding. They didn't need to apologize for failing to register every conceivable word, usage, and context. It was a difficult enough job merely to follow the trusty dictum told to all aspiring storytellers, "Write what you know," when this material needed to be chaperoned by tired and humble caveats, by "obscures" and "origin uncertains."

Britain's radio and dictionary offices were home to liberal, kindly groups of colleagues.* No member of their staff looked a bunch of L.A. teens in the eye and said their words didn't belong under the umbrella of English. As far as Lord-something & Company could see, two parallel meanings of "English" might live side by side without wrestling or hurting each other. By nailing down the rules of Broadcast English, the BBC boss aimed to "stem modern tendencies to inaccurate and slurred speech," but not in a violent way, and though he expressed a hope that his radio station's accent would eventually be common to "most educated persons," he

* Actually, Lord-something was a Nazi sympathizer. But on other topics he could be very charming.

also felt no ambition to dictate how the hoi polloi of the English-speaking world should talk. By "educated," I suppose he meant people reared in a particular way, and by that, I guess he meant polite society, although "educated," like "English," may convey different things to different people at different times.

For linguists in the twentieth century, the word "English" shone as much darkness as it did light, sometimes naming the speech habits of Lord-something but not of the young Hampton Hawes, and vice versa at other times, or else referring to both people at once as if the difference in their voices didn't matter. To sound more organized (as they viscerally desired to be), the students of language looked for a new vocab. Scholars working in the Caribbean came up with the labels "acrolect," "mesolect," and "basilect," after trying to straighten out the chaos of talk on those islands. The words matched the knobs on a stereo's three-band EQ – high, medium, and bass – and referred to who earned what, and how. The visitors noticed that high-income Caribbean residents spoke an English that Lord-something might feel comfortable with, while the poor made any number of strange, local noises. In Jamaica, people with low-incomes said "nyam" where the rich would say "eat," or "nana" where polite society said "granny." Middle-income earners fell in the middle, roughly speaking, and might say "nana" but not "nyam," and so on. Even different pronunciations of the same words came with a dollar value attached. Worldly, wealthy Guyanese English-speakers said, "eye gayve him wun," while their provincial cousins said, "mi bin gee am wahn," for instance.* It's odd, considering how easily a person can make either sound, that the former costs so much more than the latter to say. "Acrolect," "mesolect," and "basilect" sounded more scientific than "rich," "average," and "poor," while also conveying a fuzzy and unwelcoming tone to outsiders, so they suited scholarship's requirements and soon found plenty of employment within the private language of experts.

Like most of us, Lord-something had a head full of wrong ideas, some of which were, simultaneously, quite right. No one *would* deny the great advantage of a standard pronunciation of English, a language's answer to accountancy's GAAP – a Generally Agreed-upon International Accent (GAIA), or whatever. It would be like a Garden of Eden, a place where order can rule and chaos can't intrude. Unfortunately, while people can move their voices closer to GAIA, they never quite arrive. An accent comes loaded with a life story, a birthplace, a training period, a mentor, a series of obstacles, a coming of age, and in some cases, a marriage of the unconscious animus with the anima. Accents can be picked up or dropped freely, and, at the same time, they cannot be. They are determined by routine, as well as fears, such as that a nearby person might tease or frown, or desires such as that the person might get friendlier, for instance, or else go away. Many experts have long suspected that the much-hunted common denominator of English – whether united on sound, meaning, or structure – is a fiction, a conceit imported from the asterisk reality that doesn't belong down here amid our mobs and crowds and tribes.

* These spellings were written by linguists imagining the vowels of a Canadian-born newsreader working for a major U.S. television network.

What young speakers want to mimic is someone visible to the naked eye, such as a parent at first, then some colleagues, who will confer in the manner of an advisory committee and decide that the motherfucker with a Cadillac seems quite cool. This is why real people tend to speak a more local, Mutually Agreed-upon Motherfucker Accent (MAMA), not a GAIA. Apart from influencing our social lives, MAMAs can hold a controlling stake in what we plan to do for a living, and what we expect to earn doing it. But even when we see our MAMAs placed in a hierarchy, sketched by somebody else into a pseudo-scientific arrangement – and even if this act is performed by a scholar with the help of an *x* and *y* axis – the free-thinking among us will rarely agree that our own MAMA isn't as good as someone else's MAMA. It is perhaps the truth closest to universal acknowledgement that a slight insult on this topic ought to be enough to get our ganders up.

The link between someone's wealth and the cosmopolitanism of his or her accent only holds for certain times and places, such as within colonies or former colonies of the British Empire during the mid- to late-twentieth century. In places where groups of families could enjoy growing their riches without moving very much or dealing directly with foreigners, the noises made by the upper classes might sound as bizarre and provincial as those of the poor. As the word "acrolect" gained caché among the professional storytellers of English, it took on a double meaning. In some contexts, it meant the way rich people talk. In others, it referred to the semi-fictional, imperfectly defined worldwide standard form of the language. Many people had an idea of what this acrolect looked like, in terms of its grammar, vocab, and (on paper) spellings, but nobody had seen it for certain. To speak it out loud, using noises that united one's MAMA with the theoretical GAIA, was one of those ambitions that could only make a person miserable.

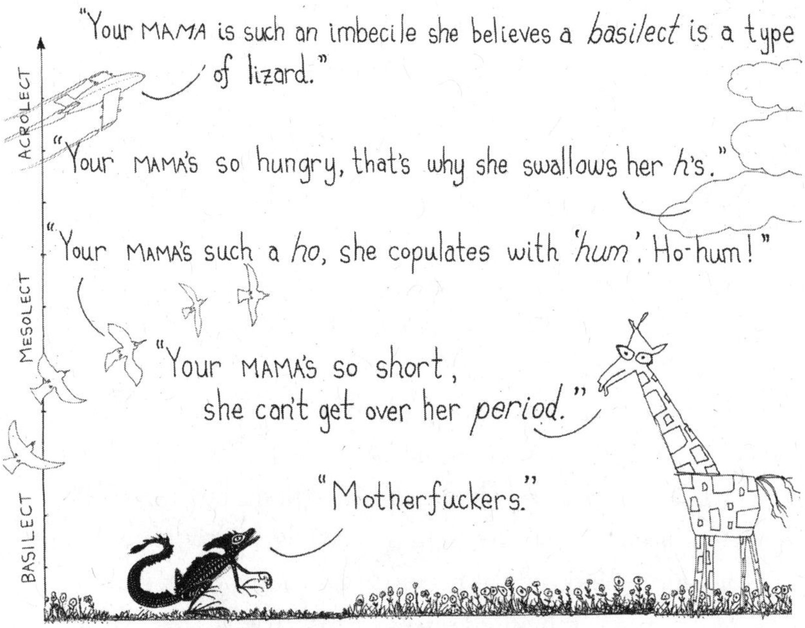

*Figure 4.3* – Mutually Agreed-upon Motherfucker Accents, like our other habits and behaviours, may be "inscribed" or "watermarked" with implicit criticisms of other groups.

In practice, if you wanted to sound international, mimicking Lord-something's radio announcers wasn't a bad plan, as long as you avoided sounding like you were reading the news. Matching another person's style of language often comes across as polite and puts them at ease, which is a smart move if that person has extra money. A better plan might be to talk like a rich American, since after World War II they tended to have more discretionary income than even the British. Business, as the saying goes, is conducted in the language of the customer, although the key exception would be the English-teaching business, whose customers wanted to learn how to make themselves agreeable to the U.S. purchasers of labour and products. Hence, a multi-billion-dollar industry spiralled up, like an airstream rising.

As a native speaker, schooled by a centuries-deep canon of books and a background in lobbying for English-language-only policies throughout Britain's former empire, Hengest ought to have easily netted a gig at the more comfy end of this rich trade. Not the *teaching* part, obviously – that job meant earning zilch and sleeping on somebody's floor – but perhaps an executive post, a consultancy or at-large role, something that kept him on the dinner circuit. Thanks to SAD, the hero already knew all the angles, so to speak. I've read stories about the porous membrane between global charities, multinational non-governmental groups, governments, and corporations – which seem to exist in a parallel universe where a lobbyist is also a diplomat, and a private executive can also be a public one, and so on. It's tough to pin these people down, and the conspiracist in me thinks that the situation may be deliberate. The company or organization for which Hengest worked probably had a brand no mortal ever heard of – the truly powerful ones never tell you their name – and the specifics of Hengest's work, like these heady echelons of society, are opaque to me. All I feel capable of asterisking, based on the little I can grasp from down here, is that if Hengest entered the stratosphere of the English-spreading business after World War II:

(1) he would stop riding boats and start flying in airplanes, such as the Boeing Stratocruiser;
(2) he would suffer frequently from jetlag; and
(3) his memos and other reading material would contain a lot of acronyms.

It is an irony, for a sector whose business is teaching English, that its reports and other documents make little sense to fluent native speakers. Roughly every third word is an acronym. Staying on top of these was probably the toughest part of Hengest's job (whatever it was). I expect a helpful junior staffer would slip him a fresh memo before each important meeting to remind the old man what the latest ones meant.

| **Full Name** | **Nickname** |
|---|---|
| English | English |
| Business English | BE |
| English as a Lingua Franca | ELF |
| Business English as a Lingua Franca | BELF |
| English as a Foreign Language | EFL |
| English as an International Language | EIL |
| English as an African Language | EAL |
| English Dialects | ED |
| Teaching English as a Foreign Language | TEFL |
| Teaching English as a Second Language | TESL |

| | |
|---|---|
| Teachers of English to Speakers of Other Languages | TESOL |
| Test of English as a Foreign Language | TOEFL |
| English Taught in Hard or Eccentric Locations | ETHEL |
| American English as a Lingua Franca in Rare Ideal Circumstances | AELFRIC |
| English as a Native Language | ENL |
| World English | WE |
| U.S. English | USE |
| Native Speaker English | NSE |
| Non-Native Speaker English | NNSE |
| General American | GA |
| General Electric | GE |
| Received Pronunciation | RP |
| Refined Received Pronunciation | RRP |
| Live Action Role Play | LARP |

In case you are wondering whether experts in this field talk with a straight face about speaking ELF, and also if they pronounce the word as "elf," I can confirm that yes, they do.

"You want me to speak *what*?" Hengest probably asked one day, rudely, at a meeting late in the century. As he ought to have known, ELF was arguably the world's most important new global tongue.

"The new language which is rapidly ousting the language of Shakespeare as the world's lingua franca is English itself – English in its new global form," David Graddol probably said, if he was at this meeting.*

*I am pencilling this asterisk based on Graddol's *English Next* report of 2006.

"What is distinctive about ELF is that, in most cases, it is a 'contact language' between persons who share neither a common native tongue nor a common (national) culture," Dr. Seidlhofer might have said, ignoring the hero of English's snorts as she read from her research paper. A language that can only be spoken by those who don't know too much of it – I expect the thought was more poetic and paradoxical than the hero's warrior brain could handle.

What goes up must come down, or it usually seems to. Throughout the twentieth century, Hengest's career rose to new-found heights (measured in paycheques) by piggybacking on his Anglocentric assets. However, an asset in one context is a liability in another, just as the ex-warrior's sword, long ago, became a burden to his old age. If Hengest hadn't snoozed through the rest of this meeting, he would have heard that speakers of English as a Lingua Franca set little value on a person's long-acquired familiarity with the ancient lives of certain English words. Their business is of-the-moment, and in most cases that moment belongs to business.

A person cannot pick up ELF by memorizing special ELF words, although the Elves do tend to share certain habits, such as not adding an "s" or "th" sound in phrases like, "Da woman kill da dwarf." If ELF were as simple as learning to do that, Hengest could adapt his personal English to fit this new one, as he'd done many times before, whenever it really meant a difference to his dinner plans. The hero had swallowed hundreds of changes since he was a boy. What makes ELF tricky to learn is that the little bugger never stays still.

Elves pick up or drop letters on the fly, partly to confuse the Dwarves, but mostly to match wits with other types of Elves. They avoid long sentences (sometimes). They don't get hung up (generally) on the difference between "who" and "which," or the need for a past passive conditional instead of a present continuous. They're paradoxical spirits, though. For instance, though they often seem to detest pre-cooked metaphors or obscure words, since these tend to waste effort or break spells of meaning, if two Elves happen to see eye to eye on a pun, they're (usually) delighted.

"As accommodation plays such a critical role in ELF, it is not viable to present learners with a single all-purpose model," said Dr. Jenkins, another ELF follower, in another paper. She didn't mean "accommodation" in the hotel sense, obviously, although hotels play a critical role in ELF too, since it's primarily a language of international trade. Jenkins meant the older sense, "to adapt or adjust." Good ELF-speakers offer accommodation rather than demanding to be given it. This crucial, inner spirit of ELF squarely contradicts a lifelong habit of Hengesty people. Many experts talk nowadays about a demise of the native speaker, characterized as the monolingual anglophone who hoped to get by without learning foreign languages, and who considers his or her fluency with connotations and wordplay a strength, not a handicap, when speaking or writing in English. Specifically, those experts mean the demise of Hengest.

As I understand it, when people enter a certain sphere of wealth and power, they cease to obey the rules that apply to normal human beings. A person of Hengest's rank never exactly gets fired. When he becomes obsolete, his colleagues gently nudge him off the airplane with a golden parachute attached to his back, and a word such as "emeritus" attached to his name. Apparently, the retirement process may involve a yacht. I don't know exactly how it all works. In any case, Hengest, the old NSE-model machine, might have found himself put out of service as ELF waxed past him, but the hero isn't likely to have come to a full stop, just another period. No doubt his bank accounts looked handsomely plump, tucked up in the Cayman Islands. His was surely going to be a soft landing.

## 10. HINDSIGHT, 2020 AD

The future is another country. They will do things a bit differently there. The past is the same way, or so I'm told. And as for the present, if it ever existed at all, it's no longer with us. This leaves a significant heap of unknowns.

If the story of English follows our language into death then it won't end for many decades yet. During the twenty-first century, perhaps, Arabic will sweep the world as the Chinese–African economic axis generates a new global hegemony and chooses the Middle Eastern tongue for the role of lingua franca. Anybody can make up stories. But then maybe Arabic, having scored that gig, will acquire marriage potential for English, and ALF and ELF will hook up and get it on. One mustn't forget that we have an environmental apocalypse to organize at some point before 2100 AD, and on top of that, there is an unnerving point of coincidence between our concept of meteors and our laws of probability, after which all bets may be off.

"What has spread around the world is not English so much as bilingualism with English, and ESL is only as good as its last deal," wrote the scholar Nicholas Ostler in *The Last Lingua Franca.* He said this language might be looking at a retirement soon – not a death, in any sense of the word, but a pulling back, a retreat from certain outposts.

By the way, those words, "retire" and "retreat," both came from the French. They got a bit mixed up after wandering into English, poor dears, and somewhat lost track of who they were, what they meant, and whatever had happened to their car, such that each ended up with some of the other's former baggage.

"The senses of the French word 'retirer' (and hence of the English word) show many points of connection with those of 'retraire' (retreat)," explains the *Oxford English Dictionary*, with the calm competence of a nurse. "In modern French the meanings 'to leave employment' and 'to withdraw (something) from service' are usually expressed with 'retreat' rather than with 'retire.'"

If I ever see the word "retirement" in person, I'd like to give it this helpful dictionary entry, which I would write out on a sheet of old-fashioned paper in large letters.

"Here you go," I'd say. "This is all you know, and all you need to know. Try to keep it with you."

**retire**

- fall back or give ground esp. when confronted by a superior force; to retreat

- take a step backward in fencing
- move a person or thing away, esp. for safety or storage
- remove a person from a place of danger or hardship
- hide
- retreat to privacy
- return frequently for rest and relaxation
- go to bed
- move to another place
- retract
- disappear, vanish from sight (chiefly poetic)
- appear to recede
- leave a courtroom to deliberate
- pull back from an idea or subject (obsolete)
- dissuade a person from an action, opinion
- get back
- recover
- settle a debt
- leave employment permanently
- stop working
- remove from office
- leave the field after being dismissed (cricket)
- withdraw from a game
- put out
- withdraw a person from use

To be honest, I had no idea "retirement" was working so hard. I'm often struck by how tenuously I know my own language, which is why I like to look words up in dictionaries – for the sense of reassurance that somebody out there has been keeping track of it all. No one has, of course, not completely, but efforts are ongoing, and that's a start. And the fact that dictionary writers are only human is a *good* thing, considering the alternative.

I don't want to know how English dies, but I would like to find out more about its hero. If my line of asterisks has brought us anywhere near the truth, I suppose he's still out there now, on his yacht, probably joined by Horsehair – or is that last part wishful thinking? Most thinking is, but still, it seems likely to me, in the academic sense, that she soured on her charity work (due to its disheartening results) and returned to poetry and the penning of anonymous works. Perhaps she edits Wikipedia, or spawns memes. Apparently the inventor of LOLcats is still unknown, for example. Does it not seem odd that a regular human being could claim such a major cultural contribution yet refuse to speak up? The mother of English should number among the suspects, I feel.

Some time ago, I mentioned two problems with the story of the English language. There is a third: the facts are hard to check. Even if the near-infinitely improbable came true and I managed to meet Hengest and Horsehair in the flesh – and even after they welcomed me aboard their yacht, offered me a deckchair and a beer, and told me about their soft spot for wastrels and wanderers – I would still be wracked with doubts.

"Are these serial killers?" I'd wonder, for instance.

Then, having pushed that thought out of my head, other question marks would pop up, regardless of what the old couple did. Hengest might tell me about his trick with the sword in the stone. Horsehair could explain SAD's organizational structure. I'd continue to feel suspicious. Their biographies should probably turn out to have wildly different plots from the ones I asterisked, and if they don't, it will enter my head that I've met two pranksters who have read *The Rude Story of English* and are taking me, literally, for a ride. I suppose I could test them with trick questions. If the couple's awareness of history seems greater than typical general knowledge, or their methods of filling gaps in the tale smell highly plausible, I might conclude they aren't amateur comedians, but must be professional historians or even scholars of language. That would be an alarming thought, and might suddenly revive my fear of getting killed.

"How do you know so much?" I would most likely ask. Worried.

Their answer would depend a great deal on who they are, of course, but luckily for future-me, this scenario is premised on having met the real-life Hengest and Horsehair, not a pair of psycho linguists.

"The question is, how do *you* know so little?" Horsehair will ask, I suppose.

Now, that will be unfair of her. Horsehair has lived longer than I have, and much of her time has been unstructured. Besides, to spend half of a regular human lifetime within reach of the collected works of our species' wisdom, with free access to virtually all books ever written (most of them translated and in searchable formats), and surrounded by people and dinners from every patch of dirt on the planet, while persisting nevertheless to have certain knowledge of next to nothing, might be considered an achievement.

Sometimes while killing time on Google Earth, I like to look, ridiculously, for their boat. It's astonishing, and mundane too, that I can see where they would need to land having snuck into, say, Hermit Bay near Sydney, a place I can't afford to visit from my home in Canada. There's a sandy spot in the bay that looks ideal, in a private backyard property where someone has left an old bucket (though the object will be gone by 2020 AD, I'm almost sure). By pulling in here, or someplace like it, Hengest and Horsehair would spare themselves a downtown moorage fee. They might be rich, but as I understand it, all retired couples look out for money-saving options when possible. If they wanted to visit Sydney proper, I expect they could scramble up that hill and through that person's garden without being accosted. Then it would be a matter of walking nonchalantly onto Carrara Road, where they could catch the 325 bus, if it's still running in those days, toward the city centre.

Knowing much while simultaneously knowing little seems to be a permanent state, or so I'm propelled to believe by my "peculiar enquiries" and "temporary theories," to borrow J.R.R. Tolkien's words (while altering them). The famous professor didn't want his own knowledge to be quite so peculiar or temporary as it insisted on being, which is why the man worked harder than most in a struggle to make sense of difficult things. I imagine such a life choice could feel disheartening because ignorance is a condition with no antidote. What we have instead are anecdotes and, by definition, they never supply the whole story. Their gaps dwarf their contents. However, anecdotes can offer comfort if taken as intended – for therapeutic purposes only – because at least *they* are knowable, by which I mean that a person may learn to tell them, and tell them again, over and over, a little differently each time.

*Figure 4.4* – Hengest and Horsehair, mother and father of the English language, 2020 AD

## ACKNOWLEDGEMENTS

Thanks to Helen Guri, who gave to this book more than any writer should be asked to give to another's work. Thanks to Gabe Foreman for being so talented and fun to work with. Thanks to the poets whose books have inspired me, woken me up, kept me wandering about language, and so on. Thanks to Eleanor Wachtel and Jacqueline Kirk for forbearance in the workplace. Thanks to parents, siblings, in-laws, nephews, and niece, for accommodation, entertainment, and other types of support. Thanks to all the Jutes, especially Anna Jensen, for reminding me about Hengest and showing me Gorm's immense grave.

Thanks to Jenny Bradshaw at Random House for her insights and patience. Thanks to C.S. Richardson for the clever cover. Thanks to Linda Pruessen for copy-editing. Thanks to typesetter Terra Page for handling the eccentric and fiddly text. Thanks to Valentina Capuani for producing the book, and to Shona Cook for telling people about it. Thanks to Suzanne Brandreth for the instigation, to Susan Renouf and Trena White for the suggestion, and to Dean Cooke for taking on such a silly author.

## A NOTE ON THE TYPE

*The Rude Story of English* is set (for the most part) in Adobe Caslon, a digitized typeface based on the original 1734 designs of William Caslon. Caslon is generally regarded as the first British typefounder of consequence and his fonts are considered, then as now, to be among the world's most "user-friendly" text faces.